# Catholic Social Teaching and the Market Economy

# Catholic Social Teaching and the Market Economy

PHILIP BOOTH

With Contributions From

Samuel Gregg
Robert Kennedy
Kishore Jayabalan
Michael Miller
Denis O'Brien
Dennis O'Keeffe
Anthony Percy
Robert A. Sirico
Thomas Woods
Andrew Yuengert

ST PAULS

First published in Great Britain in 2007 by
The Institute of Economic Affairs
2 Lord North Street
Westminster, London SW1P 3LB
in association with Profile Books Ltd

The mission of the Institute of Economic Affairs is to improve public
understanding of the fundamental institutions of a free society, by
analysing and expounding the role of markets in solving economic and
social problems.

Second edition published by
©2014 St Pauls Publishing
187 Battersea Bridge Road – SW11 3AS London

ISBN 978-0-85439-837-9

Typeset by David Exley at www.beamreachuk.co.uk
Production and Cover Design: DX Imaging, Watford, Herts, UK
Printed by Martins The Printers, Berwick upon Tweed, UK

A CIP catalogue record for this book is available from the British Library.

*ST PAULS is an activity of the priests and brothers of
the Society of St Paul who proclaim the Gospel through
the media of social communication*

# CONTENTS

# PART ONE:
# ECONOMIC WELFARE AND
# THE ROLE OF THE STATE

# PART TWO:
# BUSINESS, THE CONSUMER AND
# CULTURE IN CHRISTIAN LIFE

# PART THREE:

# SUBSIDIARITY AND SOLIDARITY – THE ROLE OF THE INDIVIDUAL, THE COMMUNITY AND THE STATE

# The Authors

## Philip Booth

Philip Booth is Editorial and Programme Director at the Institute of Economic Affairs and Professor of Insurance and Risk Management at the Cass Business School where he was formerly Associate Dean. He has an undergraduate degree in economics from the University of Durham and a PhD in Finance. He is a Fellow of the Institute of Actuaries and of the Royal Statistical Society. Previously, Philip Booth worked for the Bank of England as an adviser on financial stability issues. He has written widely, including a number of books, on investment, finance, social insurance and pensions, as well as on the relationship between Catholic social teaching and economics. Recent publications as co-author or editor include: *Verdict on the Crash, Modern Actuarial Theory and Practice, The Road to Economic Freedom* and *Christian Perspectives on the Financial Crash.* He is editor of the journal *Economic Affairs* and on the editorial boards of various other academic journals.

## Samuel Gregg

Samuel Gregg has written and spoken extensively on moral questions in law, medicine and finance. He has a Doctor of Philosophy degree in moral philosophy from Oxford University and has authored several books, including *Morality, Law, and Public Policy* (2000), *On Ordered Liberty* (2003), *Ethics and Economics* (1999), *A Theory of Corruption* (2004), *Banking, Justice, and the Common Good* (2005), and *The Commercial Society* (2007). He also publishes in journals such as *Law and Investment Management, Oxford Analytica, Journal des Economistes et des Etudes Humaines, Economic Affairs, Evidence, Markets and Morality*, and *Policy*, as well as newspapers including the *Wall Street Journal Europe*, the *Washington Times*, the *Australian Financial Review* and *Business Review Weekly*. He is Director of Research at the Acton Institute, an Adjunct Professor at the Pontifical Lateran University, a consultant for Oxford Analytica Ltd, and general editor of the Lexington Book Series *Studies in Ethics and Economics*. He was elected a Fellow of the Royal Historical Society in 2001, and a Member of the Mont Pèlerin Society in 2004.

## Kishore Jayabalan

Kishore Jayabalan is Director of Istituto Acton, the Acton Institute's Rome office. Formerly, he worked for the Vatican's Pontifical Council for Justice and Peace as an analyst for environmental and disarmament issues and desk officer for English-speaking countries. Kishore Jayabalan earned a BA in political science and economics from the University of Michigan, Ann Arbor. In college, he was executive editor of *The Michigan Review* and an economic policy intern for the US Chamber of Commerce. He worked as an international economist for the Bureau of Labor Statistics in Washington, DC and then graduated with an MA in political science from the University of Toronto. During his graduate studies, Kishore was baptised and received into the Roman Catholic Church by Pope John Paul II in Rome in 1996. He later worked as a student campus minister at the university's Newman Centre, which led to his appointment to the Permanent Observer Mission of the Holy See to the United Nations in New York in 1997. Two years later, he returned to Rome to work for the Pontifical Council for Justice and Peace. Kishore became director of Istituto Acton in 2005 and organises the institute's educational and outreach efforts in Rome and throughout Europe.


*Robert Kennedy*

Robert Kennedy is a full professor and chair of the Department of Catholic Studies at the University of St Thomas (St Paul, Minnesota) and co-director of the University's Terrence J. Murphy Institute for Catholic Thought, Law, and Public Policy. He also holds a joint appointment (as professor in the Department of Ethics and Business Law) in the College of Business, where he served as Chair of the Faculty in 2004/05. He received his PhD in medieval studies (with a concentration in philosophy and theology) from the University of Notre Dame, and also holds master's degrees in biblical criticism and business administration.

## *Michael Miller*

Michael Miller is a Research Fellow and Director of Acton Media at the Acton Institute. He received his bachelor's degree from the University of Notre Dame, has an MA from Nagoya University's Graduate School of International Development (Japan), an MA in philosophy from Franciscan University, and an MBA in International Management from Thunderbird (The American Graduate School of International Management). Before coming to Acton, he spent three years at Ave Maria College of the Americas in Nicaragua where he taught philosophy and political science and was the chair of the philosophy and theology department. He has almost 10 years of international experience and has lived and travelled in Europe, Asia, Africa, and Latin America. He has been published in the *Washington Times*, The *Detroit News*, the *Los Angeles Daily News*, and *Crisis*. His research interests include political economy, moral philosophy, economic development, and political theory.

### Denis O'Brien

D. P. O'Brien was educated at Douai School and University College, London. He was Professor of Economics at Durham from 1972 to 1997. Prior to that he taught at Queen's University, Belfast. His publications are mainly in the fields of industrial economics and the history of economic thought.

### Dennis O'Keeffe

Dennis O'Keeffe was educated at St Benedict's School, Ealing, and at the universities of Durham and London. He is Professor of Social Science at the University of Buckingham and Senior Research Fellow in Education at the IEA. He has written widely in the area of education and social theory. He is also well known as a broadcaster and journalist. His latest work includes *Economy and Virtue*, a collection of essays for the IEA, and a translation for Liberty Fund of Benjamin Constant's *Principes de Politique*.

### Anthony Percy

Father Anthony Percy is rector of the Good Shepherd Seminary, in the Archdiocese of Sydney. He was ordained to the priesthood in 1990 and has served as an assistant priest, administrator and now parish priest in the archdiocese. He obtained his doctorate from the John Paul II Institute for Studies in Marriage and Family, in Washington, DC. He is author of *Theology of the Body Made Simple*. Father Percy also has a master's degree in Finance from the University of New South Wales.

## Robert A. Sirico

Father Robert A. Sirico is president of the Acton Institute for the Study of Religion and Liberty. His writings on religious, political, economic and social matters are published in a variety of journals and he is often called upon by members of the broadcast media for statements regarding economics, civil rights and issues of religious concern. He is a member of the Mont Pèlerin Society, the American Academy of Religion and the Philadelphia Society. Father Sirico also served on the Michigan Civil Rights Commission from 1994 to 1998. He is also currently pastor of St Mary Catholic Church in Kalamazoo, Michigan. Father Sirico's pastoral ministry has included a chaplaincy to Aids patients at the National Institute of Health and the recent founding of a new community, St Philip Neri House, in Kalamazoo, Michigan.

*Thomas Woods*

Thomas E. Woods, Jr, is a senior fellow at the Ludwig von Mises Institute in Auburn, Alabama. His books include *How the Catholic Church Built Western Civilization, The Church Confronts Modernity, Meltdown* and *The Politically Incorrect Guide to American History*, a *New York Times* bestseller. He won first place in the 2006 Templeton Enterprise Awards for his book *The Church and the Market: A Catholic Defense of the Free Economy*.

*Andrew Yuengert*

Andrew Yuengert holds the John and Francis Duggan Chair of Business at Seaver College, Pepperdine University. Before coming to Pepperdine twelve years ago, he was a research economist at the Federal Reserve Bank of New York. He is the author of two recent books: *The Bound-aries of Technique: Ordering Positive and Normative Concerns in Economic Research*, from Lexington Press, and *Inhabiting the Land: A Case for the Right to Migrate*, published by the Acton Institute.

# CATHOLIC SOCIAL TEACHING – 'AS RADICAL AS REALITY ITSELF'

Somewhat over thirty years ago I was working on the remote East Coast of Sri Lanka in a joint Methodist–Jesuit project – perhaps the only one on the planet. One of our enterprises was to manufacture industrial starch. The Jesuits' secret formula meant that we beat the competition out of sight. But the government textile and paper manufacturers had their own cosy deals with other suppliers. So we had to rail-freight tonnes of our stuff across the country, and sell it to Muslim traders in the back streets of Colombo. We prospered, while the country suffered many of the ills associated with the suppression of the market. When the region was plunged into the horrors of race war, we went bust.

This book is a splendid attempt to bring the weight of Catholic social teaching to bear on this and many other harsh realities. It now seems obvious that an effective and competitive market contributes immeasurably to human well-being, especially for the world's poor. It was not always so. But that view, with many necessary qualifications, is the burden of the argument of *Centesimus annus*. It now seems clear that this epochal document is largely coherent with *Rerum novarum*. These are the great peaks of Catholic social teaching, and their shared vision appears ever more remarkable.

At the time of *Rerum novarum*, the Holy See found itself embattled by the modernism of the new great European States – Italy, Germany and the French Third Republic. Britain and America were no less problematic, but less pressing. Pope Leo kept his nerve, and answered the claims of modernity in its own language, but on the Church's own terms. Secular modernity gave us the catastrophic conflicts of the twentieth century, waged on the back of that unbridled state power against which *Rerum novarum* warned. That story needs to be retold, now that socialism has vanished and the world-wide significance of religion is daily more evident. A modern gloss on this extraordinary document might be that it is only in a free society that the Catholic Church can claim the space to be herself.

*Centesimus annus* appeared in a world in which communism had collapsed and the shape of the future was unknown. Over two decades on, we find that the future which ensued bears remarkable resemblances to the past – a world of globalising prosperity despite the financial crash, the erosion of Victorian values in the naughty nineties, when even the English decided to have fun – and a world armed to the teeth, both with weapons and with ideological prescriptions for their use.

Amongst its other contributions this book contains two modest proposals which will ruffle feathers in some places. The first of these is that Catholic education should be more...well, *Catholic*. The second is that the busy scribblers of Eccleston Square should pay more attention to the fundamentals of Catholic social teaching when they formulate documents on today's vital topics, as for instance on taxation, the environment and the European Union. As a former busy scribbler of nearly twenty years' standing, I might say in our defence that it is sometimes difficult to resist the conventional wisdom of the day, especially when it comes in an authoritative package. The hardest thing is 'to be as radical as reality itself', as was remarked by Pope Leo's younger contemporary, V. I. Lenin. In that high calling these papers largely succeed. The first edition most certainly achieved its objective of furthering understanding of Catholic social teaching and the benefits of a market economy. This new and expanded edition is even more relevant and covers topics of contemporary importance.

One suggestion seems worthy of further study – that somehow the market cannot be held responsible for the hedonism that is associated with it. Capitalism does come with its own culture. We once knew how to employ the moral disciplines of poverty in a world of scarcity. How do we now create the ethical framework that will serve a world of prosperity? Perhaps this is the question that arises most sharply from this volume – and which was raised also by *Caritas in veritate* – and makes it therefore doubly welcome.

**Reverend John Kennedy**
*Methodist minister, formerly Secretary for Church and Society at Churches Together in Britain and Ireland, and Secretary for Political Affairs of the Methodist Church*

# Acknowledgements

In the compilation of an edited book such as this, one owes a great debt to many people, in particular to the authors. I would like to give special thanks to Dr Samuel Gregg of the Acton Institute, who has provided help and advice well beyond the call of duty as an author. I would also like to thank the anonymous referees who provided a number of helpful comments.

# Preface

As Christianity spread across the Roman world, it was considered distinctive for its emphasis on compassion and on the dignity of human labour. After two thousand years, compassion and the dignity of human labour remain important to Catholic social thought.

Religious and lay Catholics continue to minister to peoples around the world. The twentieth century, however, witnessed major new developments. One is the growth of the state in Western societies. The tendency of government to tax resources has made governments a favoured place to propose the expression of compassion. While there is continued private charity by ordinary individuals and by wealthier persons, there has been a redirection of means and ends in the political world.

Studies in the UK, Australia and the USA have described how the introduction of government unemployment and pension programmes earlier in the twentieth century contributed to the decline of the fraternal societies. The wide participation in the insurance programmes of the fraternal societies and associations represented a healthy level of member participation in administration and mutual aid. The government's introduction of universal coverage in order to aid a small minority not covered by fraternal insurance had the unintended consequence of devaluing important intermediate institutions and undermining subsidiarity. This consequence was warned against by the major Catholic fraternal and mutual organisations at that time.

In the USA, historical research has demonstrated the cohesion of the black family in the nineteenth and early twentieth centuries. Unemployment in the Great Depression was a strain on the black family. But legislation to relieve such strains sometimes had long-term negative effects. General minimum wage legislation meant there was no provision for lower wage rates for youths who did not have any work experience. The consequence was widespread youth unemployment, particularly in the black community, as young black people tended to have less education and thus commanded a lower wage than others. As the youth had no opportunity to gain work experience at an introductory wage rate, the black young men were condemned to general unemployment. This was an unintended consequence of a good intention.

Subsequent welfare legislation for women and children was dependent upon a man not being a member of the household. Since black men suffered unemployment owing to their not having gained introductory skills as youths, this attempt to assist women and children had the unintended consequence of undermining stable marriage. The exclusion due to legislation of black men from the dignity of labour has caused deep pathologies among the men and their families. The dignity of work for the disadvantaged has been a major casualty for them when legislation interferes with the improving process of the market economy.

Thus, many of the major advances in government social legislation have had the effect of unintentionally undermining the dignity of labour and of the family. It is a warning to us to be more careful in the application of compassion outside the decisions of individuals or intermediate groups in society. When the wealth and the power of government are applied the consequences, intended and unintended, can be heavy and ruinous. It can be the persons we most wish to help who can be injured by the compassion without intention.

The chapters in this book reflect this, and also reflect the insights of Pope John Paul II in the encyclical *Centesimus annus:*

> The activity of a market economy cannot be conducted in an institutional, juridical or political vacuum. On the contrary, it presupposes sure guarantees of individual freedom and private property, as well as a stable currency and efficient public services. Hence the principal task of the state is to guarantee this security, so that those who work and produce can enjoy the fruits of their labours and thus feel encouraged to work efficiently and honestly... (*Catechism*, para. 2431)

Pope John Paul II's *Centesimus annus* was a celebration of the one hundredth anniversary of the encyclical of Pope Leo XIII, *Rerum novarum*. These two giants of the social doctrine of the Catholic Church deserve to be studied together.

The chapters in this book recognise the reality that the budgetary crises of the developed countries require the withdrawal of the state from many activities undertaken in the confusions of boundless expectations. Indeed, the interlude between the first and second editions has seen the crises become even more urgent. The new realities mean a return to self-involvement of citizens in the affairs that affect their health, retirement, and so on. Of the many areas studied in this book, education may be the most important. It is the education of our children upon which the future of the economy and of the resources for the health and pensions of the older generation will depend. Yet the recognised shortcomings of the state education system, especially for the disadvantaged for whom it was especially introduced, seem the most difficult to resolve owing to entrenched structures.

Among the private initiatives in the 21st century will be increased attention to charity by the better off. In the USA there continues to be an expansion of charity. Those with middle as well as higher incomes and wealth observe the private institutions that are offering assistance and make their charitable judgements on the basis of their attention to these institutions. Many people are participating as volunteers in the assistance programmes. Some are dedicated to moving the disadvantaged from static welfare to the dynamic of self-help. The Christian is motivated by compassion to assist the disadvantaged to achieve the dignity of labour. This confirms one of the themes of a number of chapters of this book – where the state withdraws it gives room for voluntary, Christian initiative to 'breathe'. This is so not just in the spheres of welfare and charity, but in the cultural sphere too – and perhaps also in the field of financial regulation discussed in one of the chapters which was written following the financial crisis of 2008. Consumers and business people must respond to their Christian calling in all areas in which they are active.

This book makes an important contribution to our understanding of the dangers of conflating compassion with government action; it helps us understand the Christian case for a more limited role for government; and it helps us to see the true Christian vocation in the context of a smaller state that allows more room for private and voluntary-collective initiative in the economic, charitable and cultural areas of life. The second edition of this book is most welcome, especially after the success of the first edition.

**Professor Leonard P. Liggio**
*Executive Vice-President*
*Atlas Economic Research Foundation*

**Catholic Social Teaching and
the Market Economy**

# 1

## Introduction

# UNDERSTANDING CATHOLIC SOCIAL TEACHING IN THE LIGHT OF ECONOMIC REASONING

### *Philip Booth*

The authors of *Catholic Social Teaching and the Market Economy* were asked to achieve one or more of three objectives. The first objective was to apply economic theory, evidence and reasoning to the analysis of policy issues that are of particular concern to Christians. Thus, for example, there is a requirement for Christians who take an interest in public policy matters to be particularly sympathetic to the position of the poor, or to ensure that families can access education. Neither the Catholic Church, however, nor other Christian denominations suggest specifically how these objectives should be achieved. Economic analysis must be one of the tools used to help inform the views of all Christians on such policy matters.

It might be thought that economic considerations should feature only in a minor way in a Christian analysis of policy. Moral, philosophical or theological considerations may be regarded as paramount. To think this way would be a serious mistake. Some Christians seem to wish to assume away certain economic laws when developing policies in areas such as the minimum wage or the provision of foreign aid. This is as sensible as assuming away the laws of gravity when considering the moral case for punishment by hanging. It is true that, if the demand for labour were not to decrease as wages increase, then a minimum wage might well help the poor. It is also true that, if the law of gravity did not exist, hanging might be regarded as a morally justified punishment by those opposed to the death penalty, because hanging would then lead only to inconvenience for the criminal rather than to death. But to proceed in such a way, by ignoring important economic laws when articulating the case for 'rights' in the economic sphere, is facile and ignores the fundamental nature of man as both a rational and an imperfect being.

We should also be careful before casually using words such as 'moral' and 'just' to describe our favoured political policies. Those words have a powerful meaning and they should not be used without care. This is particularly so in the analysis of economic and political policies requiring compulsory redistribution of income or wealth through taxation. The issues are much more subtle than we may think. As the philosopher H.B. Acton put it, 'there is no morally defensible reason at all for forcing some individuals, irrespective of their incomes or circumstances, to give pecuniary help to beneficiaries whose incomes and circumstances have not been inquired into. In this way benefits are provided for people who may not need them by people who may not be in a position to afford them' (Acton, 1993: 81). This does not mean that the state should not provide for the poor. It also does not mean that policies to help the poor do not have a moral characteristic. We should be cautious, however, before using the words 'moral' or 'just' to describe such policies, not least because they always involve using coercion by taking the freely and properly acquired property of one individual in order to give it to another. We should also be cautious before we proceed to implement such policies lest we undermine the love and charity present when assistance is provided to those in need through an act of free will, uncoerced by the state, a process described so lucidly by Pope Benedict XVI in *Deus caritas est*.

Rigorous economic analysis of policy issues is a complex process. Even economists do not agree on the results of such analysis. As the Catholic French economist Frédéric Bastiat pointed out, however, without proper analysis there is always the temptation to take account of the 'seen' effects of economic actions and ignore the second-round or 'unseen' effects. The authors of this book try to address this particular problem. Notwithstanding this point, Christians should not necessarily feel that they need to be fully informed about economic issues. It is perfectly reasonable for Christians to reserve judgement on certain issues or to vote or speak according to their own experiences, without taking full account of the economic analysis that lies behind a proper appraisal of policy alternatives. We cannot all be experts in every field. It is not acceptable, however, for Christians to speak with absolute certainty, as if their perspective were the only perspective compatible with Christian belief, if they have not properly considered the economic principles that implicitly underpin their policy statements. One purpose of this book is to help Christians underpin their analysis of policy issues by a more rigorous understanding of the related economics and political economy.

## Understanding policy issues in the light of Catholic Social Teaching

Our authors were also asked to examine Catholic social teaching to help us understand better how it can be applied to policy issues. There is always a danger when examining the social teaching of the Catholic Church in this way that aspects will be selectively chosen to fit an author's own line of argument. Thus, in the case of the authors of this book, criticisms of the market economy might be ignored and elements of Catholic social teaching promoting individual freedom, autonomy of the family and private property might be selected as being representative. I believe, however, that this problem has been avoided. In British writing important aspects of social teaching that favour the market economy are frequently ignored, or hidden under a bushel, and it is right that this text corrects that tendency. The authors have not been afraid, however, to engage Catholic social teaching and criticise it when they believe that it is wrong or that its application would undermine the very objectives it seeks to achieve. This is notable particularly in the chapters on foreign aid and on the just wage. Catholic social teaching is provisional and it is accepted that Catholics can agree to disagree about it. In disagreeing with teaching on economic and social matters the authors are not, in any sense, undermining the teaching authority of the Church in those areas of morals and theology where she claims special insights of truth.

## Challenges to theologians and Christian politicians

Finally, our authors were asked to raise new questions or to take a fresh look at areas of policy that have both an economic and a moral aspect to them. The chapters on foreign aid, consumerism, the environment and the responsibility of business, for example, raise important moral questions for Christians and for the Church's social teaching. How should we proceed to help poor countries if the structures of government in those countries are such that development aid will bolster the bad governments that keep the poorest people poor? How should Christian consumers, and business people, respond to a materialistic climate that can develop in capitalist societies? Some of these questions are discussed briefly below and all are tackled fully in the main chapters.

## The scope of *Catholic Social Teaching and the Market Economy*

This book does not pretend to look at all sides of the argument or consider all topics. Certain topics have been omitted. Free trade, the provision of healthcare and a general treatment of globalisation are three important subject areas not covered in detail – though they are covered in the context of the analysis of other issues. This second edition has been extended to cover new fields such as the environment, the financial crash, corporate social responsibility and the social teaching of Pope Benedict XVI. Also, while some authors do engage anti-free-market arguments, and some chapters are very balanced in their approach, other authors have analysed their subject area from a rigorous free-market perspective. There are important reasons for this. First, the book is intended to be relatively brief and succinct. There are other, more expansive, reference works that take in a broader range of subjects and lines of argument (see, for example, Charles, 1998). Also, rigorous economic analysis tends to lead in a pro-market direction: certainly the great debate between the opponents and proponents of central planning is now settled. Despite this, there is a relative dearth of literature that examines economic policy issues from a Christian perspective while taking proper account of free-market economics. On the other hand, Christian socialist perspectives on policy matters are abundant.

Nevertheless, the economic analysis of the issues presented here should be of value to people on all sides of political and economic debates. It should help Christians inclined to a free-market perspective to understand issues more clearly. It should also help Christians of a socialist perspective to understand better the obstacles that stand in the way of a socialist solution to problems such as poverty. The book may convert a few from that way of thinking; it may help others sharpen their arguments. The authors hope that it will, at least, cause them to pause for thought.

The authors were asked to limit their analysis to *Catholic* social teaching. Again, this was because we wanted incisive analysis of particular aspects of Christian theology and economic policy, rather than a broader text. But this book is intended to be useful for Catholics and non-Catholics alike – and indeed for non-Christians. The problems that are addressed should interest any person involved with public policy. Furthermore, the problems considered are not only of concern to Catholics. Indeed, Catholic social teaching has seeped into the thinking on economic policy of most Christian denominations. Catholic social teaching has also influenced the thinking on economic and political issues of non-Christians, just as non-Christian thinking on economic matters has influenced Catholic social teaching. Thus these new perspectives on Catholic social teaching are relevant to all who wrestle with the same policy problems and examine them from more or less the same moral perspective. Like all IEA books, this text has been peer reviewed. Non-Catholic academics were involved in that process.

## Fundamental messages

It is now generally accepted that the market economy is more efficient at producing and allocating economic resources than alternative forms of economic organisation. This argument is important: less efficient economic systems produce less while using more resources; people are poorer as a result; and the poor tend to be much poorer in socialist economic systems than in market-oriented ones. There are, however, deeper messages that the authors wish to convey in this book.

## Community, society and government

One such deeper message of the authors is this: the fallacy that sees the provision of welfare by government as an extension of the charitable activity of the Christian community should be rejected once and for all. The main purpose of government is to protect individuals, families and communities, and their property, from harm. Government must also provide the legal framework that allows us to plan our economic and social life, allows us to provide for our welfare, and so on. If a government does not perform these functions then civilised and developed economic life is impossible, as we see in so much of the world today. In other words, government must provide the juridical and political framework within which human flourishing is possible. Even a government of a distinctly Christian character should not, however, take upon itself the duties of Christian communities to share goods, provide welfare and look after the aged and sick, except where efforts to provide these functions outside the government sector have failed. If a government goes beyond its remit in this respect, it undermines the free will, dignity and genuine love and charity of individuals within their communities: government action in these fields crowds out voluntary action and the innovation and personal response that are key characteristics of voluntary action motivated by true love.

In this respect it is interesting to consider the words of the Acts of the Apostles on Divine Mercy Sunday (the first Sunday after Easter) in Year A of the Catholic missal: 'The faithful all lived together and owned everything in common; they sold their goods and possessions and shared out the proceeds among themselves according to what each one needed.' It is tempting for Christian socialists to argue that the state should bring this ideal to fruition and does so through the welfare state. But for many reasons the Catholic Church strongly opposes that view. It is for the state to provide the conditions in which human flourishing can take place. In order for sharing to take place – if this is the ideal in all Christian communities at all times – private property is a prerequisite. There cannot be sharing or generosity without private property. The Christian community cannot behave in the way suggested in the Acts if the state takes substantial portions of people's income in taxation and attempts to undertake the functions described in the Acts itself. As we see in a number of chapters in this book, the attempt by the state to take on the functions of the community has led to a serious undermining of human flourishing.

The subtle but crucial distinctions between community, society and government can be better understood by thinking of the situation of many underdeveloped countries. It is often said, no doubt correctly, that in many African countries there is an important sense of community that has been lost in the West. That sense of community is, however, clearly distinct from the political structures that frequently exhibit the worst forms of corruption, violence and the abuse of power. Furthermore, attempts to generalise the sense of community that is apparent within and between families, within churches and so on, through the democratic control of economic resources via a socialistic political system have been catastrophic for African economies.

The democratic political process is absolutely necessary to resolve certain problems peacefully. But the whole point of the democratic process is that it is used to settle disputes between people whose views and interests are different. The losers in elections agree to abide by the result because they know that the winners would have done so had they lost. This tacit agreement holds if the government performs a limited range of functions. All the different communities, each made up of individuals and families, can then pursue their aims by working within the framework set by the democratically elected government.

## Self-interest in the market and self-interest in the political system

The application of free-market economic principles is often criticised by Christian socialists because of the suspicion of the forces of self-interest that motivate decisions in free economic systems. Self-interest is often, incorrectly, regarded as synonymous with greed or selfishness. One counter-example is sufficient to show that this parallel drawn between greed and self-interest is fallacious. Every day I travel to work by train, rather than by car; and I cycle to the station rather than take a taxi. Both those decisions are motivated by self-interest, but it would be ludicrous to regard their motivation as manifestations of greed or selfishness. A market economy tends to put self-interest to good use because market transactions require agreement between transacting parties. It is in the self-interest of a shop to provide me with clean and reliable products. In other words, the shop provides for consumers by discovering what consumers wish to pay for while working in the self-interest of its own shareholders. This is an economic process wholly compatible with the natural human condition. In particular it is compatible with the Christian understanding of the human person as a being who lacks perfect knowledge and who is imperfectible. We lack the knowledge to plan centrally the allocation of economic resources effectively and, being imperfectible, it is important that our economic system ensures that the natural human desire for self-betterment is put to more general benefit.

It is worth noting that, as *Caritas in veritate* (published between the first and second editions of this book) pointed out, not all economic actions are motivated purely by self-interest. Some economic actions will be motivated by love and charity and some by a sense of reciprocity. Often all these motives will be important in particular economic actions. Philosophers and theologians can try to unravel the different motivations but, for economists, the important point is that a market economy allows people to pursue their objectives purposefully, whatever those objectives may be.

As far as economists are concerned it is especially important that, as has been noted, where self-interest (or even greed) is motivating economic action, the pursuit of one's own interests will generally be compatible with the promotion of the welfare of society as a whole. This is because voluntary exchange must benefit both parties. On the other hand, greed and self-interest pursued through the political process can be destructive because government achieves its objectives by coercion. Christian socialists seem to assume away the forces of self-interest and greed when it comes to an analysis of the political process. Yet, if we allow the state to allocate economic resources, then voters, bureaucrats and politicians who are motivated by the forces of self-interest can seek the redistribution of resources through the political system in their own interests. How often do we see a Member of Parliament campaigning for the closure of a hospital in his own constituency because it will release resources for other hospitals that may be in greater need? The allocation of economic resources through the political system can simply lead to resources being allocated to the politically powerful and the articulate. We should therefore, as Christians, seriously question a system in which 50 per cent of the income of Christian families is taken from them to be spent by a secular state. Could we not do better with that money ourselves – both to provide for our own families, but also to aid the welfare of those who are less well off than ourselves?

Thus, if we accept that the human person is imperfectible in the sense of tending to sinfulness, it is the market economy that ensures that good can come from self-interest and it is when economic power is vested in the state that self-interest and greed is at its most destructive. It is certainly wrong to decry a market economy because its actors are motivated by self-interest yet to simply ignore that possibility when considering the actions of politicians.

The issue of imperfectibility in the sense of human persons having limited cognition is also worth further discussion. Human persons are not omniscient. The knowledge that is held by economic actors cannot be centralised within government planning authorities. Government planners can never even know the objectives of individuals and voluntary communities never mind the costs and benefits of different ways of achieving those objectives. That is the lesson of the great socialist experiments but that lesson can be applied to the milder forms of socialism too. The nature of the created human person makes socialism – even in its milder forms – not just undesirable but impossible.[1]

## The market allocates resources by agreement

It is worth dwelling further on the point that the market allocates resources through voluntary contracts or agreements, yet the government allocates resources through the force of law. To

---

[1] Pennington (2010) makes this argument from a very rigorous non-religious perspective.

a Christian, the former should be intrinsically attractive. Not only is the process of voluntary contracting most compatible with free will, it also ensures that economic resources are distributed by a process of peaceful voluntary cooperation and agreement. On the other hand, the governmental and political control of economic resources results in resources being allocated through processes that can inherently lead to conflict, unless there is broad consensus in society. It is not a pretty sight to see protests by young people, farmers, the old and so on in France and other EU countries, all campaigning for more resources to be allocated to them through the political system. In the case of farmers, those resources come from the poorest people in the underdeveloped world as protectionism is used to bolster the incomes of EU farmers. Those who point to greed and materialism in the UK at the current time – and those are certainly moral issues that must be faced by all Christians – seem to forget the violent conflicts and strikes of the 1970s as groups competed for resources to be allocated to them through the political system.

## The common good, solidarity and subsidiarity

In the tradition of Catholic social teaching the fundamental purpose of public policy is the promotion of the common good or 'the sum total of social conditions which allow people, either as groups or as individuals, to reach their fulfillment more fully and more easily'.[2] This is certainly not

---

[2] *Catechism* paragraph 1906 (Catholic Church, 1994): originally from

contrary to a view that regards the most important economic functions of the state as providing the framework within which contracts and private property are enforced. Such a situation generally provides the framework within which individuals and voluntary communities can fulfil their economic, cultural and spiritual needs.

The concept of solidarity is important because individuals are born into societies with a duty to care for other members of society. Solidarity is a virtue which involves a deep-seated concern for others. Solidarity should not be a pretext for politicians to command the resources of individuals and families to create over-arching welfare states: 'Solidarity is first and foremost a sense of responsibility on the part of everyone with regard to everyone, and it cannot therefore be merely delegated to the State' (*Caritas in veritate*, 38).

The development of solidarity is, of course, an aspect of the preferential option for the poor. From the starting point that most nations find themselves in today, a thriving market economy would be the preferential option for the poor. The concentration of economic power, tendency to cartelisation and the absence of business opportunities that tends to exist in countries that suppress the market economy leads, in many cases, to utter destitution.

This is not to say that all government intervention is illegitimate. When should the government intervene to help the poor or for other purposes? Townsend, writing in Spencer and Chaplin (eds) (2009) tries to square the circle. He argues that,

*Gaudium et spes.*

when sins of omission lead to situations whereby human flourishing is impossible, the government may wish to intervene. This may include, for example, providing an income sufficient for basic needs if charity is insufficient.

There is then the question of how the government should intervene. Here, the principle of subsidiarity is helpful. A richer interpretation is required than the common interpretation that subsidiarity is the delegation of government powers to the lowest level. Instead, subsidiarity involves government intervention at the lowest level and in such a way that the intervention *helps* the lower order communities fulfil *their* legitimate objectives in the pursuit of the common good. For example, in the field of education, there is no need for the government to build and provide schools and teach everybody according to a state-controlled curriculum. Instead, the government can help the poor afford an education by contributing to the cost.

There are, of course, times in history when problems arise that appear to be the result of the free-market economy. Sometimes these problems arise because government is not performing its own legitimate functions properly. This occurs in many less-developed countries where exploitation of individuals or resources by multinational corporations can occur because governments do not fulfil their crucial roles of protecting and enforcing property rights and contracts.

But even where the outcomes of a market economy seem undesirable to a Christian, there are many possible responses. Sometimes Catholic teaching calls for moral restraint and the creation of a more Christian culture by those operating in the market. This was certainly one of the messages of *Caritas in veritate*. Such moral restraint and a Christian culture complements and supports the market economy, it does not undermine it. We should be wary of the state having too much of a role in 'creating' our culture. If we have a predominantly Christian society, a Christian culture should develop. If we do not have a predominantly Christian society and we give the state too much of a role in developing society's culture then that culture is likely to be one that is indifferent to or hostile to Christianity. Government needs to leave room for culture to evolve and to breathe. Christians would do well to spend more time influencing their culture rather than influencing government to influence their culture.

## Distinction between the free economy and the market economy and the relationship to the 'Big Society'

The authors of this book are also keen to stress the 'depth' of the market economy. We sometimes think of the market economy as a simple process of earning and then spending on consumer goods. This is unfortunate. Economics is not about consumption or about producing the maximum number of material goods at the minimum price. Economics seeks to explain how human action leads to the use of scarce resources to fulfil our needs and desires. The economic sphere is, of course, distinct from the religious sphere, but the former goes far deeper than the pursuit of material satisfaction. It is legitimate to use economics to seek to examine why South Korea is a producer of cars for export and New Zealand is a producer of lamb for export and why they may then trade with each other. But economics is also a subject that can be used to examine other forms of decision. The decisions to home-school rather than to work longer hours to earn money to pay school fees or to help out at the local Scout troop rather than going to watch horse-racing also have economic aspects to them. There may be a moral, charitable, reciprocal and altruistic dimension to such decisions too, but they are decisions about how we use our scarce resources in the pursuit of our legitimate ends.

Again, it was H. B. Acton who described how the market economy appears much shallower than it really is, or should be, because of the expansion of the remit of the state. For example, between one third and one half of the population have decisions about housing, pensions, unemployment and disability insurance and many other essential services taken for them by the state in the UK. For over 90 per cent of the population decisions in relation to healthcare and education are taken by the state. It is no wonder that, for so many people, a market economy looks like a process of earning money for conspicuous consumption: we are not allowed to take decisions about how we provide for less overtly material needs.

We should ask whether taking away responsibility from families for essential services such as education, healthcare, savings, insurances and housing actually undermines the development and flourishing of the human person. It certainly prevents the market economy from deepening and intertwining with the structures of voluntary communities to the extent that it could. This makes the market economy appear to be a much cruder institution than it really is and, arguably, limits the capacity of communities to provide for their most important needs. This was a theme that was taken up – at least implicitly – in *Caritas in veritate*. For the same reasons, as has been noted, it is important that the state does not try to supplant those good things that are provided by a sound culture in a developed society.

We could summarise this problem by suggesting that there should be a large free economy outside the market economy. It is perhaps this free economy outside the market economy that ought to comprise the 'Big Society' that the current UK government wishes to develop (though the current government's policies are rather interventionist in that the government seems to want to 'organise' the big society).

Nevertheless debates between Christians on the appropriate scope of the market and the domain of the state in economic life are legitimate. The Catholic Church and scripture certainly do not exhibit a bias in favour of the use of socialised, political mechanisms to achieve the sorts of objectives (protection of the poor, provision of health and education, and so on) that Christian communities and others hold dear. Indeed, political mechanisms should be regarded as a last resort when other mechanisms have failed. In the words of the recently published *Compendium of the Social Doctrine of the Church*: 'Experience shows that the denial of subsidiarity, or its limitation in the name of an alleged democratization or equality of all members of society, limits and sometimes even destroys the spirit of freedom and initiative ... state action in the economic sphere should also be withdrawn when the special circumstances that necessitate it end' (Pontifical Council for Justice and Peace, 2005: paras 187 and 188). There is legitimate debate to be had on what those special circumstances are and when they have ended. The authors of this book make an important contribution to that debate.

## Mercy, compassion and the market

Given the central part that mercy and compassion play in Christian social relationships, I have sometimes been asked what role there is for mercy and compassion within a free economy. Economic action can have many motivations as was discussed in *Caritas in veritate*. It can be motivated by self-interest, charity or reciprocity. Sometimes all these motivations can be present and it is difficult to untangle which is dominant.

It is difficult to understand how mercy and compassion can be at the heart of economic action when governments are responsible for resource allocation. Compassion means to 'suffer with' and mercy often involves the suspension of the normal principles of justice. Sometimes this might be appropriate (for example, when letting somebody out of prison towards the end of their life). However, when a government employee

42

takes a decision that appears to be motivated by mercy or compassion, it is not the decision-taker who bears the consequences but other (normally unseen) individuals in society. For example, if there is legislation that prevents banks foreclosing on bad debts in a recession, the shareholders of the banks will bear the cost (who are, for example, potential pensioners) and they may be pushed into penury as a result. If politicians wish to raise taxes to assist the poor, they cannot be said to be exercising mercy or compassion because the suffering is borne by others (taxpayers). The politicians may be right or wrong to help the poor in this way, but mercy and compassion are not being exercised.

For this reason, mercy and compassion are exceptional acts in the context of government – that is not a criticism of government, merely an observation that government has a particular function which does not, in general, involve the exercise of mercy and compassion. Actors within a free economy can, however, exercise mercy and compassion liberally. They will not always do so, but they are always free to do so; on the other hand government servants are not free to exercise mercy and compassion liberally – their role is generally to deliver justice. Indeed, in a free economy, mercy and compassion are exercised more than we might think. Every person who gives up a lucrative career to help a housebound relative, for example, is exercising compassion.

The acts of mercy and compassion are not just individual decisions. Such acts can also be taken by communities acting freely, with those communities freely choosing to bear the costs of those actions (for example, a local church community may choose to help pay off the debts of an indebted widow or give huge amounts of time or money to victims of an earthquake). Mercy and compassion can be community acts but, to be genuine acts of compassion and mercy, they should be acts that are freely undertaken by people who, by and large, bear the responsibility for the decision to help others in this way.

## New expressions of 'distributism'

In recent years, distributism has become fashionable again within policy circles. The most well known proponent is Anglican Phillip Blond. This view tends to hold that both a free economy and the government sector of the economy tend towards monopoly and undermine communities: both business and government become more distant from those they should be serving, it is argued.

It is difficult to see the rationale for this thesis both in theory and in practice. Certainly, government is able to create enduring monopolies because it relies on coercion and can put its own service providers in a privileged position. For example, those who do not wish to use state education have to pay fully for private education despite receiving state education free at the point of use. On the other hand, most private businesses have to ensure that they attract customers from alternative providers. Of course, there are examples of industries that tend towards a situation of predominance of large suppliers – though not, in general, monopolies with anything like the coverage of the UK National Health Service. Big companies are important in a market economy, but that does not mean that their market power is unchallenged. Companies that are household names in one generation are rarely household names two generations later.

Secondly, there seems to be confusion in the minds of distributists between 'monopoly' and 'bigness' which ignores 'market definition' – a crucial concept in competition economics. One of their proposals, for example, is to penalise supermarkets to help local high street shops. Such high street shops are often monopolies in the context of a very small market. Large supermarkets, on the other hand, may be very large companies which serve huge markets whilst competing with other supermarkets.

Thirdly, distributists tend to be vague in terms of their policy prescriptions and assume away the 'knowledge problem' which Christians ought to understand very acutely. If, for example, large supermarkets are penalised for the benefit of small shops, how do we know that this will increase human flourishing? It may, on the other hand, reduce the time people are able to spend with their families by making shopping less efficient; increase the time that people spend working to pay higher food prices; reduce employment opportunities for the unskilled; and so on. In a market economy, people can express their preference for the sorts of institutions that distributists admire by paying higher prices if they wish.

Finally, it is generally the case that the types of commercial institutions that distributists admire waned because of government intervention. This is not the only reason for their diminishing importance but the academic evidence suggests that it is a very important reason. In fact, distributists do accept that the state has tended to take over the functions of community-based and non-profit institutions in the field of welfare provision. But, in the field of finance, the state has had a much more subtle – though equally important – role that is simply not recognised by distributists. Here, the academic evidence suggests that the increase in financial regulation has undermined mutual in favour of proprietary ownership. This is because mutuals often existed to resolve conflicts of interest that are now resolved by regulation. The implicit state guarantees to large financial institutions also make the evolution of large financial institutions almost inevitable.

To many formerly socialist-sympathising Catholic NGOs, distributism seems like an acceptable 'middle way'. To the extent that distributism has helped such people become sceptical of the 'big state' it may have played a useful function. However, there is a lack of cogent economic analysis and certainly a lack of detailed understanding of economic history that seems to underlie the position of the distributists. There are other criticisms that could be made too (see Woods, 2005). In particular, many of their policy prescriptions could lead markets to be much more 'exclusive' institutions with fewer opportunities for 'outsiders' arising from free competition. However, to be fair to the modern distributists, represented by thinkers such as Phillip Blond, this is not such a strong characteristic at it was in the thinking of earlier generations of distributists.

## The main themes

The book is divided into three main parts, preceded by two introductory chapters (including this one). All the chapters are self-contained and can be read individually without reference to earlier or later chapters.

The next introductory chapter, by Kishore Jayabalan, summarises the main themes of Catholic social teaching before briefly describing the contents of the main social encyclicals. This is an invaluable introduction to the topic.

The first part of the book is entitled 'Economic welfare and the role of the state'. It consists of chapters by Father Robert Sirico on welfare, Philip Booth on foreign aid, Thomas Woods on the just wage and Philip Booth on taxation and the role of the state. These chapters examine specific policy issues on which Christians often wish to speak from a moral perspective, informed by economics.

The just wage is an issue that has concerned Christians for many centuries. There are several aspects of this subject. Should businesses be forced by law to pay a minimum wage? Do businesses have a moral obligation to provide a living wage? If businesses do not pay a living wage, should income enhancements to the poor be given through transfers via the state? Woods concludes that mandating a minimum wage simply harms the people it is intended to help. It might be desired by some to assume away the economic laws that lead to this being the case, but it is not within our power to do so. We should have more humility than that!

The second part is on 'Business, the consumer

and culture in Christian life'. The ills of materialism surround us in very obvious ways and these are discussed by Andrew Yuengert in the first chapter in this section. Capitalism is very effective in providing material goods. This provides moral challenges to Christians as consumers because we can become materialistic in outlook. But it is simply shirking moral responsibility to resolve this problem by undermining the enterprise economy. Indeed, materialism is not specific to an enterprise economy. Socialist systems are explicitly materialistic as they attempt to raise the condition of the person through the provision of material goods. Those who allocate resources within socialist systems are not, of course, immune to the temptations of materialism. Thus, we have to think of materialism as being intrinsically a moral rather than a political problem. As such, the problem should be addressed by moral and cultural renewal rather than, in the first place, by recourse to the political system. It is important that the political sphere allows more space for the cultural sphere to assist us in making sound moral choices.

The second chapter in this section is a wider examination of the contributions and responsibilities of business by Robert Kennedy. Businesses, like entrepreneurs, are essential components of the economic system. They allow individuals to use their talents creatively to fulfil their own needs and the needs of others. We should recognise the immense contribution that business activity has made to economic and social well-being and not restrain it from performing its vital functions. Nevertheless, Christian business people have a particular moral calling which they should not ignore. They cannot allow materialistic motives to override their consciences.

Father Anthony Percy writes about entrepreneurship. We often think about the needs of workers in our prayers and when considering policy issues, but what about the needs of entrepreneurs? Just as some workers struggle to make ends meet, entrepreneurs struggle too. In addition, they take risks; they frequently cannot find unemployment insurance; and they rarely have their positions 'protected' by regulation. Entrepreneurs face the same moral dilemmas as workers – should I open the shop on a Sunday if much of my trade is at the weekend? Entrepreneurs, like other workers, have to decide whether to work harder and spend less time with their families. Presumably St Joseph was an entrepreneur. Entrepreneurs are, of course, workers too, but there are other aspects of their vocation that we should consider. We should pray for entrepreneurs; we should think about their needs in our church community and the special contribution they can make; and we should consider their needs when formulating economic policy. Entrepreneurship is, indeed, a noble vocation. On the whole, when entrepreneurs become rich, they have done so by taking risks and providing goods and services of value to the community. Of course, many entrepreneurs, having become rich by meeting the needs of consumers, then further help society by giving away their wealth to others.

Philip Booth examines environmental problems in the context of the principles of subsidiarity and solidarity. Radical environmental movements are often anti-Christian in their underlying principles yet receive support from Christian voters. Booth proposes a way in which policy towards environmental issues can be developed from Catholic social thinking.

In the following chapter, Michael Miller examines the topic of 'corporate social responsibility' (CSR). Secular treatments of CSR tend to be value-free and often simply give carte blanche to managers to pursue objectives that are not shared by the owners of businesses. Michael Miller proposes a different way forward, arguing that one of the responsibilities of business is to make the case for the market economy as well as to behave in an objectively morally right manner. It might be thought that businesses need no encouragement to make the case for the market economy! On the contrary, however, large businesses in particular often prefer the market economy to be regulated to reduce competition and entry by small firms; alternatively, they petition the government for implicit or explicit subsidies; or promote forms of crony capitalism. In many respects it is the market that is the preferential option for the poor. As such, business has a responsibility to make the case for the market economy whilst behaving ethically – even if it is not in the self interest of particular businesses.

Dennis O'Keeffe examines the role of the Catholic school in passing on the faith, including the way in which Catholic schools communicate the Church's teaching. He suggests that Catholic schools are not necessarily valued these days because they are Catholic but because they are successful in human terms – providing a good education, a safe environment, and so on. Catholic schools have an important role in shaping culture, however, which itself has been noted as being important in shaping the space in which business and the consumer operate. The teaching materials exist today to help Catholic schools to do a better job in shaping a vital Catholic culture, but Dennis O'Keeffe is not convinced that schools can do this given the current institutional framework within which they operate.

One area where questions have been raised about the moral context in which market participants operate in recent years relates to the financial sector. Indeed, *Caritas in veritate* addressed these issues in part. The last chapter in this section deals with the financial crash.

The final part of this book, 'Subsidiarity and solidarity: the role of the individual, the community and the state', discusses the basic principles that were important in analysing the specific issues covered in Part One and Part Two. In doing so, it acts as a conclusion to the book.

This part begins with a new chapter written for the second edition on the social teaching of Pope Benedict XVI. This chapter contains important insights into the thinking of Pope Emeritus Benedict XVI that permeated his writing in *Deus caritas est, Caritas in veritate* and in many homilies and other writings.

Denis O'Brien's chapter on subsidiarity and solidarity makes several important points. The higher structures in society (local government, central government and, in the case of the UK, the European Union) do not exist to supplant the will of the lower structures (individuals, families, voluntary associations and communities), still less to pursue their own aims. The higher structures of government exist to serve the subsidiary structures in the pursuit of the latter's own legitimate aims. Thus, for example, governments should not provide education except, perhaps, as an absolute last resort. Rather, they should assist families, if it is necessary to do so, in obtaining education for their children. This is very different from the concept of subsidiarity that is supposed to operate within the European Union, where the higher governmental structures determine aims and then are supposed to require the lower structures to pursue those aims. O'Brien also examines documents produced by the England and Wales Bishops' Conference and finds that they do not give the same emphasis to subsidiarity that is evident from papal encyclicals. Furthermore, the England and Wales hierarchy's understanding of solidarity often seems to bypass the most crucial vehicles of solidarity – the family, voluntary associations and the community – and jump straight to the state. It thus frequently recommends political action at the highest level of government, including the EU level, when sound economic analysis and the application of the principle of subsidiarity would recommend a different course. O'Brien has strong words to say about the public statements of the England and Wales Bishops' Conference. Not all will agree with those strong words. Nevertheless, an examination of documents produced by the Conference certainly suggests that more careful thinking on economic issues might lead to different policy prescriptions. It is worth noting that, since the drafting of this chapter for the first edition, the Bishops' Conference of England and Wales produced a document to inform debate in the 2010 general election which was much more analytically rigorous than previous documents.

Finally, the second chapter by Sam Gregg specifically deals with the question of the role of the state, the community and the individual as defined and discussed in Catholic social teaching. He stresses the crucial importance of the state keeping within its own legitimate space to prevent it from crushing the development of other instruments of socialisation. A large state will also prevent human flourishing. The state is an imperfect instrument, so a belief in God, argues Gregg, must lead us to believe that the power of the state should be limited because the 'infinite necessarily limits the finite'.

Overall, these contributions, by learned scholars from three continents, provide fresh thinking and challenge the paradigm within which so many of these issues are currently considered.

## References

Acton, H. B. (1993), *The Morals of Markets and Related Essays*, Indianapolis, IN: Liberty Fund.

Charles, R. (1998), *Christian Social Witness and Teaching: The Catholic Tradition from Genesis to Centesimus Annus*, Leominster: Gracewing.

Pennington, M. (2010), *Robust Political Economy: classical liberalism and the future of public policy*, Cheltenham: Edward Elgar.

Pontifical Council for Justice and Peace (2005), *Compendium of the Social Doctrine of the Church*, London: Burns & Oates.

Spencer, N. and J. Chaplin (eds), (2009), *God and Government*, London, UK: SPCK.

Townsend N. (2009), 'Government and social infrastructure', in Spencer N. and J. Chaplin (eds), *God and Government*, London, UK: SPCK,.

Woods, T. E., Jr (2005), *The Church and the Market: A Catholic Defense of the Free Economy*, Lanham, MD: Lexington.

## Annexe: a note on referencing

All the chapters in this book were written independently. All authors have used the same framework for referencing. Many of the references that are discussed by a number of authors cannot easily be listed in a standard way, however. While the editor has tried to maintain consistency, he has not wished to stand in the way of an author expressing himself in his own style, and thus there are some minor inconsistencies in referencing. Major papal and Church documents are not listed in the references at the end of each chapter. They have been introduced within each chapter in which they are mentioned. Subsequent references to such documents within chapters are then generally made by the document's initials rather than the full title. References are given to the paragraph numbers of such major papal and other Church documents. In the Appendix there is then a list of all the major papal and other related documents, with the date of publication and author (where appropriate), as well as a note of where they can be obtained free of charge. It was felt that this approach would allow the reader to have access to a list of all the major papal and related documents in one place within the text. Different authors have quoted from different versions of Church documents, thus there will be slight differences in quotations. For example, some versions from which authors quote are in American rather than British English.

## 2

# THE CATHOLIC SOCIAL ENCYCLICAL TRADITION

*Kishore Jayabalan*

The body of teaching by the Catholic Church on social and economic matters is alternatively called Catholic social teaching or Catholic social doctrine.[1] This teaching is developed primarily in encyclical letters of the Pope, addressed to his brother bishops all over the world, the Catholic lay faithful and sometimes to 'all people of good will'. The first social encyclical was published by Pope Leo XIII in 1891, with subsequent encyclicals often coming on anniversaries and dealing with similar themes as those raised by Leo.[2] Leo did not,

---

[1] The terms 'Catholic social teaching' and 'Catholic social doctrine' are generally interchangeable, though one could assert that social teaching pre-dates the modern era and originates in Christ's commandment to love God and neighbour, with the official doctrine formulated more recently. It is worth noting that the Church speaks of social and economic rather than political; the former would seem to be sub-political and less determinative, if we mean political in the widest sense of the word, as opposed to partisan. As will be seen, ideological and partisan categories originating from the French Revolution such as 'right' and 'left' are very difficult to apply to Church teaching as a whole, which is not to say that there are no partisan interpretations of the teaching by the partisans themselves. On some issues, the teaching will seem 'progressive', on others, 'reactionary', but it will always remain Christian if it takes the Gospels' as its source.

[2] An unexamined question in this paper is what makes a particular encyclical

---

however, invent this social teaching; he developed what the Church had taught on society from its origins into a more coherent body, and it is the cumulative nature of Catholic social teaching that other popes have built upon, now comprising a 'doctrine'. It is therefore fitting to speak of the tradition of these encyclicals, through which the papacy has applied long-standing principles on human nature and public life to (often rapidly) changing circumstances, a reading of 'the signs of the times' by the popes.

This chapter will highlight the main points of this tradition by putting forth the most salient principles of Catholic social teaching and then presenting a summary of each of the social encyclicals, ranging from Pope Leo's *Rerum novarum* (1891) to Pope Benedict XVI's *Caritas in veritate* (2009). Because of this chapter's summary nature, there is no way to present all the historical circumstances that make up the background of the papal letters, especially since some of the encyclicals only implicitly refer to these circumstances. But it is still necessary to place the encyclicals in their historical context in order to give the reader some idea of the motivation of the popes to address this or that particular issue, and how Catholic social doctrine has developed over time.

---

'social', in as much as any papal document on public matters would be based on the Church's social teaching. This is particularly true of many of Leo's 'non-social' encyclicals, several of John Paul II's, and the first two of Benedict XVI's pontificate. The most commonly used classification of social encyclicals completely neglects Pius XII's writings, including those on the threat of Nazism, a neglect for which the Church has paid a great price in the realm of popular opinion.

## What is an encyclical?

Before looking at the basic principles of Catholic social teaching, one should understand what an encyclical letter is. As the name suggests, it is a letter 'circulated' by the Pope, usually to the other Catholic bishops of the world. The main audience for encyclicals has been the world's Catholic bishops due to their authority and duty to spread the encyclical's teachings within their own dioceses. Gradually, popes have expanded the 'official' audience, that is, those explicitly mentioned on the title page of the letter, to the lay faithful and even those outside the Church. The growth of modern communications has made it much easier for the encyclicals to reach a wider audience across the globe, as has the Church's interest in inter-religious, inter-denominational and cultural (i.e. including the world of non-believers) affairs. Most importantly of all, the main reason the encyclicals are addressed to a universal audience is the original mandate given by Jesus Christ to the apostles to make believers of all nations of the earth. Social teaching is, therefore, an integral part of and in the service of the Church's evangelical mission.[3]

Encyclicals are just one means of expressing papal teaching on a variety of matters; there are also instruments such as Apostolic Constitutions, Apostolic Exhortations, and Apostolic Letters or

---

[3] See: 'The Church's Mission and Social Doctrine', chapter 2 in Pontifical Council for Justice and Peace (2005), pp. 33–60. All citations from the *Catechism of the Catholic Church*, various papal encyclicals and other Church documents taken from the English version of the Vatican website: www.vatican.va

Motu Proprios (meaning 'on his own impulse'). Encyclical letters tend to have wide-ranging themes and are less concerned with a particular matter of internal Church governance, which makes them a more appropriate vehicle for transmitting the Church's social teaching. All encyclicals are written in the Pope's name, regardless of whether the Pope himself is the original author of the text or whether there have been other contributors and consultants involved. The encyclicals have Latin titles that are usually taken from the first words of the letter and have some significance to the occasion or subject matter of the letter.

The principles enunciated in these letters form a part of the ordinary magisterium of the Church. The 'ordinary magisterium' is the body of teaching of the Catholic Church exercised by the Pope and the bishops, either separately or in unison. It is distinguished from the 'extraordinary magisterium', which is issued specifically *ex cathedra* solely on matters of faith and morals, concerning divine revelation, by the Pope or by the Pope and bishops in unison, and is by definition infallible, requiring the 'full assent of faith' of Catholics. Specific teachings of the ordinary magisterium may or may not be infallible, depending on the doctrine in question. They are infallible when they are so defined, taught definitively, or belong to 'the inheritance of the deposit of faith'. They must also be 'universal': i.e. not issued solely by a local bishop but by all bishops in unison and in union with the Pope. Non-infallible teachings of the ordinary magisterium are considered authoritative and require the 'religious submission of intellect and will' of Catholics. It would appear that the principles of most social teachings of the Church fall under this latter category. [4]

As a part of the Church's ordinary magisterium and in the service of the Church's evangelical mission, social encyclicals are emphatically not works of political science, economics or social theory, though the teachings will have some impact on these and many other 'secular' subjects. Encyclicals are the result of the Church's theological and philosophical reflections over the centuries, some of which may have been disputed at some point in history but have since become settled teaching. Once again, it is the Church's universal scope and mission to invest all aspects of human life with Christ's saving grace that is the primary motive for the writing of these encyclicals and the propagation of social teaching.

Over time, the objectives of social encyclicals came to be more precisely defined. By 'providing principles for reflection, criteria for judgment and directives for action',[5] the encyclicals are meant to help Christians and others build a more just, fraternal society that reflects God's love of man and our subsequent duty to love God and neighbour. The encyclicals do not endorse any particular order as *the* Catholic model or propose a 'third way' between liberalism and socialism. Instead, Catholic

---

[4] See: Second Vatican Council Dogmatic Constitution on the Church, *Lumen gentium*, n. 25., Congregation for the Doctrine of the Faith, Doctrinal Commentary on the Concluding Formula of the *Professio fidei*, n. 9.

[5] Congregation for the Doctrine of the Faith, *Instruction on Christian Freedom and Liberation, Libertatis conscientia*, n. 72, Paul VI, Apostolic Letter, *Octogesima adveniens*, n. 4; John Paul II, Encyclical Letter, *Sollicitudo rei socialis*, n. 41.

social teaching presents itself as a 'leaven' in society, a soul or animating principle in a living body. The 'worldly' or secular application of many of these principles can and does vary, and is therefore the particular responsibility of the lay people who have the necessary expertise and authority to apply the teachings to particular realities.

## Basic principles of Catholic Social Teaching

There is some debate within academic circles as to the number of principles contained in Catholic social teaching, but there is general agreement on these four basic ones: human dignity; the common good; subsidiarity; and solidarity.[6] All the social encyclicals make explicit or implicit references to these principles.

The importance of human dignity is the result of every human person being created in the image and likeness of God. Every human person is endowed with a spiritual and immortal soul, reason and free will; the human person is a unity made up of the material (body) and the spiritual (soul).[7] This dignity is further enhanced by the Incarnation of Jesus Christ: God became man, took on human flesh and was like other men in all things but sin. Christ's redemptive sacrifice for all men in all times also carries great importance for the Catholic understanding of human dignity – all people have

---

[6] Additional principles often mentioned are the universal destination of created goods; the preferential option for the poor; and participation. See Pontifical Council for Justice and Peace (2005), ~ Chapter 4, 'Principles of the Church's Social Doctrine'. Most of these can be derived from one or more of the four principles dealt with in this chapter.

[7] See Catholic Church (1994) pp. 355–384.

been redeemed by Christ through no merit on their part: therefore human dignity is a fact of nature, a God-given gift, and is explicitly not the result of the use of reason, free will, a healthy body, or other qualities.

While human dignity has this ontological dimension, it also has a moral one: dignity is enhanced and further realised by the practice of virtue by 'embodied persons' who are not simply thinking, willing autonomous beings but ones created for a final end – eternal life in union with God the creator of all.[8] As a result, Christian instruction and exhortation are a necessary aspect of Christian moral and social teaching, which aims at character formation in conjunction with the moral law and with the help of grace that comes as a gift from God, as well as the structural reform of society that will inevitably be carried out by these same persons. Human dignity is therefore a given as well as a calling; while all human persons have inherent dignity, not everything humans do is necessarily 'dignified' and therefore worthy of acceptance and respect.[9]

The common good is the end of all political life and results from the social nature of man. The Second Vatican Council defined the common good as 'the sum total of social conditions which allow people, either as groups or as individuals, to reach

---

[8] See Benestad (2011) pp. 35–51.
[9] Sin in all its forms is the most obvious example. In theological terms, God desires that all people be saved, despite our own sins and defects, which God understands and forgives. But due to our freedom and pride, not everyone accepts God's invitation; some are therefore damned by their own refusal of God's mercy.

their fulfilment more fully and more easily',[10] with the implicit understanding that this fulfilment is ultimately spiritual and transcendental. The spiritual aspect makes this notion of the common good a substantial one, rather than an instrumental good that serves a collection of individual interests of material well-being and happiness. Given its spiritual end, the realisation of the common good is not entrusted solely to political authority but involves all members of society and the Church itself.

The principle of subsidiarity states that 'the true aim of all social activity should be to help individual members of the social body, but never to destroy or absorb them ... It is wrong to withdraw from the community and commit to the community at large what private enterprise and industry can accomplish themselves'.[11] Subsidiarity has both a negative (the community should not interfere) and a positive function (help, *subsidium*, is required from the community when individuals cannot accomplish their legitimate goal). Always these goals should be understood in the context of the pursuit of the common good. It therefore opposes *laissez-faire* individualism and social Darwinism, as well as unrestrained bureaucratic centralisation in social and political life; it promotes self-government along with individual and social responsibility. The opposition to individualism does not necessarily imply opposition to particular forms of government characterised, for example, by very

---

[10] Second Vatican Council, Pastoral Constitution of the Church in the Modern World, *Gaudium et spes*, n. 26.
[11] Pius XI, Encyclical Letter, *Quadragesimo anno*, n. 79.

limited regulation. Rather, it implies opposition to the idea that the pursuit of individual freedom is the only end of political society and opposition to an individualistic moral attitude within society.

Solidarity is a moral virtue defined as the 'firm and persevering determination to commit oneself to the common good'.[12] It is based on the unity of the human family, irrespective of nation, race or class, and widens the notion of civic friendship found in cohesive societies to a universal level: while our primary responsibilities are to those closest to us, they are not limited by affinity or proximity. It is perfected by the gift of self, whereby persons find their fulfilment in love of and service to others.[13]

## Summary of the social encyclicals

### *Rerum novarum* 'On New Things' (1891)

In terms of sheer authorship, Pope Leo XIII had one of the most prolific pontificates in history, writing 86 encyclicals during his reign of over 25 years. He followed the contentious papacy of Pius IX and the violent Church-States battles in the wake of the French Revolution and the Italian Risorgimento. Rather than trying to regain papal political power (which would have been difficult as a 'prisoner of the Vatican' as the Pope was called at the time), Leo emphasised his teaching authority, of which *Rerum novarum* is perhaps the most prominent example.

The 'new things' referred to in the title are the social changes brought about by the industrial revolution, and especially the plight of the working

---

[12] John Paul II, Encyclical Letter, *Sollicitudo rei socialis*, n. 38.
[13] *Gaudium et spes*, n. 24.

classes, which became known as 'the social question'. These workers often left the stable – if stagnant – rural lives, where Church and extended family and social relations comprised the norm, for more solitary lives in the crowded urban settings of manufacturing industries. Karl Marx's critique of industrial Britain launched the revolutionary movement of Marxism, which threatened not only industrial capitalism but also the Christian faith, already under siege from the more stridently anti-theological liberals and industrial modernisers. Marx and his followers called religion the 'opiate of the masses' that needed to be eradicated if 'false consciousness' was to be overcome and truly revolutionary change was to take place.

While Leo clearly recognised the social misery that came with the Industrial Revolution, he also condemned the errors of socialism, namely, the eradication of private property and the institutions of marriage, the family and organised religion in the name of the working classes. Leo went so far as to call the right to property 'sacred and inviolable',[14] a stronger defence than the one made by St Thomas Aquinas,[15] which had been traditional Church teaching for several centuries. The threat posed by socialism was so grave as to justify an extremely liberal stance on property. *Rerum novarum* also criticised the notion of class conflict that formed the basis of Marxist thought. That the interests of capitalists, i.e. the owners of

---

[14]  Leo XIII, Encyclical Letter, *Rerum novarum*, n. 46.
[15]  Thomas Aquinas, *Summa Theologica*, II-II q. 66. See Fortin, 'Sacred and Inviolable: Rerum Novarum and Natural Rights' in Benestad (eds) (1996) pp. 191–222.

the means of production, and workers would be in permanent opposition deeply contradicted the principle of solidarity and the unity of the human family. Instead Leo emphasised the dignity of the worker and the complementarity of labour and capital. Both Marxism and certain versions of liberalism relied on a heavily materialistic and atheistic view of human nature which was opposed to the Christian view of man and which Catholic social teaching could not but reject.

### *Quadragesimo anno* 'The Fortieth Year' (1931)

Pope Pius XI began the tradition of commemorating *Rerum novarum* with a social encyclical of his own, *Quadragesimo anno*, in 1931. The encyclical is best known for its definition of the principle of subsidiarity that would come to be a bedrock principle of Catholic social teaching.[16] Writing during the popular movement fostered by Benito Mussolini in Italy, Pius contrasted Christian solidarism with fascist corporatism. He qualified Leo's defence of property and returned to a more Thomistic understanding by referring to property's social function, while also bluntly stating that 'no one can be at the same time a good Catholic and a true socialist'.[17] All the good promised by socialism (equality, solidarity) was already contained in Christianity, while all the bad in it (materialism, no recognition of the person or property) is directly opposed to Church teaching.

---

[16] See note 11 above.
[17] Pius XI, Encyclical Letter, *Quadragesimo anno*, n. 120.

*Mater et magistra* 'Mother and Teacher' (1961)

For the seventieth anniversary of *Rerum novarum*, Pope John XXIII looked at new aspects of the social question first raised by Leo: specifically, how the problems faced by the working classes in Europe took on an international scope and merged with the problems of developing countries. Issues such as agriculture, transportation, communications and health found their way into a Catholic social encyclical for the first time. John XXIII was especially prescient in warning about the temptation to resort to population control measures to 'fix' the problem of development by limiting the rights and freedoms of the poor.[18]

*Pacem in terris* 'Peace on Earth' (1963)

In *Pacem in Terris*, John XXIII became the first pope to address a social encyclical not only to the bishops, priests and religious and lay faithful of the Catholic Church but also to 'all men of good will'. This expansion of the audience showed that the Pope recognised not only the growing interdependence of countries in the 20th century and the global voice of the papacy, but also that social encyclicals could serve as evangelical tools by bringing the message of Christ to those outside the Church. The encyclical expanded the notion of the common good beyond the local or national level and spoke of a universal common good that would also require some kind of a universal political authority for direction and

---

[18] John XXIII's warnings about the population control movement were soon confirmed by secular economists such as Julian Simon and Peter Bauer, who criticised the reigning orthodoxy in development economics for failing to credit human creativity and ingenuity as the solution to poverty.

order. John XXIII reiterated Catholic teaching on human rights by tying them to human duties and responsibilities to others and to the moral order. His concern for authority and order can also been seen in the encyclical's passages on disarmament and deterrence, and his recognition of the serious moral problems of communism.

### *Gaudium et spes* 'Joy and Hope' and *Dignitatis humanae* 'Human Dignity' (1965)

While these two documents are not social encyclicals authored by an individual pope, they are considered important developments of Catholic social teaching by the Second Vatican Council. *Gaudium et spes*, also known as the Pastoral Constitution of the Church in the Modern World, emphasised the importance of Christian anthropology as the basis for Catholic social teaching, while *Dignitatis humanae* examined the roots and consequences of human dignity, especially with regard to religious freedom. Both developed the principle of the primacy of the human person and the role of individual conscience in the Church's social doctrine, combining a subjective understanding of human experience with the objective requirements of the common good and the natural law. The Second Vatican Council also coined the term 'universal call to holiness' to insist that all the faithful, including those who were tasked with putting social teaching into practice and not limited to priests and religious, could reach Christian perfection in their fulfilment of their daily tasks.[19]

---

[19] Cf. Second Vatican Council, Dogmatic Constitution of the Church, *Lumen gentium*, chapter V.

### *Populorum progressio* 'The Progress of Peoples' (1967)

Pope Paul VI, whose pontificate began as the Second Vatican Council was taking place, penned his first social encyclical on the theme of integral human development. In using this term, the Pope hoped to expand the scope of discussion among international development agencies, which was normally limited to material living standards in the aggregate and neglected the spiritual and religious dimension of the human person. Like John XIII before him, Paul VI strongly criticised the population control movement, which pushed the neo-Malthusian ideology that population growth would necessarily outstrip the earth's resources and humans' ability to develop adequately. In an era of rapid de-colonisation, the Pope also called for increased foreign aid from richer to poorer countries, not only as reparations for past injustices but also as a manifestation of charity towards the poor. That foreign aid could be the vehicle for population control and other ideological schemes and aid's deleterious effects on economic development were not examined, making *Populorum progressio* one of the more controversial social encyclicals to date.[20]

### *Octogesima adveniens* 'The Eightieth Year' (1971)

Officially an apostolic letter rather an encyclical, *Octogesima adveniens* recalled the legacy of *Rerum novarum* on its eightieth anniversary and continued

---

[20] See, for example, Peter Bauer, 'Ecclesiastical Economics: Envy Legitimized' in Bauer (2000) and Robert Royal, 'Reforming International Development: Populorum Progressio', in Weigel and Royal (eds) (1993). This issue is discussed in detail elsewhere in this book.

the discussion started in *Populorum progressio* about post-colonialism and some of the prerequisites for a functioning democracy. The historically remarkable shift of the Church as a notorious opponent of liberal democracy in the 19th century to its most insightful supporter by the end of the 20th century became more apparent, especially as Catholic countries such as Spain, Portugal and their former colonies in Latin America started to move from authoritarian to democratic governments and societies.

### *Laborem exercens* 'On Human Work' (1981)

Pope John Paul II's first social encyclical on the ninetieth anniversary of *Rerum novarum* was noteworthy for several reasons. As someone whose hands knew manual labour in his native Poland, as well as being artistically and culturally astute, Pope John Paul looked at the subject of work from the inside out. Having suffered through the Nazi and Soviet occupations, he also knew how easily work can become misguided when it is based on a faulty anthropology: the Nazi slogan above the gates of Auschwitz, 'Work will set you free', and the permanent class conflict between capital and labour expounded by the Marxists came at a heavy human price in Poland and throughout central and eastern Europe. In *Laborem exercens*, John Paul developed a 'spirituality of work' and examined the 'subjective' dimension of human existence, by which work affects man's character and being. He did not shy away from appropriating the Marxist term 'alienation' to describe what happens when man is disconnected from his work. Unlike the Marxists, the encyclical revealed a rich, ethical, and deeply Catholic understanding of work, rather than putting forward a plan of social or political action.

### *Sollicitudo rei socialis* 'On Social Concern' (1987)

In his second social encyclical, John Paul II addressed a world that was still deeply divided by the Cold War but one that was about to change dramatically. This encyclical tried to bridge some of the ideological rivalries between the right to economic initiative and the common good and address the problems of thinking in terms of partisan blocs. Like his two immediate predecessors (whose names he took for his own), John Paul also avoided a narrow conception of development of the type that was often proposed by both Marxists and secular liberals. The errors of socialism would soon become evident to all, while those of secular liberalism were less apparent, as few besides John Paul were able to see at the time.

### *Centesimus annus* 'The Hundredth Year' (1991)

The hundredth anniversary of *Rerum novarum* was momentous, coming two years after the fall of the Berlin Wall, which saw the end of a divided Europe; the complete collapse of Soviet communism would follow shortly thereafter. The entire context in which modern Catholic social teaching had been situated was changing. Echoing and expanding upon the teachings of his predecessors, John Paul II ascribed the failure of socialism to its erroneous anthropology. He was able to take a new look at the virtues and vices of the liberal market economy, while reminding the world, and especially Europe, of its spiritual vocation to make good use of this hard-won political and economic freedom. *Centesimus annus* contained a scathing critique of the welfare state and the dependency it created among the poor on centralised state bureaucracies. Rather than criticising market economies or democratic governments for the misuse of freedom, John Paul instructed his readers to look to the broader ethical and cultural environment that often shapes and influences the choices made in a free society.

### *Caritas in veritate* 'Love in Truth' (2009)

Pope Benedict XVI's first social encyclical had been meant to commemorate the fortieth anniversary of Paul VI's *Populorum progressio* but was delayed two years, supposedly due to the massive financial crisis that struck the USA and Europe in 2008.[21] A document intended to revisit the subject of international development instead had to address aspects of a complicated banking crisis brought on by the crash of the sub-prime housing market in the USA and its ripple effects. This is not an easy task for specialists, let alone for one of the world's foremost theologians,

---

[21] The 40th anniversary of *Populorum progressio* would have been 2007; the financial crisis began in the second half of 2008. It is more likely that the difficulty of revisiting the issues of foreign aid and other outdated issues were responsible for much of the delay.

Joseph Ratzinger.[22] As a result, it is advisable to read *Caritas in veritate* 'theologically': Christian charity and our social activities for the poor have to be based on the truth about God and man. It should also be read in conjunction with Benedict's previous two encyclicals, *Deus caritas est* ('God is Love', published in 2005) and *Spe salvi* ('Saved in Hope', published in 2007). Though neither of those encyclicals were proper social encyclicals, each explains the relationship of theological virtues such as charity and hope to social life, and warns against becoming overly enamoured with the partial truths of human wisdom. Read accordingly, *Caritas in veritate* further develops what Pope Paul VI first called integral human development and builds upon the rich tradition of Catholic social thought.

## Future challenges in Catholic Social Teaching

The principles of Catholic social teaching have remained constant, as each pope and each encyclical are shaped by the particular strengths and weaknesses of attempts to understand the issues of the day as they are taking place. Since Catholic social teaching is constantly under development and often influenced by reigning academic and policy orthodoxies, it is worth asking, what are some of the political, social and economic trends this tradition may have to address in the near future?

---

[22] *Caritas in veritate* was especially criticised for its proposals for increased foreign aid and structural reforms of the financial industry and the United Nations. In this regard, at least, the encyclical was a worthy heir to *Populorum progressio*. At the same time, the encyclical criticised existing foreign aid programmes.

The demographic crisis would seem to be a top priority, given the great emphasis placed on the family from Leo XIII forward, and the rapidly declining global birthrate. While there is no single cause for this decline, the explanations tend to range from the industrialisation and atomisation of society, the increasing educational and professional opportunities for girls and women, and the availability of contraception, abortion, sterilisation and other medical procedures. Most of these have been subjects of Catholic encyclicals. What else can the popes, or perhaps better, the Church, do besides instruct and exhort people to respect life and the family? What kind of societal changes would have to occur to reverse these trends, which affect not only family life but also have a substantial impact on health care, long-term care for the elderly and pensions. How do these trends inform our discussion of the relative role of the state and the family and the roles of state transfers and saving in providing for health needs, pensions and personal care for the elderly?

The internationalisation of economic life, also known as globalisation, has been an increasingly important factor in the life of nations. While Catholic social teaching has traditionally defended the labour movement, workers' right to free association and collective bargaining, fewer and fewer employees are actually members of trade unions. International capital and labour flows have become more prevalent, making any kind of national or local social policy regulation more difficult to enact effectively. Catholic social teaching has traditionally highlighted the duties of the host countries as well as immigrants, multi-national corporations and foreign investors to care for the common good. This teaching will have to account for the changing expectations people have for work, leisure, family life and the faith, in the workplace and beyond.

At the time of writing, the European Union is struggling to maintain its currency union in the midst of a sovereign debt crisis affecting national governments and banks alike, and keener observers within the EU are voicing concerns over the lack of a substantial identity for Europe.[23] With the Catholic Church having moved from critic to friend of liberal democracy, what will it have to say about the future of the nation-state or other forms of political organisation? Or is the Church's support for democracy based on a more 'humanitarian', personalist, apolitical view of the world? Are there drawbacks to this approach? The differences in perspective are revealed in the different understandings of 'global governance' and 'global government'. Can there be governance without government? Where is the proper locus of political authority responsible for the universal common good? What do the alternating sentiments of apathy towards political institutions and concerns over their lack of transparency and accountability mean for self-government and global authority?

Finally, when the Catholic social encyclicals speak of human rights, they always maintain

---

[23] See Pierre Manent, 'Making Sense of the West: Political History and Political Philosophy', John Marshall lecture at Boston College, 1 November, 2011.

the close connection between rights, duties and responsibilities towards others. Yet, generation after generation, especially in but not limited to the West, has seen a steady erosion of the sense of obligation found in liberal societies and increasing demands for 'entitlements' from rent-seeking interest groups.[24] How can Catholic social teaching help correct tendencies that damage not only respect for the Church but also for society at large? In thinking about human rights, will Catholic social teaching surrender to the temptation to give the *demos* whatever it wants, whenever it wants it? Or will it perform the more unpopular but necessary function of denying the sustainability of entitlements and 'rights' that no authority can reasonably guarantee?[25]

No pope or encyclical can be expected to provide immediate answers to these questions. Future popes, using their own intellects and under the guidance of the Holy Spirit, will have to develop Catholic social doctrine accordingly, avoiding the extremes of overly-technical policy prescriptions and utopian visions of a world without sin. If there is one quality the Catholic Church has shown over the centuries, it is the ability to weather political and social storms and have her voice of moral conscience heard, if not always fully assented to by the world. Whether her message is ultimately heeded may depend as

---

[24] See Heclo (2008).
[25] See, for example, Pope Benedict's December 2011 address to the Roman Curia which refers to the loss of faith and the resulting loss of a willingness to sacrifice for others.

much on the faith and docility of the recipient as on the eloquence and *modus operandi* of the deliverer.

## References

Bauer, P. (2000), *From Subsistence to Exchange and Other Essays*, Princeton, NJ: Princeton University Press.

Benestad, J. Brian.(2011), *Church, State and Society: An Introduction to Catholic Social Doctrine*, Catholic University of America Press.

Benestad, J. Brian (ed.) (1996), *Human Rights, Virtue and the Common Good: Untimely Meditations on Religion and Politics*, Lanham, MD: USA: Rowman & Littlefield.

Catholic Church (1994), *Catechism of the Catholic Church*, London: Geoffrey Chapman.

Heclo, H. (2008), *On Thinking Institutionally*, Boulder, CO, USA: Paradigm Publishers.

Pontifical Council for Justice and Peace (2005), *Compendium of the Social Doctrine of the Church*, London: Burns & Oates.

Weigel, George, and Robert Royal (eds) (1993), *Building the Free Society: Democracy, Capitalism and Catholic Social Teaching*, Grand Rapids, MI: Wm. B. Eerdmans Publishing Co.

Part One

# ECONOMIC WELFARE AND
# THE ROLE OF THE STATE

# 3

# RETHINKING WELFARE, REVIVING CHARITY: A CATHOLIC ALTERNATIVE

*Robert A. Sirico*

## Introduction

Let us consider the topic of welfare by analogy with religious practice. In the West today, a system of religious liberty properly understood, with no entanglement in religious sectarianism by the state, is considered the system most compatible with human flourishing and the one most likely to permit a flowering of faith in society. This is a hard-won lesson, one on which there has only recently emerged a consensus that what used to be dismissed as an 'American system' is the best all-round approach to the issue of religion in society. After all, the USA is one of the most religious societies in the world, and one reason is precisely because this sector of society was left to society to develop and grow, and not left to the state.

This is a counter-intuitive conclusion. Let us say that a person who knew nothing about the modern experience sought to design a pious society where everyone attended religious worship, where there was a church near every lightly populated neighbourhood, and where there were plenty of ministers to serve people's needs. One might suppose that the political apparatus needs to be deployed on behalf of the cause: building churches, putting ministers on the payroll and enforcing a moral code on everyone through legislation.[1] A laissez-faire policy would not be the first choice, mostly for the fear that one cannot know with certainty what the outcome of free decisions will be.

This approach to religion was, after all, the historical choice that tended to prevail among Christians from the time of Constantine through the Reformation and all the way to the American experiment in religious pluralism. Who today would seriously suggest that it was theologically coherent for a Christian church to be headed, at least formally, by a head of a nation-state? Even today, remnants of the old world still survive in Europe, where there are state churches in many countries, where ministers and churches receive public subsidies, and where citizens are asked to declare their religious affiliation for the purposes of the tax rolls. Even as recently as the Second Vatican Council, the issue of religious liberty was a hotly debated topic within Catholicism.

Before the Council, much debate had been sparked by the publication of the American

---

[1] It is, however, clear that it would be very difficult for churches and religious communities to grow without a state that underpins basic constitutional and institutional elements, such as an independent judiciary and the rule of law, which are necessary for any society that does not want to lapse into anarchy.

Catholic theologian John Courtney Murray's book *We Hold These Truths* (Murray, 1960). Murray, a Jesuit priest who devoted many years of study to the American founding, the place of natural law in that founding and the role undertaken by Catholics and other Christians in shaping the theological and philosophical underpinnings of that founding, is best known for articulating a classic Christian and natural law argument for limiting the state. As Murray puts it, 'the American thesis is that government is not juridically omnipotent. Its powers are limited, and one of the principles of limitation is the distinction between state and church, in their purposes, methods, and manner of organization' (ibid.: 68).

Murray served as a theological adviser to American bishops participating in the Second Vatican Council. American bishops, ranging from Cardinal Spellman in New York to Cardinal Meyer of Chicago, were determined to see the Council address the question of religious liberty, but without leaving the Church open to the charge of endorsing religious indifferentism or the notion that anything could be justified on grounds of religious liberty. Thus it was not surprising that certain aspects of Murray's idea were taken up and authoritatively elaborated upon in the Second Vatican Council's *Pastoral Constitution on the Church in the Modern World, Gaudium et spes*, which states: 'As for public authority, it is not its function to determine the character of civilization, but rather to establish the conditions and to establish the means which are capable of fostering the life of culture among all …' (GS 59). It also notes that 'Rulers must be careful not to hamper the development of family, social or cultural groups, nor that of intermediate bodies or organizations, and not to deprive them of opportunities for legitimate and constructive activity …' (GS 75).

Though Murray's treatise on religious liberty does not discuss economic questions at any length (aside from describing the basic institutional protections necessary for property inherent in a regime respecting the natural law), his book does contain an oblique endorsement of the free economy. 'The most obvious growing end of the free society has been its business system,' Murray states. 'Behind its enormous growth', he adds, 'has lain the pressure of the people's needs, wants, desires, dreams, passions, and illusions' (Murray, 1960: 99).[2] The Catholic Church in America, Murray wrote in 1960, 'has accepted this thing which is the American economy. Her life, the life of grace, is tied to it in multiple respects'. In particular, Catholic charities and public schools are wholly dependent on the productive energies of the free market. This market has created enormous wealth, and 'a wide distribution of wealth', without

---

[2] Murray adds, however, with characteristic humility, that he 'has no competence' to engage in economic theorising. He does so only briefly, but then with an uncharacteristic lack of clarity. He uses the language of 'power' to describe the role of corporations in society which 'direct' the activities of the 'economic-political system'. These passages could be understood on behalf of economic liberty if we construe these corporations as those that enjoy a privileged legal status from the state, and thereby do indeed exercise unwarranted power. But I make no claim that this is in fact what Murray meant to describe. If he meant to suggest the corporation itself exercises 'power' merely because it provides consumers goods and services they desire, and investors a return on their savings, then he is adequately answered by Novak (1982: 237–358).

which the exercise of these Catholic virtues would be 'impossible' (ibid.: 180).[3] Murray further warns that alterations in the structure of the economy in the direction of 'state socialism' would 'subtly alter the relation of the Christian people to the institutions of the Church' (ibid.: 181).

Contrary to popular perception, Pope Benedict XVI was always thoroughly convinced of the necessity of religious liberty. Certainly the Catholic Church has always insisted that people should choose to order their freedom to the truth made known through faith and reason so that they might realise the ultimate freedom to which St Paul says all Christians are called. While Pope Benedict continued to emphasise this point to a world that commonly mistakes freedom for licence, he wrote of the 'real gift of freedom that Christian faith has brought into the world. It was the first to break the identification of state and religion and thus to remove from the state its claim to totality; by differentiating faith from the sphere of the state it gave man the right to keep secluded and reserved his or her own being with God ... Freedom of conscience is the core of all freedom' (Ratzinger, 1988: 202–3).

## The welfare issue

At this point, we may consider an analogy between religious liberty and the welfare state. It is indisputable that the obligation to care for those in need is an integral part not only of the

---

[3] As *Centesimus annus* says, 'not only is it wrong from the ethical point of view to disregard human nature, which is made for freedom, but in practice it is impossible to do so' (CA 25).

Christian faith but also of any modern notion of what it means to live in a good society. Whether the justification is based on a notion of secular justice or Christian love, hardly anyone is prepared to say that the poor ought not to be cared for, the disabled neglected, and the aged forgotten. Because of a notion of justice that seems innate to human nature, we want to live in societies where people who are victims of unfortunate circumstances are assured some modicum of care.

And yet the same points noted above about the religious sphere apply also to the welfare sphere. Many have come to believe that the only way to ensure a flourishing of such support is through an elaborate state apparatus. Throughout the West and especially in western Europe, we have created massive systems of social support for the aged, children, the disabled and many other groups perceived to be victims of society. The public is taxed heavily, bureaucracies are created, and political elections often turn on the management of these large systems of social insurance. Almost all economically advanced countries are in the throes of reforming these systems to make them less expensive and less easy to manipulate through electoral politics. But the question as to whether these systems ought to be re-thought entirely is hardly ever raised.

We are at the first stages of considering a very radical question: whether the care of the poor ought to be treated in the same way that religion in society ought to be treated: that is, as something to be kept out of politics and immunised from political intervention, not because it is a lesser social priority but rather because it is of such high social priority that we dare not permit the state to dominate this area. Just as religion flourishes best when it is left to the free association of individuals and groups, so too perhaps the care of the less well off in society ought to be the first responsibility of society to manage on its own, and with the same counter-intuitive conviction that such an approach will yield more effective systems of support.

Within Catholicism, it was John Paul II who especially emphasised and clarified the importance of freedom in this sensitive area. He wrote the following strong words in his encyclical *Centesimus annus*:

> In recent years the range of such intervention has vastly expanded, to the point of creating a new type of state, the so-called 'Welfare State.' ... excesses and abuses, especially in recent years, have provoked very harsh criticisms of the Welfare State, dubbed the 'Social Assistance State.' Malfunctions and defects in the Social Assistance State are the result of an inadequate understanding of the tasks proper to the State. Here again the principle of subsidiarity must be respected: a community of a higher order should not interfere in the internal life of a community of a lower order, depriving the latter of its functions, but rather should support it in case of need and help to coordinate its activity with the activities of the rest of society, always with a view to the common good. (CA 48)

When the state becomes the primary and first caretaker of children, through well-intentioned laws designed to enhance their welfare, it tragically reduces the responsibility of parents and the value of children to parents. A particular problem occurs when the state subsidises behaviour that should be discouraged if we want to retain strong families. A good example is out-of-wedlock births, which have dramatically increased anywhere the state has chosen to give an excess of money to women in this position. When the state intervenes in this manner, it sends a signal to fathers that it is not necessary for them to stay in their roles as husbands and fathers, resulting in an increase in single parents (usually female).

Among the vulnerable in any society are the poor, whether in our own families or in the wider community. When this issue is usually discussed, the matter of inequality of wealth inevitably arises. But it is not the issue of inequality of wealth which should concern us primarily. After all, inequality can always be reduced by making everyone equally poor. The issue is poverty itself and the human suffering that accompanies it.

After several decades of an almost obsessive concern with issues of distribution, more and more Catholics have declined to remain locked in a 1960s approach to economics and have come to realise that the best solution to material poverty is wealth creation and a growing economy. It provides jobs, better pay, better working conditions, more opportunities, and growing opportunities for everyone to achieve. A growing economy requires that the market economy be allowed to function without the kind of excessive interruption, regulation and intervention that diminishes overall wealth.

Of course, there are cases when even a growing

economy, and all its requisite institutions, leaves some people out. The causes can be many, ranging from personal misfortune to lack of initiative. A note of caution, however, should be recorded: so long as trade is voluntary, the state remains limited, and people can freely contract with each other, the cause of poverty cannot be the wealth of others, as Marxism would have us believe. That is why the temptation towards a policy of mere redistribution in the name of charity should be avoided. No benefit accrues from this policy to anyone but the radical egalitarian, whose impulses should not be allowed to drive public policy in a good and just society. Instead, we should strive to continue to expand the pie rather than fight over the various ways in which the pie can be sliced up.

## Bureaucracy does not help the poor

In thinking about ways to help the poor, the virtue of prudence suggests that we must consider the costs and benefits of various strategies. If we turn to the government as a response of first resort, particular dangers arise. Government policies can create impersonal bureaucratic institutions with which the poor will be forced to deal, which can be demeaning (Niskanen, 1973). In addition, bureaucracies have a tendency to expand their own payrolls and, as Max Weber famously detailed, pursue their own agendas of self-preservation and expansion instead of focusing on serving others. Instead of staying within fiscal constraints, they invariably take a greater and greater share of private wealth. This means that the benefits of state aid to a specific group might well be outweighed by indirect and longer-term costs to the whole community.

State bureaucracies have demonstrated a lack of ability to fully understand the nature of the problem of poverty. Bureaucracy tends to be notoriously imprecise in targeting assistance to those in need. Public agencies cannot make the necessary distinctions between legitimate need and illegitimate demands. And they tend to impose heavy burdens of debt on future generations, which are best avoided. As John Paul II explains:

> By intervening directly and depriving society of its responsibility, the Social Assistance State leads to a loss of human energies and an inordinate increase of public agencies, which are dominated more by bureaucratic ways of thinking than by concern for serving their clients, and which are accompanied by an enormous increase in spending. (CA 48)

Even the worker in the bureaucracy himself is given attention by Pope John Paul II in his first social encyclical, *Laborem exercens*:

> [Dignity is] extinguished within him in a system of excessive bureaucratic centralization, which makes the worker feel that he is just a cog in a huge machine moved from above, that he is for more reasons than one a mere production instrument rather than a true subject of work with an initiative of his own. (LE 45)

Long-term poverty is more than a condition of lacking material goods; it is a condition that involves deeper and more structural problems that require personal attention. This kind of attention is best given by individuals, families and churches rather than by agents of the state, which have all too often proved not to be the friend of the poor. That is why the assertion of rights – to a job, to healthcare, to a good living – is such a serious business. Special care should be taken to prevent open conflicts between rights. Stating that everyone has a right to a job may implicitly oblige those in a position to hire to act in a way that violates their right to economic liberty as well as the stability of their enterprise, by which others are employed.

Jesus commands his followers to be charitable. It must be exercised in accordance with his will, and nowhere does he suggest this obligation can be passed on to public employees. Nor can the obligation be discharged by lobbying the government to take on new social welfare functions. Although it may tempt some, the existence of the welfare state and various forms of social regulation is not the fulfilment of Christ's commandment to care for the poor. Indeed, forms of charity that keep people in an unnecessary dependency relationship to the state actually do more harm than good. In this case, a person following the Gospel of Christ might have an obligation to speak out against the system or programme that is the source of the problem.

Historically, the most charitable societies in the world have been the wealthiest, and the wealthiest societies have also been the most free. When people have more disposable income, they can invest more in charitable causes. Only a free economy can generate this kind of wealth. Prosperity permits people to spend more time in leisure rather than work, which allows them to spend more time volunteering for community activities and service to the poor. A free economy allows for growing levels of voluntary free time to make this possible.

Daniel M. Hungerman of Duke University provides some very revealing data to back up this intuition. Before the Great Depression and the advent of the New Deal social assistance state, the US charitable sector was immense, spending up to six times as much money on charitable services as government spent. During and after the New Deal, church benevolence fell dramatically.

> We find strong evidence that the rise in New Deal spending led to a fall in church charitable activity. Our central estimate suggests that each dollar of government relief spending in a state led to three cents less church spending. This is a small level of crowd out in dollar terms, but it is large in proportional terms, since church spending at the start of this period amounted to only 10 per cent of the ultimate size of the New Deal. Relative to this baseline, there was a crowd out of at least 30 per cent, which can explain the time series decline in church benevolence over this period. (Gruber and Hungerman, 2005)

This study covers only one period of history, even if a decisive one that took place during the advent of the modern welfare state. How big might the charitable sector have grown in the absence of state intervention? How much wealth has not been voluntarily redistributed owing to the imposition of forced redistribution? And how much more efficiently, and with greater personal care, might all this have been done? These are the unseen effects that cannot be measured.

We should also remember that even the most competent helper of the poor does not discharge his whole duty to God because the poor are made better off. The 'preferential option for the poor' is not to be understood exclusively. This, John Paul II wrote in *Ecclesia in America,* is 'in part because of an approach to the pastoral care of the poor marked by a certain exclusiveness that the pastoral care for the leading sectors of society has been neglected and many people have thus been estranged from the Church' (EA 67). The preferential option for the poor, moreover, may never be construed as a legal preference for one class over another (Leviticus 19:15). In understanding assertions regarding the supposed inherent moral superiority of one class, we must remember the call to universal salvation issued by the same Gospel. As believers, love and service of God should always be our primary focus, and the obligation to others flows from that. When charity and concern for others become secularised and taken over by the state, they thereby become less of an instrument in the service of God.

## True Christian charity

In many ways, John Paul II's writings on this topic can be seen as a development of Leo XIII, who wrote in *Rerum novarum* in 1891 that 'No human devices can ever be found to supplant Christian charity' (RN 30). That remains true today, though we are more confused than ever about what constitutes genuine charity. Some believe that paying taxes suffices to discharge our duties to our neighbours, because the state has undertaken so many activities to care for the well-being of those in need. Others think that charity comes from voting for political parties that support redistribution.

Benedict XVI is fully aware of this confusion, which is why his encyclical *Deus caritas est* sought to clarify the Christian teaching on charity by calling for a new civilisation of love – not one based on a superficial secularist understanding but one rooted in classical Catholic theology. The state cannot be the source by which this love is realised.

> There is no ordering of the State so just that it can eliminate the need for a service of love.... There will always be suffering which cries out for consolation and help. There will always be loneliness. There will always be situations of material need where help in the form of concrete love of neighbour is indispensable. The State which would provide everything, absorbing everything into itself, would ultimately become a mere bureaucracy incapable of guaranteeing the very thing which the suffering person – every person – needs: namely, loving personal concern. We do not need a State which regulates and controls everything, but a State which, in accordance with the principle of subsidiarity, generously acknowledges and supports initiatives arising from the different social forces and combines spontaneity with closeness to those in need ... This love does not simply offer people material help, but refreshment and care for their souls, something which often is even more necessary than material support. (DCE 28)

There are a number of important insights here. The Pope engages in a *reductio ad absurdum*, speaking of the state that absorbs everything into itself, because this is precisely the tendency of the state that purports to care for the poor, the weak, the elderly and the sick. It becomes the cradle-to-grave state that knows no limits and for which no aspect of social management is off limits. The state's activities in this regard tend to crowd out the need for Christian charity in three senses: they bind the recipient to a dependency relationship to the state, one that tends to be more materially generous than private charity (and thus providing a moral hazard to the recipient); secondly, they encourage an attitude among potential charitable workers and donors that their charity is not needed – 'I gave at the office'; thirdly, the sheer expense of the welfare state is paid out of the reserve capital of a country's wealth, which might otherwise go towards building up a robust charitable sector.

Even in the case of such a crowding out, Benedict XVI reminds us in *Deus caritas est* that the Church has a positive obligation that it can never forgo:

> The Church can never be exempted from practising charity as an organized activity of believers, and on the other hand, there will never be a situation where the charity of each individual Christian is unnecessary, because in addition to justice man needs, and will always need, love. (DCE 29)

## Defining and dividing responsibilities: solidarity and subsidiarity

As for the tendency of the state to expand and encroach on aspects of the Church's obligation, consider that the whole of society is made of spheres, which are both distinct and intertwined. The state is distinct from society, society from locality, locality from community, community from church, church from family, and family from individual. Each is essential. Each has a function to fulfil. The function is most efficaciously accomplished when each sphere stays within its own domain as much as possible. We should not want the state, for example, to assume the task of facilitating spiritual renewal: that is the task of the Church. Correspondingly, we should not want the Church to assume the task of secular law enforcement, for this is the state's responsibility.

We do well to consider, then, which social functions are best addressed by which sphere and to establish protections for the resulting domains. This is not to say that the spheres cannot overlap. Business, for example, is the place for enterprise, but a family business can be among the most efficient. The community can engage in charitable work that complements the work of the Church. But we err if we forget that each institution has a primary function often exclusive of others.

Thus the state's primary purpose is the enforcement of the rule of law and the administration of justice. With regard to other social and individual human problems, we should not regard the government as the problem solver of first resort. Establishing that a moral obligation exists – to help the poor, for example – does not also establish that government should become the normative agency to fulfil that obligation. Allowing for the encroachment of one function on another should be carefully thought out, but a special danger exists when the state is made to interfere with functions that are not its own.

'Power tends to corrupt' (Acton, 1988: 519) precisely because the state has a legal monopoly in its use of coercion.

Just as the social functions should be distinguished among institutions, the principle of subsidiarity must be brought to bear for the common good of the community. This principle says that social issues are best addressed by those closest to the problem, and that higher orders should be enlisted only in cases of obvious failure. The care of the aged and poor, for example, is best left to the lower order of the family, church and community, and not the higher orders of the nation and state. Subsidiarity also warns the higher orders against intervening unnecessarily in the affairs of the lower order. Indeed, as the *Catechism of the Catholic Church* states, 'the principle of subsidiarity is opposed to all forms of collectivism. It sets limits for state intervention. It aims at harmonizing the relationships between individuals and societies' (Catholic Church, 1994, para. 1885).

The principle itself is not satisfied unless the lower orders themselves take care to address the needs that most closely and directly fall within their purview. The unfortunate temptation raised by the existence of centralised state welfare provision is that these responsibilities may be shoved aside by lower order groups. The principle also establishes an ordering of responsibilities, so that we understand our primary responsibilities are to God, our families (immediate and extended) and to our community of faith.

This manner of approaching social issues ensures that governments consider carefully what powers legitimately belong to them and whether their exercise would increase or reduce the capacity for responsible decision-making at lower levels. Governments, and those who advise them, need to recognise the considerable limits of governments in addressing human problems. Government can be effective as an instrument of coercion, but not usually as a force for compassion.

Here we ought to recall that the principle of solidarity is not intended as a countervailing force to that of subsidiarity, but rather its complement. If subsidiarity helps us to identify the respective responsibilities of each individual and social group vis-à-vis others, solidarity represents the interdependence of all of society's individuals and institutions. 'Today perhaps more than in the past', Pope John Paul II wrote in his second encyclical, *Sollicitudo rei socialis*,

> people are realizing that they are linked together by a common destiny, which is to be constructed together, if catastrophe for all is to be avoided. From the depth of anguish, fear and escapist phenomena like drugs, typical of the contemporary world, the idea is slowly emerging that the good to which we are all called and the happiness to which we aspire cannot be obtained without an effort and commitment on the part of all, nobody excluded, and the consequent renouncing of personal selfishness. (SRS 26)

Interestingly, some Christians fail to see that the free economy promotes the formation of cooperative associations, business firms, mutually beneficial exchange, charitable actions and institutions, families and civic associations, and also encourages everyone's participation in shaping political institutions consistent with the dignity of the human person. Solidarity, then, presupposes freedom of association, opportunities for exchange and enterprise, and material abundance to ensure that intermediating forces between the individual and the state can form and thrive.

Thus in the USA, which has one of the world's freest economies, 89 per cent of households give to charity, with the average household giving $1,620 or 3.1 per cent of income. Some 42 per cent of households report doing voluntary work with no remuneration on top of this, for a total of 15.5 billion hours at a value of $239.2 billion. Among those who volunteer, charitable giving is even higher, up to $2,295 per year.[4] The largest motivation for giving is religious, with the rich giving far more than anyone else. The total size of the private charitable sector in the USA, including foundations and labour time, approaches half a trillion dollars per year (Brooks, 2006).[5]

Can the private sector replace the public sector in terms of total dollars spent? It is doubtful; nor is it necessarily desirable. Public sector provision can be too generous in some areas and not so generous in other areas. The main problem, however, is that those resources too often go towards bureaucracy, not to true human assistance. Private sector charity is more efficiently employed towards desirable ends. It can better discern the needs of the poor, avoid the problem of dependency and be accountable to the

---

[4] See *Giving and Volunteering in the United States*, The Independent Sector, Washington, DC, 2001.
[5] Among many findings herein reported is that people who attend worship services are far more giving than those who do not.

donor base. Thus private charity simply does not need the same resources as public sector welfare provision to achieve the desired results.

There is nothing inherent in the mechanism of the free economy that somehow causes people to extend a hand of charity to the less fortunate. The impulse to do this stems from religious and cultural motivation that can exist or not exist within any system of economics. The advantage of the market economy lies precisely in its ability to generate the vast wealth necessary to create the means to live out moral obligations and ideals. It is precisely the market economy which provides the means that allow people to carry out charitable activity in a way that other economic systems cannot.

Ultimately the source of an authentic social conscience must come from outside the market. It is from a personal knowledge of our Creator – mediated, Catholics believe as a matter of faith and reason, through the Catholic Church established by Christ – that we gain those virtues that enable a productive economy to thrive and assist all the members of the community. Only then is it possible to recapture an integrated and settled sense of the reality of man's origin, dignity and ultimate destiny.

## Conclusion

There is probably no one in the Catholic Church who does not know the story of the Good Samaritan. This is invariably drawn upon as a model of Christian charity. But what does it say about the specific option of public versus private aid?

The following fact is unavoidable: the Samaritan was not an agent of the state. He was a private individual. He helped of his own volition. This is his virtue, along with the fact that he transcended ethnic boundaries. He was not acting as a public servant. He used his own money. It was a sacrifice of the Samaritan's own time and resources. His actions were not only good for the poor suffering soul on the street; they also contributed to his moral flourishing.

'When I return', said the Samaritan, 'I will reimburse you for any extra expense you may have'. This is generosity. This is charity. It is exercised by individuals acting on their own impulses as informed by ethics and good morals. There is no substitute for that. This is one of the many wonderful lessons of this beautiful parable, and points to a true model of charity in a free and virtuous society.

A final objection: how can we know for sure that the poor will be cared for in the absence of a welfare state? I would like to substitute the following rhetorical question as a way of refocusing the debate: how can we know for sure that people will be religious in the absence of a state-imposed religion? Let us trust in freedom – that 'product of the Christian environment' (Ratzinger, 1988: 162).

## References

Acton, J. (1988), *Essays in Religion, Politics, and Morality*, Indianapolis, IN: Liberty Classics.
Brooks, A. (2006), *Who Cares*, New York: Basic

Books.

Catholic Church (1994), *Catechism of the Catholic Church*, London: Geoffrey Chapman.

Gruber, J. and D. Hungerman (2005), 'Faith-based charity and crowd out during the Great Depression', Working paper, Meetings of the Association for the Study of Religion, Economics, and Culture, 6 November 2005: www.religionomics.com/.

Murray, J. C., SJ (1960), *We Hold These Truths: Catholic Reflections on the American Proposition*, New York: Sheed and Ward.

Niskanen, W. A. (1973), *Bureaucracy: Servant or Master?*, Hobart Paperback 5, London: Institute of Economic Affairs.

Novak, M. (1982), *The Spirit of Democratic Capitalism*, Washington, DC: American Enterprise Institute.

Ratzinger, J. (1988), *Church, Ecumenism, and Politics*, New York: Crossroad.

# 4

# AID, GOVERNANCE AND DEVELOPMENT

*Philip Booth*

## Introduction

Throughout mid to late twentieth-century Catholic social teaching there was a consistent articulation of the position that the developed world should transfer economic resources to the developing world through government-to-government aid financed by the tax system. The tenor of the teaching has been unambiguous, though at certain times a different emphasis has been put on the role of charity and the role of transfers through taxation.

It is easy to see why there might be an inclination towards this position. Certainly the parable of the Good Samaritan implies that charity should not respect national boundaries; similarly, it could be argued, the use of government aid, financed by taxation, to provide for those in great need or to assist the process of development should not respect national boundaries. The argument is less clear, however, with regard to government aid than with regard to charity. If the notion of national sovereignty is to be respected, it may, in practice, be impossible for one country to ensure that the conditions for development are nurtured in another country – in other words, it may be impossible to ensure that aid benefits its intended recipients. When examining appropriate policies in relation to government aid, it is important to have an understanding of what does and does not work, underpinned by theoretical and empirical economic examination.

In this chapter we will subject Catholic teaching on aid to scrutiny from an economic and political economy perspective. Important questions are raised for Catholic social teaching. For example, if the provision of aid makes the economic situations of countries worse, if it increases the power of corrupt governments, or if it centralises power and economic resources rather than disperses power and resources among those in need, how should developed countries respond?

Catholic social teaching stresses the importance of 'good governance'. But how should we proceed if the structures of governance in an aid-recipient country are such that poor government may be bolstered by the provision of aid? In other words, if the systems of justice in a recipient country are failing, how does a potential donor country meet its obligations in social justice, as they are described in Catholic social teaching? It is not possible to answer this question in detail in this brief chapter. It will be raised, however, as a fundamental question that Catholic economists and political theorists should attempt to answer if they are to make a meaningful contribution to raising the condition of the poor through aid.

This chapter will begin by examining some statements in Catholic teaching on the economic position of developing countries. These will then be contrasted with teaching on the fundamental structures that are necessary for a market economy to prosper and for justice to be administered. The economics and political economy of the case for aid will then be analysed. The focus is on development aid and not on disaster or famine relief.

## Catholic exhortations to the developed world to finance 'aid'

### A false premise

We will see from our discussion of taxation (see Chapter 6) that the Church does not regard property rights as sacrosanct in situations where some individuals do not have the means for basic living. It is therefore not surprising that the Church exhorts better-off nations to help poorer nations by taxing its own citizens to help those of other countries. This could be regarded as appropriate in order to respond to 'sins of omission' – that is insufficient charity – where those sins of omission are such that they prevent others from having sufficient to meet their basic needs (see Townsend in Spencer and Chaplin (eds) 2009). Before discussing these issues, it is worth noting that Church teaching on these matters is, to some extent at least, based on a false premise that seems to go unchallenged within its teaching documents. This false premise is articulated, for example, in

Pontifical Council for Justice and Peace (2005):[1]
'In fact, there are indications aplenty that point
to a trend of *increasing inequalities*, both between
advanced countries and developing countries,
and within industrialized countries. The growing
economic wealth made possible by the processes
[of globalization] described above is accompanied
by an increase in relative poverty' (para. 362, italics
in original). In *Populorum progressio*[2] it is stated that
'the poor nations remain ever poorer while the
rich ones become still richer' (PP 57). *Sollicitudo
rei socialis*[3] speaks of 'hopes for development, at
that time[4] so lively, today appear very far from
being realised' (SRS 12) and '... the first negative
observation to make is the persistence and often
widening of the gap between the areas of the so-
called developed North and the developing South'.

These statements are, at best, superficial. It is
true that there are certain countries, sometimes
described as 'failed states',[5] that have not shared
in the economic growth arising from globalisation
because they have not participated in the process
of globalisation. As other countries have grown
richer, partly as a result of globalisation, people
in failed states whose incomes have only grown
slowly, or have perhaps shrunk, become relatively
poorer. But this arises because of the failure of such
states to participate in globalisation, not because
of inherent faults in the process of globalisation.

---

[1] That is, in the *Compendium of the Social Doctrine of the Church*, also referred
to as the *Compendium* below.
[2] Published by Pope Paul VI in 1967.
[3] Published by Pope John Paul II in 1987.
[4] That is, at the time of the publication of *Populorum progressio*.
[5] See Wolf (2004).

This point is certainly not recognised in the *Compendium*, which, quoting from the encyclicals of John Paul II, explicitly talks about countries being left behind *as a result of* globalisation.

It is also worth noting that the *Compendium* focuses in the statement above on *relative* poverty. The emphasis on relative poverty in the *Compendium* is out of place. Catholic social teaching has generally emphasised meeting basic needs as the motivation for charity and government intervention. Though relative poverty was a theme of Pope John XXIII's encyclical *Pacem in terris*, the reduction of relative poverty would appear to be a misplaced aim for many reasons. Firstly, it is inherently materialistic. If some communities wished to carry on meeting basic needs, but go no further, whilst the rest of the world becomes richer, relative poverty will increase.[6] But why should we be concerned? Perhaps those who focus on material goals become worse off in other respects as a result. Secondly, if a large part of the world's population were able to meet basic needs as a result of globalisation, whereas they could not do so before, but, at the same time, other countries become richer still, it is possible for relative poverty to increase. But why should this be a concern? Individuals should not be encouraged to measure their living standards by comparison with others as that can foster envy and materialism.

As it happens, relative poverty has decreased during the process of globalisation and absolute

---

[6] I refer here to a situation of voluntary choice of individuals and groups of individuals. People in religious orders are, of course, the most obvious example. There may, however, be other communities whose members freely choose a more simple way of life, uncoerced by government.

poverty has decreased dramatically. In particular, the gap between countries that have only recently seen rapid growth and those countries that have been relatively well off for many decades has narrowed significantly. Stylised facts do not prove the point but they provide sufficient information to seriously question the premise that globalisation is leaving the poor behind. In China, 400 million people have been pulled out of 'dollar-a-day' poverty in the last decade or so. It is inconceivable that this would have happened without China's participation in the process of globalisation. The same could well happen in India in the next decade if the country continues to liberalise its economy and allows trade to develop – indeed absolute poverty has already begun to fall sharply. The income of poor countries has not, in general, grown more slowly than that of rich countries during the recent episode of globalisation. For example, India, Sri Lanka, China, Chile and Pakistan have all grown faster than the world average over the last ten years, whereas each of the six biggest economies in the world ten years ago has grown more slowly than the world average. Today the average Indian is twice as well off as ten years ago while the average Japanese or German is barely better off at all. China's GDP has more than doubled relative to that of the USA in the last 25 years. Taking a longer period, the growth rates of the poorest fifth of countries[7] from 1950 to 2001 were not significantly different from those of the other 80 per cent of countries (Easterly, 2005).

---

[7] That is, the poorest quintile.

Indeed, for nearly the whole of human history until 1800, about 80 per cent of the world's population lived on a subsistence income or below. Then, the first phase of globalisation began and that proportion halved in 150 years. In the second phase of globalisation, beginning around 1980, the proportion of the world's population halved again to 20 per cent in just 25 years (see Griswold, 2009). The achievements resulting from the extension of a market economy have been immense – but the process is sadly incomplete.

Also notable is the advance of the global middle class (see Das, 2009) – people who live above subsistence level and have some money to save and buy consumer durables. In the 15 years from 1990, 1.2 billion people entered the global middle class from a situation of poverty, mostly in countries that have embraced globalisation normally without significant development aid. This has gone hand-in-hand with improvements in many other measures of well-being such as literacy and life expectancy. Such progress is beginning to be seen in sub-Saharan African countries, some of which have been making substantial economic progress in very recent years generally preceded by progress towards better governance and a better business environment.

In making strong statements about the widening disparity between rich and poor an important subtlety is being missed. It is possible for the gap between the richest and poorest to become greater while the number of poor shrinks, perhaps dramatically. Indeed, this is what has happened. In the last 50 years, many previously poor countries have become much better off. In more recent years, many people in some formerly very poor countries containing around one third of the world's population have become better off.

Nevertheless, there are some parts of the world – notwithstanding recent progress, this particularly includes countries in Africa – that have not grown at all. Indeed, in some cases incomes have shrunk. We will focus on those countries that are still very poor in absolute terms in this chapter.[8] If we understand that the underdeveloped world is getting smaller because many previously poor countries have grown richer, it allows us to understand better the conditions for successful development. It is a better starting point for constructive analysis than the false presumption that income disparities are widening.[9]

## Catholic Social Teaching: making the case for aid

The Church has taught clearly that development assistance and responses to extreme poverty should be given not only through voluntary sacrifice or charity but through government action too. For example, *Sollicitudo rei socialis* states: 'The obligation to commit oneself to the development of peoples is not just an individual duty, and still less an individualistic one, as if it were possible

---

[8] That is not to say that there are not serious problems, including significant income differences, within countries in Asia and South America which do not suffer from the absolute poverty of Africa. They are not, however, the subject of our discussion.

[9] Indeed, it has been recognised in more recent encyclicals that development should be aimed at aiding other countries to develop rather than transferring income from rich to poor. This, implicitly at least, should lead us to focus on the inhibitions to development, many of which lie in the policies of underdeveloped countries themselves.

to achieve this development through the isolated efforts of each individual. It is an imperative which obliges each and every man and woman, as well as societies and nations' (SRS 32). The absolute requirement that solidarity should not recognise international borders is also made clear (para. 39). This international vision of the principle of solidarity is rooted in the parable of the Good Samaritan – though this is a parable about charity, of course, not of international political and economic relationships between governments.

The Vatican II document *Gaudium et spes*, following on from Pope John's encyclicals *Mater et magistra* and *Pacem in terris*, emphasised the need to see 'solidarity' in global terms. Concern was expressed about inequalities in economic outcomes: 'For excessive economic and social differences between the members of one human family or population groups cause scandal and militate against social justice...' (GS 29); this theme then continues at the beginning of Chapter III of the document. Chapter I finishes with the statement that 'solidarity must be constantly increased until that day on which it will be brought to perfection'. While there is a case made for aid in *Gaudium et spes*, the background for 'home grown' development is also made clear: 'technical progress, an inventive spirit, an eagerness to create and to expand enterprises ... all the elements of development must be promoted' (GS 64). The collective organisation of production was also criticised (GS 65). Nevertheless, paragraph 69 makes it clear that both individuals and governments should share their goods to relieve suffering and to help peoples develop themselves. In paragraph 84, the importance of international organisations in fostering development was stressed. The document then went on to be critical of political systems that did not foster private property and sound money and promote the virtues of what today would be called 'good governance'.

*Populorum progressio* expanded the analysis of *Rerum novarum* to apply it to world problems – particularly those of development. As in *Gaudium et spes*, conditions of good governance and the conditions for development are spelled out. The importance of private property and free competition is emphasised. Planned and collectivised economies are criticised. The aid agenda is made explicit, however – and it is promoted as an agenda for governments rather than just an activity of charity. Nations as well as individuals are told they must partake in the process of building solidarity. People are told that they must accept higher taxes to finance distributions to poorer countries. An increased role for international institutions, particularly the United Nations, was proposed. Development is described as a 'right' that imposes a duty on all nations, both developed and underdeveloped.

Overall, in *Gaudium et spes*, there is a mature discussion of the problem of the poorest in underdeveloped countries. The conditions for indigenous growth are understood; the responsibility of Christian groups is made clear; it is made clear that development is primarily the responsibility of peoples themselves; and the conditions necessary for long-term development are understood and effectively articulated. However,

*Populorum progressio* was to a much greater degree influenced by the fashions of interventionist development economists in the 1960s. Nevertheless, in both documents there is a responsibility put on the governments of developed countries and on international organisations (generally financed by developed countries) to finance aid both for relief and development.

It is not asked in this encyclical whether development aid granted to countries in which the conditions of good governance do not exist could actually do harm. This observation is interesting given the context of *Populorum progressio*. It was strongly influenced by a visit by Pope Paul VI to India (Charles, 1998). India is possibly one of the best examples of a country that failed to develop because of policies of poor governance and of central planning. It is reasonable for a Christian to suggest that aid should be granted to countries even in such circumstances if the aid benefits the poorest, or even if it does no harm. But the question remains, what should Christians do if government-to-government aid, of the type proposed by *Populorum progressio*, actually acts to strengthen the institutions that have brought about the failure to develop in the first place?

The *Catechism* (Catholic Church, 1994) makes a distinction between the provision of aid to address particular problems and assistance given for development: 'Direct aid is an appropriate response to immediate, extraordinary needs caused by natural catastrophes, epidemics, and the like. But it does not suffice to repair the grave damage resulting from destitution or to provide a lasting solution to a country's needs' (para. 2440). To achieve the latter, argues the *Catechism*, requires reform of institutions. The *Catechism* states that 'Rich nations have a grave moral responsibility towards those which are *unable* to ensure the means of their development by themselves or have been prevented from doing so by tragic historical events' (para. 2439, my italics). Of course, this may include those who are prevented from prospering as a result of the policies of their own governments, but the *Catechism* emphasises the importance of personal responsibility for development, where individuals are allowed to take such responsibility.

Catholic social teaching documents do regard aid as an imperfect response and put the primary responsibility for development on underdeveloped nations themselves (see below). In other ways, the discussion of aid has become more nuanced in recent years. *Caritas in veritate* was intended to mark the fortieth anniversary of *Populorum progressio* – though it was not published until 2009. Integral human development – not just economic development – is the main theme of the document. The word *aid* is mentioned 19 times and the word *development* over 250 times. However, though the document makes one exhortation for governments of richer countries to provide aid, on 15 of the 19 occasions on which the word 'aid' is used, Pope Benedict is critical of aid agencies, the way in which Western governments provide aid or the way in which recipient governments use aid. For example, Pope Benedict writes: 'International aid has often been diverted from its proper ends through irresponsible actions' (CV 22) and that:

'Aid programmes must increasingly acquire the characteristics of participation and completion from the grass roots' (CV 58). Pope Benedict criticises tied aid, warns about the problem of aid dependency and suggests that trade should be the principal form of assistance. The key theme, reiterated throughout the document – though not taken up in detail here – is that development requires the correct moral orientation: charity cannot be separated from truth.

## Catholic Social Teaching: the relationship between aid and governance

Interestingly, comment by local Church leaders on issues such as foreign aid almost never links aid with governance. One of many examples of this problem is Cardinal Keith O'Brien's comments at the 'Make Poverty History' rally in Scotland in 2006, together with his associated press articles. In the *Scotsman* (1 July 2006) he said: 'They came from all over Britain and further afield to ask for more and better aid for the world's poorest countries, cancellation of their unpayable debts and trade rules that will help their economies grow. Acts not of charity, but of justice [sic].' This raises two questions. Firstly, which should come first, charity or justice?[10] And, secondly, what precisely does justice mean in this context if the mechanisms for achieving the 'just' result are not within the control of those desiring to

---

[10] We will not discuss this further – there is more discussion of this issue in Chapters 1, 3 and 6. I think, however, it would have been more appropriate to say 'relieving the needs of the poor is a duty of justice if charity fails'.

deliver justice? If the transfer of resources from government to government either does no good or actually does harm for reasons discussed below, how should a potential donor nation respond? It may not be within the power of the donor nation to achieve the aim of justice as defined by Cardinal O'Brien. To describe aid, in such circumstances, as an essential part of justice is therefore meaningless and unhelpful. Indeed, if the political institutions in recipient countries follow the forms laid down by Catholic social teaching, the need for aid may well disappear.[11]

Until *Caritas in veritate*, the problem of providing aid where there are imperfect political structures is mentioned in social encyclicals, though the implications for aid policies are not drawn out. The problems of imperfect political and economic structures are regarded as important issues in aid-dependent countries. For example, in *Sollicitudo rei socialis* it is stated that extreme poverty in underdeveloped countries happens, 'not through the fault of the needy people, and even less through a sort of inevitability dependent on natural conditions or circumstances as a whole'

---

[11] Not only is there no reference to issues of governance in Cardinal O'Brien's articles and speeches, quite the opposite is the case. He strongly opposes promotion of policies by donors that can encourage economic growth and good governance, such as sound fiscal polices and privatisation. Clearly it is a matter of opinion whether such policies are beneficial, but to dismiss them out of hand as the Cardinal does is wholly inappropriate, particularly given the disastrous environmental consequences of state ownership and subsidisation of energy and water supplies. The Cardinal also suggests that budget cuts mean that poor countries have less to spend on healthcare and education – but if such services are paid for only by deficit financing the consequences are generally catastrophic for poor countries – particularly for following generations.

(SRS 9). More specifically John Paul II then refers to 'grave instances of omissions on the part of developing nations themselves, and especially on the part of those holding economic and political power' as being responsible for the deterioration in the position of underdeveloped countries (SRS 16). Furthermore, John Paul then goes on to mention the problem of aid being misused: '... investments and aid for development are often diverted from their proper purpose and used to sustain conflicts'. The accent here, however, is not on misuse due to internal decisions but as a result of directions from donors – particularly in the context of the 'cold war'.

Pope John Paul then further examines the background in which development assistance is given. He comments on the structures of social sin, rooted in individual sin, that cause underdevelopment. Again, however, many of the problems identified relate to donor communities rather than the political systems of recipient countries – still reflecting the cold war period when aid was often used as a tool to obtain political influence. Responsibility is, however, thrust upon the leaders and peoples of developing countries: 'Development demands above all a spirit of initiative on the part of the countries which need it' (SRS 44); 'Other nations need to reform certain unjust structures, and in particular their political institutions, in order to replace corrupt, dictatorial and authoritarian forms of government by democratic and participatory ones' (SRS 44). Underdeveloped countries are then exhorted to open their trade to other underdeveloped countries. There is a clear emphasis here on creating the economic conditions to allow growth and development to take place.

The importance of the wider institutional background necessary for economic development and prosperity is stated clearly in the *Catechism*, which reaffirms the message of *Centesimus annus*:

> The activity of a market economy cannot be conducted in an institutional, juridical or political vacuum. On the contrary, it presupposes sure guarantees of individual freedom and private property, as well as a stable currency and efficient public services. Hence the principal task of the state is to guarantee this security, so that those who work and produce can enjoy the fruits of their labours and thus feel encouraged to work efficiently and honestly. (*Catechism*, para. 2431)

Thus it is clear that the Church has not ignored the institutional and political requirements that are necessary for economic development and prosperity. Indeed, *Centesimus annus* goes further in making clear that those countries that *have* developed are those that have participated in 'international economic activities' (i.e. trade in goods, services and capital). This is an important move forward and change of emphasis from the encyclicals of the 1960s, which tended to emphasise income transfers; perhaps the later encyclicals responded to the better understanding of the economics of development and the economics of institutions that was prevalent by the time *Centesimus annus* was published. *Caritas in veritate*, recognises this problem more explicitly when it states: 'The focus of *international aid*, within a solidarity-based plan to resolve today's economic problems should rather be on consolidating constitutional, juridical and administrative systems in countries that do not yet fully enjoy these goods.'

Even this analysis, still leaves open, however, the issue of how we should respond if the political, legal and economic environment is not only hostile to economic development but also such that aid will be wasted and may be used to centralise power within corrupt political systems. The existence of this possibility should at least make us hesitate before calling automatically for increased aid either to promote development or to help those on low incomes in underdeveloped countries.

## The Bauer critique of papal encyclicals

Peter Bauer was severely critical of the teaching of the Catholic Church on issues such as the concentration of wealth and development aid in the 1960s and 1970s (see the essay 'Ecclesiastical economics: envy legitimized', presented to the American Enterprise Institute, published in Bauer, 2000). From *Populorum progressio* (published in 1967), for example, Bauer quotes sections, such as 'God intended the earth and all that it contains for the use of all human beings and peoples' (PP 22) and 'You are not making a gift of your possessions to the poor person. You are handing over to him what is his. For what has been given in common for the use of all, you have arrogated to yourself. The world is given to all, and not only to the rich'[12] (PP 23). On government planning,

---

[12] Originally from St Ambrose.

he cites *Populorum progressio* (PP 33): 'It pertains to the public authorities to choose, even to lay down, the objectives to be pursued in economic development, the ends to be achieved, and the means of attaining them, and it is for them to stimulate all the forces engaged in this common activity.' Bauer then quotes *Octogesima adveniens* (published by Pope Paul VI in 1971) as stating that there is a major problem as a result of 'the fairness in the exchange of goods and in the division of wealth between countries'.

Bauer raises some important issues. In particular, it is certainly possible that the tone of *Populorum progressio* and *Octogesima adveniens* has aided the arguments of many leading figures in the Christian community who have proposed wholesale reform of capitalist economies, international trade, financial institutions, aid policies and so on as the solution to problems of poverty. Bauer also argues that the encyclicals have given succour to those who argue that the rich become rich at the expense of the poor.

Charles (1998), in turn, criticises Bauer's analysis. Charles points out that Catholic teaching does emphasise that the burden of development belongs with underdeveloped nations themselves. He then suggests that Bauer's critique is inappropriate because he is unable to provide a fully argued case showing how underdeveloped nations can achieve development themselves without help from the outside. He thus suggests that Bauer effectively argued why the popes, and the experts on whom they relied, were wrong, but never articulated 'the right' (pp. 455–6). But this leaves an open question.

If a country is poor because its basic economic, legal and political structures do not allow economic and political freedom to give rise to human flourishing, might it be possible that little can be done through political systems external to the country concerned to rectify this situation? It is perfectly reasonable for academics to point out that proposed solutions to particular problems will do more harm than good while still being unable, themselves, to resolve the problems. *Populorum progressio* argued that in good conscience we must support policies of higher taxes to finance aid – a notion strongly criticised by Bauer. *Sollicitudo rei socialis*, however, put it rather differently. This document suggested that if we know how to alleviate poverty and choose not to do so this is a moral failing.[13] Bauer believed that the developed world does not have it in its power to resolve the problems of the underdeveloped world, and this view would not contradict this sentiment of *Sollicitudo rei socialis*.

## Aid in theory and practice

If we are to accept the case for development aid as articulated in papal encyclicals and other Catholic social teaching, then those making the case must be able to demonstrate that, on balance, it is effective in promoting development. The arguments and evidence will not be discussed in detail here but a prima facie case will be made that development aid can be harmful and that the case for development

---

[13] I am grateful to Father de Souza, Kingston, Ontario, Canada, for this insight.

aid is weak. Those making the case for development aid need to challenge this argument or come up with methods of distributing development aid that will circumvent the problems discussed here. The problems with development aid presented here have been discussed at greater length by Bauer, Lal, Erixon, Collier and others.[14]

## Aid and government

The provision of development aid is, by nature, a top-down process. At a fundamental level, therefore, aid rewards the governing elites in those countries where those elites keep their people poor. Aid also makes it more likely that incompetent, corrupt or brutal government will survive because aid provides the resources for governing elites to alleviate some of the internal problems caused by poor or unjust government. Frequently, such governments have, of course, pursued policies that have included the persecution or expulsion of the most productive ethnic groups in society. The availability of aid also provides incentives for governments to pursue policies that will attract more aid.[15] Collier (2007) suggests that, in Africa, 40 per cent of military spending is inadvertently financed by aid. Aid cannot be a moral imperative, if the realities of providing aid are such.

Aid also changes lines of accountability in government. Governments become accountable to

---

[14] See, for example, Lal (2002), Bauer (2000), Erixon (2003), Erixon (2005) and Collier (2007). It should be noted that Collier is not an opponent of aid.
[15] i.e. policies that lead to high levels of absolute poverty and policies that promote government consumption and not investment – thus giving the impression that money is not available for investment, health and education.

those from whom they receive aid – either other governments or international institutions – and not to their own people. Erixon (2003) describes how in 2001 Tanzania had to produce 2,400 reports and studies on different aspects of present and future aid. A former minister of finance of Kenya estimated he had to spend 75 per cent of his time in discussions with donors.

As Bauer has pointed out, development aid leads a country's political and economic structures to orient themselves inappropriately. In many African countries aid is a significant proportion of national income.[16] Talented and entrepreneurial people within a country that receives large amounts of aid have a strong incentive to direct their efforts upwards, towards government, to become beneficiaries of aid-financed projects, instead of attempting to raise their material position through business and entrepreneurship. Thus, aid encourages rent-seeking. This whole process strengthens the hold of government on economic life, which is generally one of the most serious problems in underdeveloped countries. On a wider scale, the greater the proportion of national income and wealth that is controlled by government, the greater is the incentive for ethnic groups to engage in conflict to try to control government: if freedom of contract, exchange and private property rights are the main vehicles for transferring and upholding the control of property, fruitful economic activity rather than political activity and conflict are more likely

---

[16] In Tanzania and Kenya, for example, it reached 30 per cent of national income in the mid-1990s.

to produce increases in income and wealth for individuals and communities.

The negative relationship between economic growth and natural resources is now well established – the so-called 'natural resource curse'.[17] In economic terms, aid is very much like natural resources – it is an 'endowment' that empowers governments and makes it more worthwhile investing economic resources or even using military means to control the machinery of government. Aid can therefore nurture bad government, which is the very problem that entrenches poverty in the first place: Djankov et al. (2006) find a strongly negative relationship between the receipt of aid and the extent of democracy.

There is a tendency for aid not to be used for its intended purpose, such as health and education, but, instead, to be used to meet the aims of governing elites (often personal betterment). Erixon describes aid as being 'fungible'. The specific aid money intended for investment or health and education spending may be used for the intended purposes, in order to provide evidence for donors. But it displaces investment that otherwise would have taken place in such sectors, including private sector investment. The additional resources are then, in effect, used for government consumption. This reinforces the problems identified above – the government becomes more dominant in economic life and the source of economic betterment. The increased resources enhance the ability of government to pursue active industrial policies

---

[17] See Sachs and Warner (2001).

with the usual detrimental effects that such policies have. Increased resources also find their way into the hands of the governing elites and their supporters. Collier reports a 2004 survey that tracked aid spending in Chad that had been intended for rural hospital prospects. Only one per cent of the money reached the hospitals. In summary, aid entrenches the position of those who are rich and powerful and makes it more necessary for individuals who wish to improve their economic position to do so by developing relationships with those responsible for the spending of aid.

All these problems encourage corruption in public life. If development aid receipts are significant, the influence of government is greater, bad government is encouraged and is less accountable to the people, and the resources available to government are greater. Government functionaries and ministers have relatively more power and economic resources which they can use for economic preferment. Government officials and politicians are in a position where they control the allocation of substantial economic resources and therefore become more susceptible to corruption – particularly where legal systems are inadequate or are themselves corrupt.[18]

---

[18] This should not be thought a patronising remark about the governments of underdeveloped countries (see Senior, 2006). In any country where government officials have control of vast economic resources and significant discretion, fraud and corruption are likely to result (note the EU Common Agricultural Policy). If, however, countries are already poor because of bad governance, providing development aid can simply feed the system that keeps the country poor. It is also worth noting that vested interests are created within donor countries (government departments, consultants and those charities that receive large amounts of project support from governments) which have strong incentives to campaign for aid-financed solutions to

In an ideal world, the provision of aid might simply work to raise the income of all poor people in a country by an equal amount. People living at subsistence levels would then have more money to save, invest and provide education and healthcare for their families. Aid does not work like this, however, partly because it comes from governments of donor countries and is spent through governments of recipient countries, leading to the effects described above. But it is also not symmetrical in its effect on different economic sectors, particularly, paradoxically, if spent wisely. For example, if aid is spent on investment projects, it can lower the marginal rate of return from investment projects financed by private saving and thus reduce private saving and investment. In any event, it will raise the real rate of exchange in a country, thus reducing the competitiveness of export sectors.[19] Other non-export-oriented sectors may benefit, of course, but any structural adjustment caused by significant changes in aid flows may cause economic problems for particular sectors.

Both supporters and opponents of aid are agreed that policies to tie aid to economic reform have not succeeded where economic reform is initiated by the funding body (again, see Erixon, 2005, and

poverty in underdeveloped countries.

[19] This may seem like an esoteric point but a paper published by the NBER (Rajan and Subramanian, 2006) suggests that it can be of fundamental importance, particularly if aid flows are considerable in a country that has had little development. Gupta et al. (2006) provide a good discussion of these issues. They note that trade liberalisation should coincide with increases in aid to reduce the impact of the 'real exchange rate effect'. Pattillo et al. (2006) note that this effect can be most detrimental to the poor, though they also suggest that it can be avoided through good policy choices in other areas.

the references therein). There are many reasons for this. It is too easy for countries to demonstrate, at the time that grants or loans tied to structural adjustment are being renewed, that progress has been made – even though progress is more apparent than real. Also, lenders and donors find it very difficult to not renew loans or grants if a country has become poorer because economic reform policies have not been followed.

## Aid and development

A strong economic case for aid rests on two hypotheses. The first is that the preconditions for economic development and growth relate to a shortage of savings, problems caused by declining terms of trade, lack of education and so on that can be resolved by income transfers from rich to poor countries. The second is that, in practice, aid transfers can be managed by benign governments to resolve these problems. We have dealt with the second issue above. What about the first?

It is, in fact, hard to find a positive relationship between aid and growth; indeed, there appears to be a negative relationship. It does not follow that a negative relationship between aid and economic growth implies cause and effect, but it should, at least, lead us to reconsider whether we should regard aid as a moral imperative. After the late 1970s, aid to Africa grew rapidly yet GDP growth collapsed and was close to zero or negative for over a decade from 1984 (see Erixon, 2005). GDP growth in Africa did not start to pick up again until aid fell in the early to mid-1990s. In East Asia, South

Asia and the Pacific, one finds a similar trend. As aid was reduced in these regions from the early 1990s, national income increased rapidly. Erixon cites a number of detailed country studies that find no benefits from aid whatsoever across a range of periods and a large number of countries. In total, in the 30 years from 1970 Africa received $400 billion of aid, under different regimes, tied to different forms of economic policy and reform, yet there is no evidence of a single country developing because of aid.

If we take 1950 as a starting point, it is clear that many countries that were then poor have become relatively wealthy while others have remained poor. It is impossible to find evidence that aid was successful in helping those countries that have become rich to do so. Botswana, for example, increased its income per head thirteenfold from 1950 to 2001, while much of Africa had a zero or negative growth rate (Easterly, 2005). Botswana is regarded as having many of the important features of good governance – certainly differences in aid do not distinguish Botswana from other African countries. Easterly notes that around 40 per cent of the poorest one fifth of countries in 1985 were not in the poorest one fifth of countries in 1950. From these observations, three facts are clear: poor countries can develop without aid; countries that receive aid do not tend to develop; and countries that are relatively rich can become poor again. This is troubling for the 'aid overcomes lack of capital and promotes development' hypothesis.

The following two figures show the relationship between aid and economic growth (Figure 1) and between aid and improvements in life expectancy (Figure 2).[20] It is very clear that there is no significant relationship – indeed there is no discernable relationship at all. This is not because aid is focused on poor countries that are growing slowly, as more detailed econometric studies show.

Figure 1 Relationship between development aid and changes in national income

Figure 2 Relationship between development aid and changes in life expectancy

---

[20] With thanks to Julian Morris for providing the figures.

## Growth and governance

It is becoming increasingly clear both from studying countries that have developed (for example in Asia) and those that have not that the problems identified by aid proponents are not the crucial ones for development. The basic precondition for development is good governance, including the enforcement of private property rights, freedom of contract, enforcement of contracts, the rule of law, the authority of law and the absence of corruption. This list is not exhaustive, of course.[21] It appears that, if these preconditions are present, development and growth will generally follow. This is not surprising. Economic activity, employment, saving and capital accumulation will not take place unless there is freedom of contract and enforcement of property rights.

The problem of the absence of formalisation and security of property rights is discussed in great detail by De Soto (2000). He argues that in underdeveloped countries much capital is 'dead capital' that is not recognised by the legal system. The absence of both secure and formal property rights prevents proper business contracts developing, leads to reduced opportunities for entrepreneurship, prevents capital secured on property from being invested within businesses, leads to corrupt legal and governmental systems and to 'private law enforcement' or 'mafia gangs' becoming dominant. In such a situation, issues such as land reform, the provision of capital through aid and so on become irrelevant to development. Unless legal systems

---

[21] One could add fiscal prudence and sound money, for example.

are reformed to properly recognise freely acquired property, capital investment and land endowments for the poor will have no meaning and will not contribute to development.

Exchange relationships are clearly necessary for an economy to develop beyond subsistence level. If contracts are not enforceable in the courts or recognised by legal systems, or if corruption or violence leads them to be enforced perversely, then exchange relationships cannot develop. Similarly, if property rights are not enforced justly or are not recognised, only very limited capital investment can take place.[22]

The problems in developing exchange relationships, small businesses and entrepreneurship are well illustrated both by De Soto's findings and from regular reports by the World Bank and Economist Intelligence Unit. For example, De Soto shows how on average 15 per cent of turnover in Peruvian manufacturing businesses are paid out in bribes. For a business to become legal and register its property in Lima it takes over three hundred working days at a cost of 32 times the monthly minimum wage. A person living in a housing settlement where title was not formally registered would have to go through 728 individual bureaucratic steps to register title with the city of Lima authority alone.

India has similar problems, though liberalisation

---

[22] It is sometimes difficult for people in the West to understand the importance of this point. If contracts that one makes as a consumer, employee, business person or employer are not enforceable (including contracts for borrowing and saving) business life simply cannot take place. Similarly, if one cannot enforce property rights in one's house, land or business premises capital investment will just grind to a halt.

has brought some recent benefits to that country. *The Economist* reports that Delhi's 250,000 bicycle rickshaw pullers collectively pay bribes of 20–25 million rupees a month for the privilege of being allowed to pursue their trade. It should be noted that, in many countries, including Peru and India, these problems have eased slightly in recent years, growth has improved and poverty has reduced. In a very poor country, small improvements in the economic and political environment can lead to rapid catch-up growth. India, for example, has an eight per cent per annum compound growth rate over the last five years.

The World Bank 2010 *Doing Business* report points out that African countries have an average rank of 139 in the world for ease of doing business compared with the OECD average rank of 30 – though some African countries are now amongst the top reformers.

Gwartney and Lawson (2004) show the relationship between economic freedom and growth. One particular statistic is compelling. One hundred countries were studied from 1980 to 2000 and their legal systems rated according to the criteria established by the Fraser Institute's Economic Freedom of the World index. The top 24 countries had an average GDP per capita of $25,716 at the end of the period and average economic growth of 2.5 per cent. The bottom 21 countries had an average income of $3,094 per capita and average economic growth of 0.33 per cent. The criteria used to rank legal systems were: consistency of legal structure, protection of property rights, enforcement of contracts, independence of judiciary and rule of law principles. This suggests that development is impossible without the basic legal structures necessary for free economic activity.

There are important subtleties in this debate which are discussed by Ogus (2005). For example, it could be argued that legal systems are less effective at enforcing property rights and contracts in poor countries because such countries lack the resources to develop effective legal systems. This argument may have some validity but is problematic as a generalisation because it raises the question of how any country manages to develop. Also, it would seem that this argument should not apply to resource-rich, underdeveloped countries, of which there are many in Africa.

An interesting study by Pattillo et al. (2006) examined the economic factors that explained sustained changes in growth in African countries. The macroeconomic environment (inflation, government borrowing and so on) was important – and many of the countries with improved macroeconomic environments were part of IMF programmes. Economic and political liberalisation were important too, as was trade liberalisation. Aid and debt concessions helped long-term growth when combined with an otherwise healthy policy environment. These results are helpful for economists in analysing combinations of factors that can aid growth but they do not help political economists answer key questions such as 'Should countries give aid when recipient countries are not undergoing internal reform?' or 'Can internal reform be driven from outside?'

The discussion in this section is neither conclusive

nor comprehensive. It provides, however, a prima facie case against development aid. Those who make the case for development aid need to demonstrate how the problems discussed here can be overcome or are irrelevant. Furthermore, those who promote government development aid in the name of Church teaching should be cautious when implying that the teaching has moral backing. If development aid is damaging to the very people it is meant to help, it is difficult to see how its provision can be a moral good.

## Catholic Social Teaching tempered by realism – is there a way forward?

Insofar as there was a consensus among economists in the 1960s behind the theories that underpinned *Populorum progressio*, that consensus is now broken. Aid has not been successful in achieving its goals and it has now become clear why this is so. Economists still disagree on policies relating to the appropriate extent of government intervention in any developing country and they will always do so. It has become clear, however, that development without good governance is impossible. Furthermore, if the basics of good governance exist, countries will tend to escape from poverty without aid.

The mix of charity and political action that is appropriate is not something the Church generally lays down and proponents of aid should be careful about drawing conclusions that ignore this tenet, when using Catholic teaching to justify their position: 'For the Church does not propose economic and political systems or programmes, nor does she show preference for one or the other, provided that human dignity is properly respected and promoted, and provided she herself is allowed the room she needs to exercise her ministry in the world' (SRS 41).

It is very difficult to justify or ascribe any meaning to statements such as that by Cardinal O'Brien (see above). In an abstract sense, he could be regarded as being correct: there is something lacking 'in justice' if people do not have the basic needs to live. But the statement was made with a practical policy implication. If it is not within the power of a donor government to put in place the processes of good governance that could allow aid to meet basic needs, then how can the developed world give effect to 'justice' through increasing aid? On the other hand, if it were within the power of potential donor governments to create systems of good governance, aid might well not be needed to nurture development. It is certainly a moral failing if we know how to alleviate poverty and do not do so. It cannot be a moral failing, however, to reject a particular approach based on an honest interpretation of the evidence and theory.

It may be possible to develop ways to better distribute aid so that the problems described above do not arise. Erixon (2005) suggests that aid can complement an internal reform programme that is already developing within a country – though aid tied to a reform programme imposed from outside does not seem to be effective. Others have suggested that aid could be given if there were an established record of reform: as the study by Pattillo et al.

(2006) suggests, this might well be effective.[23] Ogus's study (2005) might be regarded as implying that aid could be useful to help develop appropriate legal frameworks that nurture economic development. Ogus also points out, however, the difficulty of transplanting particular model legal systems into other cultures. The precise form of legal systems, norms for enforcing contracts, recognition of property rights, etc., will often be culture-specific.

The report of the Commission for Africa (2005) assimilates some of the points made above and makes clear the importance of governance and trade for growth. It suggests that aid should be a complement to internal policies to promote growth and to trade liberalisation by the West. In a sense it follows recent Catholic social teaching on development. Whether it is possible to deliver aid while guaranteeing that other reforms will take place, however, and while not giving incentives for the adoption of bad internal policies, is a subjective and pragmatic question. The history of promoting growth by 'blueprint' and 'planning' from outside is not a happy one, and it is difficult to be confident that the Commission's agenda will achieve the desired results.

Bottom-up-style approaches to providing development assistance are being attempted through the US-led African Development Foundation (ADF). The ADF appraises projects and has strict

---

[23] It is to be hoped that initiatives that encourage reform, such as the African peer review mechanism NEPAD, might be helpful. The record to date does not, however, lead to much hope. It may be the case that reform of a few countries within Africa, combined with the NEPAD mechanism, might promote beneficial reforms in other African countries.

selection criteria. Thus it may have more hope of success. Of course, the conclusions drawn from any success by the ADF could not be generalised to the majority of potential aid recipients that cannot meet the strict conditions imposed by the ADF. At the time of writing there is little independent assessment of its success. If it is successful, it will have practical lessons for policy-makers but few general lessons for theologians.

Without the conditions described by Erixon being applied to the granting of aid, it is at least possible that aid does little good and that it may do much harm. Indeed, as Bauer (2000) has suggested, if aid does do the damage its opponents suggest (by entrenching the power of bad government and undermining bottom-up development) the harm that it does is serious. If, however, aid has the benefits that its proponents suggest, the evidence indicates that, at best, those benefits are marginal.

Many of these issues are clearly understood and implicit in the generality of Catholic social teaching. Their acceptance, however, has implications for the specific exhortations that have been made in social encyclicals on the issue of development. Paragraph 47 of *Populorum progressio* suggested that individuals in good conscience should not just support projects to help the needy at their own expense but should also support the raising of taxes so that public authorities could expand their work in this area. It is difficult to justify such statements given the empirical and theoretical knowledge we now have on the record of development aid. Some Catholics in good conscience might support increased taxpayer support for aid. Others, equally in good conscience, might not. Given that experience of successful development strategies imposed or even nurtured from outside a given country is relatively limited, the specific guidance that it would be reasonable for the Church to give ought to be correspondingly cautious, perhaps along the following lines:

> Extreme poverty is an extremely serious matter: Christians should try to find and promote policies that they believe, in good conscience, and in a spirit of prudence, will genuinely help the promotion of development. They should also expend both time and money to assist charities promoting development. Christian politicians should expend time and energy seeking appropriate ways to aid development and to develop international bodies that may assist development and good governance more effectively than those that exist today.

In the Catholic Church's teaching, wider problems that prevent development and which might even make aid work against the interests of the people of developing countries have been recognised. Many of the points that have been made in this regard relate to the cold war age. Others relate to the international financial and trading systems with respect to which Christians are engaged in vigorous debate on different sides of the argument. These messages are well taken and well understood. But the importance of trying to nurture good governance is also understood in Catholic social teaching. This leads to particular geopolitical issues that cannot be addressed in this chapter but which are clearly very important for Christian social scientists wishing to make a positive contribution in this area. What should be the response of governments of developed countries when human rights, property rights, basic freedoms and basic principles of justice are absent in poor countries? In what way, if any, should intervention take place in order to create conditions that are conducive to development and the productive use of both charity and government aid? It is certainly reasonable for the Church to encourage Christians to try to understand these issues better and develop policy that will genuinely aid victims of bad governance and underdevelopment.

## Charity and relief

Some of the problems that we have described with regard to aid also exist when government-to-government relief is given in times of particular need due to famine and other disasters. Despite this, the arguments favouring caution and non-intervention in such circumstances are less strong. Firstly, if there is an immediate need to be met then we should not necessarily think about the long-term consequences before deciding to meet it. Secondly, it is easier for the government to provide disaster relief using non-government agencies in the recipient country – thus, to an extent, avoiding the problem of the aid process entrenching bad governance.

Our main focus has been on *government* aid to underdeveloped countries. Charity, provided through bodies that are genuinely independent of political systems in both donor and recipient countries, is less likely to cause harm and may well do much good, even when administered in countries with corrupt and unjust regimes. Many of the problems with government-to-government aid do not apply to charity administered through voluntary agencies, particularly where those voluntary agencies administer assistance through well-established structures in recipient countries which provide not just money but personal ministering to the poor. It is important to point out that we should not wait for a just ordering of the world or good governance in recipient countries before supporting such organisations. A number of statements made in Pope Benedict XVI's first encyclical, *Deus caritas est*, stress the importance of charitable action by Christians, *regardless of the underlying causes of the need they are trying to meet*. Pope Benedict stresses that whether a just society exists here and now is irrelevant to our mission of charity: 'There is no ordering of the state so just that it can eliminate the need for a service of love' (DCE 28).[24] He also stresses that the exercise of charity is fundamental to the lives of Christians. It is then made clear that Christian charitable activity must be independent of parties and ideologies – it is an extension of the Christian mission of love not to be put at the service of political goals.[25]

Thus the duty of Christians to help those in

---

[24] This can be considered from two perspectives. Firstly, regardless of the political order, there will always be people in need who are deserving of charity. Secondly, as is made clear by Pope Benedict elsewhere in the encyclical, charity satisfies a deep human need that government bureaucracies distributing financial and material help cannot meet.

[25] This is emphasised twice in paras 31 and 33. In para. 33 it is stated that those involved in charity 'must not be inspired by ideologies aimed at improving the world, but should rather be guided by the faith which works through love'.

immediate need is clear. This duty is not conditional on the political order, the reason why help is needed or whether the help leads to some long-run benefit. Some Christians may wish to apply this reasoning to development aid provided by the state. Aid provided by the state, however, is fundamentally of a different character from that provided by charity – both morally and economically speaking. On the basis of our knowledge of the theory and evidence it is difficult to argue that, with regard to the political agenda, the Church can go further than to stress the importance of lay faithful taking the issue of how to facilitate development very seriously and that it is an issue where Christians are free to differ about the means by which desirable ends can be achieved. To go further would be to risk promoting policies that, on the balance of evidence, have clearly done little good and may well have done much harm.

## References

Bauer, P. (2000), *From Subsistence to Exchange and Other Essays*, Princeton, NJ: Princeton University Press.

Catholic Church (1994), *Catechism of the Catholic Church*, London: Geoffrey Chapman.

Charles, R. (1998), *Christian Social Witness and Teaching: The Catholic Tradition from Genesis to Centesimus Annus*, Leominster: Gracewing.

Collier P. (2007), *The Bottom Billion: Why the Poorest Countries are Failing and What Can Be Done About It*, Oxford: Oxford University Press

Commission for Africa (2005), *Our Common Interest: Report of the Commission for Africa*, London: Commission for Africa.

Das, D. K. (2009), 'Globalisation and the emerging global middle class', *Economic Affairs*, 29(3), 89-92.

De Soto, H. (2000), *The Mystery of Capital: Why capitalism triumphs in the West and fails everywhere else*, London: Black Swan.

Djankov, S., J. G. Montalvo and M. Reynal-Querol (2006), 'Does foreign aid help?', *Cato Journal*, 26(1): 1–28.

Easterly, W. (2005), *Reliving the '50s: The Big Push, Poverty Traps and Takeoffs in Economic Development*, Working Paper no. 65, Centre for Global Development.

Erixon, F. (2003), 'Poverty and recovery: the history of aid and development in East Africa', *Economic Affairs*, 23(4): 27–33.

Erixon, F. (2005), *Aid and Development: Will it work this time?*, London: International Policy Network.

Griswold, D. (2009), *Mad About Trade: Why Main Street America Should Embrace Globalization*, Washington DC, US: Cato Institute.

Gupta, S., R. Powell and Y. Yang (2006), *Macroeconomic Challenges of Scaling Up Aid to Africa*, Washington, DC: International Monetary Fund.

Gwartney, J. and R. Lawson (2004), 'What have we learned from the measurement of economic freedom?', in M. A. Wynne, H. Rosenblum and R. L. Formaini (eds), *The Legacy of Milton and Rose Friedman's 'Free to Choose': Economic liberalism at the turn of the 21st century*, Dallas, TX: Federal Reserve Bank of Dallas.

Lal, D. (2002), *The Poverty of Development Economics*, Hobart Paper 144, London: Institute of Economic Affairs.

Ogus, A. (2005), *Towards Appropriate Institutional Arrangements for Regulation in Less Developed Countries*, Paper no. 119, Centre on Regulation and Competition, Manchester: University of Manchester.

Pattillo, C., S. Gupta and K. Carey (2006), *Sustaining and Accelerating Pro-Poor Growth in Africa*, Washington, DC: International Monetary Fund.

Pontifical Council for Justice and Peace (2005), *Compendium of the Social Doctrine of the Church*, London: Burns & Oates.

Rajan, R. and A. Subramanian (2006), *What Undermines Aid's Impact on Growth*, NBER Working Paper no. 11657, Cambridge, MA: National Bureau of Economic Research.

Sachs, J. D. and A. M. Warner (2001), 'The curse of natural resources', *European Economic Review*, 45: 827–38.

Senior, I. (2006), *Corruption – the World's Big C: Cases, Causes, Consequences, Cures*, Research Monograph 61, London: Institute of Economic Affairs.

Spencer, N. and J. Chaplin (eds) (2009), *God and Government*, London, UK: SPCK.

Townsend, N. (2009), 'Government and social infrastructure', in Spencer N. and J. Chaplin, (eds), *God and Government*, London, UK: SPCK.

Wolf, M. (2004), *Why Globalization Works*, New Haven, CT: Yale University Press.

# 5

# THE UNANSWERED QUESTIONS OF THE JUST WAGE

*Thomas E. Woods, Jr*

## The limits of the Church's teaching authority

The question of the 'just wage', the level of remuneration that an employer must award his workers if he is to satisfy the demands of justice, became an especially important one in the Catholic world following the publication of Pope Leo XIII's *Rerum novarum* (1891). There the Pope condemned socialism, but he also agreed with the conventional thinking of his time that, firstly, capitalist greed had forced the working class into their miserable state, and, secondly, that wage rates reached by means of the voluntary agreement of both parties might be unjust, particularly since the workers lacked the bargaining power necessary in order to win for themselves the wages they needed and deserved.[1] Thus the document criticised the notion of wages as 'regulated by free consent, and [that] therefore the employer, when he pays what was agreed upon,

---

[1] Although the Pope does not use the modern term 'bargaining power', this point is strongly implied in *Rerum novarum* (RN 1, 3, 36, 37). The US bishops expressed the argument in modern terms in 1984: see Block (1985: 151). For a critique of the idea that workers lack 'bargaining power', see Woods (2004).

has done his part and seemingly is not called upon to do anything beyond'. Workers and employers may enter into agreements pertaining to wages, but

> there underlies a dictate of natural justice more imperious and ancient than any bargain between man and man, namely, that wages ought not to be insufficient to support a frugal and well-behaved wage-earner. If through necessity or fear of a worse evil the workman accept harder conditions because an employer or contractor will afford him no better, he is made the victim of force and injustice. (RN 45)

Pope Leo later spoke of the need to pay wages 'sufficient to enable [the labourer] comfortably to support himself, his wife, and his children' (RN 46).

It has not been easy to carry on a fruitful, critical study of this issue, since supporters of the just wage so often attempt to stifle rational debate through a simple appeal to authority: the popes, they say, have spoken. The teaching, however, is in fact quite recent, is not consistent over time, and is based on superficially plausible but dubious economic presuppositions (labour's supposedly unequal bargaining power being among those dubious presuppositions) that would appear to be debatable matters of fact rather than statements of faith and morals. The sixteenth-century Spanish Scholastics adopted a generally laissez-faire position regarding wages, arguing that no wage to which a labourer gave his consent could be unjust. If he was unhappy with the compensation he was being offered, he could terminate his employment. No one at the time reacted in horror, or declared it to be radically at odds with Catholic tradition.[2]

Catholic supporters of the free labour market, it is sometimes alleged, are no different from Catholics who dissent from the Church's official teachings on controversial topics such as abortion, medical ethics and human sexuality. This charge is completely without merit: the free-market Catholic typically objects only to instrumental rather than substantive features of the social teaching. In other words, the Catholic supporter of the free market wants to see the same good outcomes that the popes seek, but fears that the means sometimes suggested to bring about those ends will not succeed. A similar point can be made about papal teaching on development aid (see Chapter 4). While the Pope has every right to declare abortion to be a moral evil, for instance, he cannot by his *ipse dixit* make *A* cause *B* if in the nature of things course of action *A* in fact inhibits *B*. The leftist is dissenting from papal teaching on an issue involving substantial moral goods; the Catholic supporter of the free labour market is concerned simply that the Pope's recommended course of action to help the less fortunate will – contrary to the Pope's own true intention – either do no such thing or make the situation worse.

Archbishop John J. Myers recently made what should be the elementary distinction between means and ends that we are making here. While

---

[2]  It should not be thought that, at that time, there was a consensus of feeling among scholars and the ruling classes in favour of freedom of contract. Indeed, the reverse is the case. While it was recognised that the Spanish Scholastics spoke with reason, the prejudice in favour of administered, rather than market-determined, wages was probably stronger then than it is today.

with abortion 'there can be no legitimate diversity of opinion', the same is not true of economic issues, where the best approach to take in concrete circumstances is a matter of informed judgement and individual conscience:

> For example, our preferential option for the poor is a fundamental aspect of this teaching. But, there are legitimate disagreements about the best way or ways truly to help the poor in our society. No Catholic can legitimately say, 'I do not care about the poor.' If he or she did so this person would not be objectively in communion with Christ and His Church. But, both those who propose welfare increases and those who propose tax cuts to stimulate the economy may in all sincerity believe that their way is the best method really to help the poor. This is a matter of prudential judgment made by those entrusted with the care of the common good. It is a matter of conscience in the proper sense. (Myers, 2004)

Our position in no way involves the claim that the social or hard sciences are exempt from moral evaluation. They are, however, exempt from *technical critiques* on the part of the Church, since churchmen may speak only as informed individuals on such questions and not for the Church as a whole. Thus if a certain medicine could be produced only by ripping the hearts out of living human beings, the Church should condemn such a thing no matter how many doctors were in favour of producing the medicine. But if two kinds of medicines are suggested to treat a particular ailment, and no moral objection can be raised to either one, then in such an area the Church must defer to those who are schooled in that specialised science.

Another claim is that Catholic supporters of the free market have defined the sphere of faith and morals too narrowly, and that the popes' statements about the economy are a perfectly legitimate subset of those areas of life over which they have been given divine authority to instruct the faithful. The popes, this argument goes, have every right to speak out on economic matters since economic affairs are not utterly distinct or removed from moral concerns.

This argument, too, misfires. No one denies that economic activity carries a moral dimension. The Pope is obviously well within his rights to condemn theft or fraud, or to instruct the faithful on the need to be generous with their wealth. He may likewise condemn government policies that involve oppression and injustice, such as burdensome taxation or inflation of the money supply. No one in this debate contests any of this.

The real issue at stake, which is obscured by these straw-man objections, is this. Suppose a Church document recommends a particular economic policy as being morally necessary because its drafters believe it will make the poor better off. Suppose further that they consider it so obvious that this policy will improve the lot of the poor that they do not consider the possibility that it could have any other effect, that there could be any good reason for opposing it, or even simply that a trade-off exists between the good outcome they hope for and unfortunate, unintended side effects of the given policy. And now suppose that the policy will, in fact, not only *not* improve the position of the poor, but may also make it even worse. What are economically astute members of the faithful to do? Are they forbidden to observe that not even the Pope himself can make reality otherwise than it is?

The question is not whether the Pope may instruct us on our responsibilities as moral actors in the marketplace (see the chapters in Part Two). The question, instead, is whether the Pope's infallibility reaches to his empirical and theoretical statements about how the economy works. For instance, the Pope may certainly say that all morally licit means should be employed in order to improve the material well-being of families, since they are the building blocks of society and the little platoons (to borrow a phrase from Edmund Burke) from which its future members will one day emerge. But in his capacity as Pope, with the power to bind all Catholics on pain of mortal sin, may he go on to say what, from a purely pragmatic point of view, would be the best or most effective way to bring about this outcome? No orthodox definition of papal authority includes infallibility regarding such matters, and it would be rank superstition for a Catholic to hold otherwise.

A good example of this difficulty involves Pope Paul VI's 1967 encyclical *Populorum progressio* (see Chapter 4). There the Pope called for the very kind of Western-funded Third World development programmes that have proved so disastrous in practice. These programmes – as scholars such as Peter Bauer pointed out in vain at the time – served to prop up some of the most brutal regimes in the world, and shielded dictators from the full consequences of their destructive economic policies. They delayed necessary reforms, enlarged the state sector at the expense of the productive economy, and created often violent ethnic and racial tension as competing groups scrambled to gain control of the state apparatus in order to control Western grant money. The encyclical was filled with the standard criticisms of the free market, yet it was the most market-oriented of the less developed nations that wound up prospering the most, and where the lot of the poor improved most dramatically (Woods, 2005a: ch. 4).

Thus Paul VI called for the implementation of policies that few informed and responsible people, looking at their horrific and lethal record, would continue to promote or defend today. There were people at the time who predicted exactly what would happen, but who were ignored in favour of the chorus of fashionable opinion that called for massive Western funding of state-led development programmes in the Third World. Now Pope Paul VI could certainly have instructed the faithful on the moral issues at stake, urging them to be generous towards their impoverished brethren. That is what a teacher of faith and morals is expected to do. But, by any standard, whether (for example) free trade or a system of protective tariffs is more effective for a developing country – obviously a matter of legitimate disagreement among Catholics – or whether state-led development programmes are a good economic idea are not issues on which the Pope may appear to make morally binding judgements. Not only are specific policy proposals all too fallible, but when enjoying the prestige of an encyclical they can unnecessarily trouble the consciences of good Catholics, whose disagreements are based not on any perverse desire to oppose the Holy See but on specialised secular knowledge they happen to possess. That is why Pope Leo XIII once said, 'If I were to pronounce on any single matter of a prevailing economic problem, I should be interfering with the freedom of men to work out their own affairs. Certain cases must be solved in the domain of facts, case by case as they occur. ... [M]en must realize in deeds those things, the principles of which have been placed beyond dispute. ... [T]hese things one must leave to the solution of time and experience' (Burton, 1962: 171).

## The minimum wage, the plight of the poor and Catholic conscience

Paul VI, like many at the time, was sure the policies he recommended would benefit the least fortunate. It is clear from the context in which wages are discussed in the encyclicals that the popes likewise take for granted that interfering with wage rates reached voluntarily on the free market, either through legally imposed wage floors or by means of moral exhortation, can make labour in the aggregate better off. Monsignor John A. Ryan, perhaps the twentieth century's most prolific American Catholic proponent of the concept of a just wage as something distinct from the freely agreed wage, wrote his books and articles on the living wage *because he thought these proposals would make labour better off.* It is difficult to imagine an official Church document arguing that forcing wages beyond the level they attain on the free market is an end in itself, *even if it makes heads of households materially worse off* by pricing some workers out of the market. No such document exists, of course, and it is safe to assume that none will ever be issued. But this is the very crux of the matter: how is a Catholic to respond to a teaching whose stated intent is to improve the well-being of struggling workers when he knows it will do no such thing?

While it is true that the popes do not directly call for legally mandated minimum wages, the logic of their arguments leads in that direction. Since the overwhelming majority of people who have written on the social teaching, from ordinary laymen all the way to bishops' conferences, have in fact justified minimum wages and minimum-wage increases on the basis of that teaching and have never been corrected or rebuked by the Vatican, it must be safe to assume that such a position is at least a legitimate development of the teaching, and is certainly not excluded by it.

In a certain sense, though, whether or not the social encyclicals call for a *legally* mandated minimum wage or whether they simply declare the employer to be *morally* bound to provide one is largely immaterial. To a Catholic employer who believes the Catholic Church is of divine institution, there may be little practical difference between a minimum wage that is imposed legally and one that is imposed on his conscience by the official teaching of a national bishops' conference.

Of the measures we might propose in order to improve the lot of the poor, the minimum 'living wage' is very likely to be the worst of all.[3] By making unskilled workers more expensive to hire, it privileges those who are the most prosperous and skilled. This is why labour unions, which in practice tend to represent those who are semi-skilled or skilled, consistently favour minimum-wage and living-wage legislation even though their own workers earn much more than these minima and would seem to be unaffected by them. By making their low-skilled counterparts relatively more expensive, they enrich themselves at the expense of the most vulnerable workers of all. And when the living-wage measure is introduced and the job losses inevitably come, it is once again the least skilled and most vulnerable who are the first to suffer.

## The 'market power' argument

A common argument in favour of state coercion on behalf of the worker involves the issue of labour monopsony – cases in which workers cannot choose between potential employers but for whatever reason must sell their labour to a particular firm. It is often suggested that labour monopsonies were common at the time the first social encyclical was written. Labour economist Morgan Reynolds has raised a number of substantial objections to this alleged problem, all of which are relevant

---

[3] There are other measures such as welfare safety nets and social insurance that can be debated on their merits, but both of these are less likely to be damaging than the imposition of a minimum wage.

to the economies of the UK and the USA in the nineteenth century. If monopsony had been so serious and pervasive in the nineteenth century as is commonly assumed, it seems difficult to explain why wages rose for most of the century, how there could have been so much job-switching, or why large firms – more likely to hold monopsony power – paid higher wages than small firms (Reynolds, 1995: 12–13).

The major obstacles to a labour monopsony involve the tendency of new firms to enter an industry over time, attracted by the low wages offered by the monopsonist and the tendency of workers simply to move away and settle somewhere that has a friendlier economic climate and a greater diversity of employers. These incentives 'make widespread, sustained monopsony impossible in an economy like that of the United States' (ibid.: 247). The widespread availability of inexpensive transportation has now essentially buried the argument from monopsony once and for all, since workers are now able to canvass employers across a radius of at least several dozen miles.

Living or minimum wages are typically demanded on the grounds that the people who will receive them need such wages in order to support their families. That, indeed, is the very heart of the just-wage position. But suppose we argued as follows in the case of individuals supporting their families from business activity: the selling prices for most used cars are too low for the sellers of these cars to support their families. The poor in particular, since they tend to have the worst-quality cars to sell, suffer the most. Therefore, it will be illegal from now on for any used car to sell for a price below £12,000. That way, sellers of these cars will earn enough to support their families.[4]

Now, of course, what will really happen is that a great many used cars, valued in the common estimation of the market at less than £12,000, will simply not sell at all. The owners of those cars will not be able to support their families *at all*, and are much worse off than they would have been if they had been able to sell their cars for at least some amount of money (naturally, too, purchasers of cars will be harmed as well). In other words, it does not follow from the mere fact that someone needs something that it would be sensible to impose his desire by law. This is what minimum wages seek to do in the case of employed people. There is no difference in principle between the government mandating a minimum wage for employed people and mandating minimum prices for the goods that somebody who is self-employed tries to sell. If the product of the worker has a market value less than the mandated price or wage the individual will not be able to obtain employment.

Finally, it is morally relevant that there exists on the free market a natural tendency for real wages to rise over time. In a relatively unhampered market, business is free to invest its profits in machinery and other capital equipment that makes labour more productive. One person can then produce far more than he once could, and at lower cost. The economy can now produce in much greater abundance. These cost cuts are passed on to consumers in the form of

[4] I owe this example to Don Boudreaux of George Mason University: http://cafehayek.com/hayek/2006/06/testing_the_log.html

lower prices.[5] These increases in the productivity of labour, by increasing the overall amount of output and thereby increasing the ratio of consumers' goods to the supply of labour, make prices lower relative to wage rates and thereby raise real wages (Reisman, 1996: 603–72; Woods 2005a: 59–67). Leo XIII was therefore more right than he knew when he made the anti-Marxist observation in *Rerum novarum* that capital and labour were natural allies rather than antagonists. Here is the proof: both labour and the owners of capital should want the same economic policies – low or non-existent taxation, and no government discouragement of business investment – since both benefit from investment in capital equipment and the resulting increase in overall wealth.

## We cannot assume away the fact that it is the poor who will suffer from a minimum wage …

The teaching of the Church on what constitutes a just war includes the proviso that violence must be resorted to only as a last resort, when all other options have failed. The same logic might be extended to domestic issues as well (see also the chapters by Sirico on welfare and charity, Gregg on the role of government and O'Brien on subsidiarity and solidarity). Before resorting to coercion we should consider all possible alternative ways of achieving economic objectives. Indeed,

---

[5]  In an economy with a rapidly expanding money supply, these price cuts are not always apparent. The point is that prices are lower than they otherwise would have been; another point is that wages increase more rapidly than prices, since the ratio of consumers' goods to the supply of labour has increased.

according to our argument above, coercion is both unnecessary and counter-productive.

Peter Kwasniewski, a critic of the free market, is unmoved by this argument. In Kwasniewski's version of things, we can solve the problem of insufficiently high wages here and now. We want everyone to earn a decent wage? Then we can simply legislate one into existence! According to Kwasniewski, if someone claims

> that he agrees with what the Popes want (e.g., a living wage) but he thinks he knows better how to get those results, he is dodging the problems that we are facing *here and now*. Let us pretend that the magic of the free market will work things out to everyone's advantage ... *someday*. How long from now? Ten years? Twenty? Fifty? Meanwhile, do we let wage agreements contrary to the moral law simply stand unchecked, because the lives of some poor people have to be, as it were, manure to fertilize the ground for more prosperous days? It seems to me the Church is saying: The worker has to be given such and such, *here and now*. If not, mortal sin is being committed and the common good damaged. If this means inefficiency, okay; if it means a lower gross national product, okay; if it means the rich have to live more frugally, that's even better. (Kwasniewski, 2004)

Kwasniewski has dodged the entire question. He simply assumes that the poor can be made better off, with no side effects that he considers morally relevant (or, at least, no side effects, such as unemployment, that are worth mentioning as *no* potentially harmful side effects are discussed or even raised), through state coercion and mandating of a minimum wage. He assumes the very point that is to be proved. In fact, *the poor themselves* would be worse off, since his recommendation would make them less employable and, by making it more expensive and less profitable to do business in the first place, would discourage the very capital accumulation that alone can improve the lot of the poor across the board.

Had Kwasniewski lived during the Industrial Revolution we can only imagine his complaints.[6] We need 2,000 square feet per family here and now. We need the eight-hour day. We need modern amenities for all. Let us impose them through law, rather than wait for economic progress to provide these things as the miserly Thomas Woods and other believers in the market economy would have us do. In that capital-starved economy these regulations would have made just about everyone unemployable, and would have brought the inevitable (if gradual) improvement in everyone's standard of living to a grinding halt – the same effect such regulations would have today. If we wanted to be sure that the Third World never emerges from poverty, we should give them this kind of advice today. It isn't that Kwasniewski has considered what economics has to say about such policies and decided that the benefits outweigh the costs to the poor. As far as Kwasniewski is concerned, there are no costs to the poor from the pursuit of such policies. He will concede that the economy may be poorer overall – though he evidently assumes that this overall impoverishment will not appreciably

---

[6] On the Industrial Revolution and the increase in the standard of living of the overwhelming majority of people, see Woods (2005a: 169–74).

hurt the poor – or that the rich may be poorer. He is willing to live with these costs, he assures us. But are there any costs for the poor? Not a word, other than an implicit assumption of 'no'.

Economist George Reisman suggests what would have happened if nineteenth-century poverty had been addressed by forcing the rich to live more frugally, as Kwasniewski suggests is possible. The problem is that

> there was virtually nothing to redistribute. The workers of the early nineteenth century did not lack automobiles and television sets because the capitalists were keeping the whole supply to themselves. There simply were no automobiles or television sets – for anyone. Nor did the workers of those days lack sufficient housing, clothing, and meat because the capitalists had too much of these goods. Very little of such goods could be produced when they had to be produced almost entirely by hand. If the limited supplies of such goods that the capitalists had could have been redistributed, the improvement in the conditions of the workers would hardly have been noticeable. If one person in a thousand, say, is a wealthy capitalist, and eats twice as much and has twenty times the clothing and furniture as an average person, hardly any noticeable improvement for the average person could come from dividing the capitalists' greater-than-average consumption by 999 and redistributing it. At the very best, a redistribution of wealth or income would have been useless as a means of alleviating the poverty of the past. (Reisman, 1996: 653)

Not only would it have been useless, but it would also have been positively harmful. If businessmen wish to stay in business, they must reinvest the vast bulk of their profits in still further additions to their capital stock – which in turn further increase the productivity of labour, thereby increasing the supply of goods that the economy is capable of producing. These increases in the productivity of labour, by increasing the overall amount of output and thereby increasing the ratio of consumers' goods to the supply of labour, make prices lower relative to wage rates and thereby raise real wages. Kwasniewski's plan to increase the lot of the working class would sacrifice the investment in capital equipment that business must now forgo, and would lower the incentive to engage in such investment in the future, since the business community now knows the fruits of such investment will be taken away (ibid.: 653).

## Providing a living wage … as soon as possible

In light of our discussion of wages and how they are increased, we are in a better position to evaluate Pius XI's statement in *Quadragesimo anno* that all men must be paid a wage sufficient to support their families in reasonable comfort, and that where this is not possible 'social justice demands that changes be introduced as soon as possible whereby such a wage will be assured to every adult workingman'. According to what we have just argued, when *Quadragesimo anno* urges us to introduce changes in order to make a living wage available to working men, a good way to comply with that instruction would be to remove as many obstacles to investment as possible, and to eliminate taxes on capital, 'excess profits' and the like. Unfortunately, certain ecclesiastical documents seem to call for just the opposite: practically every single recommendation set forth in the American bishops' famous 1984 statement on the economy would have made workers and the poor worse off (Block, 1985: 125–60). That document, among others, is an object lesson in the need for sound economic reasoning to inform our moral conclusions. 'What was wrong with Catholic social thought in the nineteenth century', writes Father James Sadowsky SJ, of Fordham University, 'was not so much its ethics as its lack of understanding of how the free market can work. The concern for the worker was entirely legitimate, but concern can accomplish little unless we know the causes and the cures for the disease' (Sadowsky, 1983: 125).

## Non-economic arguments and the just wage

The matter of the just wage raises additional concerns beyond the merely economic. Imagine a case in which the authorities have somehow managed to pinpoint the 'just wage' as £5 per hour – and assume that the requirement is not statutory but is regarded as a moral obligation by some Christian employers. Then consider employee John, and firms A and B. Firm A, not considering John's labour worth the decreed wage, passes him over for employment. Firm B, however, willing to incur the criticisms of the wage authorities, employs John at the mutually agreed-upon wage of £4 per hour.

Consider how the 'just wage' proponent would

apportion moral approval and censure in this case. Firm *A* chooses not to employ John at all. Firm *B* employs him at £4 per hour, which is £4 per hour more than John receives from Firm *A*. Yet in the 'just wage' framework, it is Firm *B* that merits condemnation, even though Firm *A* did not even hire John in the first place. Indeed, Firm *A*'s action (or inaction) will not even be known about. Firm *B* makes the man at least somewhat better off than he had been before, while Firm *A* contributes nothing at all to his well-being. Is it morally preferable for someone not to be hired at all rather than to be hired at a wage that is somewhat below whatever has been decreed as the 'just wage'?

Roman law, in its treatment of prices, held that a thing was worth what it could generally be sold for. In the absence of any better offer for the man's labour, it is not clear on what grounds his current wage can be considered unjust. James Sadowsky poses the natural question: in the case of a worker in dire need, while 'certainly from a Christian point of view we ought to help him meet his needs, the question that *ought* to arise is this: "Why, however, should it be precisely the *employer* on whom this obligation falls, if in fact the employer is not worsening but bettering the condition of his employee?"' (ibid.: 124). If no one else can find any use for the man's labour at a price higher than or equal to what his current employer is offering, why is his current employer the only party to be morally censured? Isn't his employer doing more than literally anyone else on earth to improve his well-being? If this teaching makes the man unemployable by closing off this one employment opportunity, he is unlikely to be consoled by the assurance that at least justice has been served.

*Rerum novarum* bases some of its argument for intervention against employers and on behalf of labourers on the notion of the primacy of labour in the overall scheme of production. In the provision of commodities that the community needs, the document explains,

> the labour of the working class – the exercise of their skill, and the employment of their strength, in the cultivation of the land, and in the workshops of trade – is especially responsible and quite indispensable. Indeed, their co-operation is in this respect so important that it may be truly said that it is only by the labour of working men that States grow rich. Justice, therefore, demands that the interests of the working classes should be carefully watched over by the administration, so that they who contribute so largely to the advantage of the community may themselves share in the benefits which they create – that being housed, clothed, and bodily fit, they may find their life less hard and more endurable. (RN 34)

Leo XIII concludes by declaring it 'good for the commonwealth to shield from misery those on whom it so largely depends for the things that it needs'.

To be sure, *Rerum novarum* is correct to note the complementarity of capital and labour, since each of course needs the other. But it seems dubious to exalt the contribution of labour to the point of suggesting that 'it is only by the labour of working men that States grow rich'. Just how much could a worker produce with his bare hands, without the aid of the machinery and other forms of capital that a firm provides for his use?

Let us briefly dispense with the facile objection that capital equipment, too, requires labour for its production, and that this fact once again demonstrates the primacy of labour.[7] What this argument overlooks is that brawn alone will never produce a steam shovel, a forklift or a computer processor. Only when informed by the knowledge of inventors and supplied with the capital saved by capitalists can the average labourer produce the tiniest fraction of what he is today accustomed to producing. There is, therefore, no sense in which the position of the ordinary labourer in the overall structure of production can give him a prior moral claim on the monies of his employer (for that reason, it seems that the Pope speaks better when he says elsewhere in *Rerum novarum*: 'Each needs the other: capital cannot do without labor, nor labor without capital' (RN 19)).

Indeed, if we are going to dismiss wage rates voluntarily arrived at as potentially 'unjust', and instead apportion monies on the basis of some theoretical reckoning of each component's contribution to the production process, the outcome will not please proponents of a 'just wage'. As we have seen, it is investment in capital equipment which increases the productivity of labour and thus increases real wages. In light of that, should workers be required to hand over a portion of their salary as a kickback to their employers to compensate

---

[7] Christopher Ferrara advanced this argument in a lengthy series of articles in *The Remnant*, a traditional Catholic newspaper published in the United States, in 2004/05.

them for the capital equipment (and the abstention from consumption that made investment in that capital equipment possible), none of which was in any way earned by the worker? Free consent as a basis for wage determination would appear preferable to wages determined on the basis of highly debatable philosophical propositions and counter-propositions.

Other intractable problems seem to plague the just-wage concept. George Stigler once observed that human beings could acquire a physiologically adequate diet for a mere $8 a month (in 1950 prices) by eating, over the course of the year, nothing but 370 pounds of wheat flour, 57 cans of evaporated milk, 111 pounds of cabbage, 25 pounds of spinach and 285 pounds of dried navy beans (Stigler, 1952: 2). It is not clear how appeals to 'justice' in wage determination can resolve such practical questions on anything but an arbitrary basis. Such a diet as this would, almost certainly, be unbearably monotonous even if nutritionally satisfactory. But just how diversified a diet can we derive from justice in the abstract as morally obligatory for an employer to provide? That question, furthermore, neglects the enjoyment a worker derives from eating an occasional meal in a restaurant rather than at home, but here again justice does not disclose to us how many restaurant meals, if any, an employer bears the moral burden of providing.

We would likewise need to adjust for the widely varying circumstances in which people find themselves. Consider a father of eight compared with a celibate Opus Dei numerary. Leaving aside the virtual certainty that such a wage would render him unemployable, does the father deserve a wage eight times as high as the numerary? The numerary may be responsible for a sick relative. How would that consideration be factored in? Would the employer need to enquire into how many people live in the numerary's Opus Dei house, what their mutual obligations are, and what the needs of the house are?[8] Would he need to enquire into the father's budget for babysitters, the relative importance he places on entertainment, or the number of movie rentals he watches per month? Would movie rentals be considered a luxury or a component of a truly just wage? These questions are not meant to be facetious, but simply to illustrate the difficulties involved in calculating a just wage and of applying the concept of 'justice' to the determination of economic and material conditions.

## Conclusion

A contemporary Catholic reviewer of Monsignor John Ryan's *A Living Wage*, writing in the *Catholic University Bulletin*, tried without success to point out to Ryan that a business is not a charitable foundation but an enterprise devoted to producing some good or service at the lowest cost to the consumer. Ryan's critic concluded: 'As an individual or as head of a family, the laborer produces the same amount of work; how then could the employer as such be obliged in strict justice to take into account a condition which is of no advantage to him?' (Sauvage, 1907: 474). These were the days of Pope

---

[8] I owe this point to Sam Bostaph of the University of Dallas.

St Pius X, and at that time the *Catholic University Bulletin* never published anything that called any solemn Church teaching into question. That the publication nevertheless considered this matter an essentially open question available for rational debate is not without significance.

Pope Pius XI made an important concession in his encyclical *Quadragesimo anno* (1931). He acknowledged that limits must exist to what the moral theologian may legitimately say within the economic sphere, since 'economics and moral science employs each its own principles in its own sphere'. It is true that the Pope then went on to deny that 'the economic and moral orders are so distinct from and alien to each other that the former depends in no way on the latter'. But once it has been conceded that economics is a bona fide science possessing an internal coherence of its own, problems immediately arise for those who would claim that Catholic social teaching definitively settles all major economic matters in an absolute and binding way. As A. M. C. Waterman points out, this concession by Pius XI 'throws doubt on the authoritative character of that very substantial part of Catholic (or at least papal) social teaching which consists not of theological and ethical pronouncements, but of empirical judgments about the economy' (Waterman, 1982: 112–13).

A great many unresolved issues remain in the area of the just wage. Those who raise them are not wicked men, perversely desirous of causing mischief in the Church. Most are serious Catholics who understand that this is an evolving teaching, and one that partly depends on means–ends connections that in the nature of things are obviously open to debate. Edward Grant tells us that in the medieval university 'reason was enthroned ... as the ultimate arbiter of most intellectual arguments and controversies. It was quite natural for scholars immersed in a university environment to employ reason to probe into subject areas that had not been explored before, as well as to discuss possibilities that had not previously been seriously entertained' (Woods, 2005b: 66). Likewise David Lindberg reports that although there were broad theological limits, the medieval professor 'had remarkable freedom of thought and expression; there was almost no doctrine, philosophical or theological, that was not submitted to minute scrutiny and criticism by scholars in the medieval university' (ibid.: 220). There is no reason that the same spirit cannot continue to animate Catholic discourse now. Let the discussion be carried on in a spirit of charity, reason and faith, and let us assume the best rather than the worst about those with whom we disagree.

## References

Block, W. (1985), 'Neglect of the marketplace: the questionable economics of America's bishops', *Notre Dame Journal of Law, Ethics, & Public Policy*, 2: 125–60.

Burton, K. (1962), *Leo the Thirteenth: The First Modern Pope*, New York: David McKay Co.

Kwasniewski, P. (2004), 'This goes way beyond free markets: thoughts on the disagreement

between Woods and Storck', 5 July: http://
chroniclesmagazine.org/News/Kwasniewski/
NewsPK070504.html

Myers, Archbishop J. J. (2004), '"A time for
honesty": a pastoral statement by The Most
Reverend John J. Myers, Archbishop of Newark',
5 May: http://www.rcan.org/archbish/jjm_
letters/ATimeforHonesty.htm

Reisman, G. (1996), *Capitalism*, Ottawa, IL:
Jameson Books.

Reynolds, M. (1995), *Economics of Labor*, Cincinnati,
OH: South-Western College Publishing.

Sadowsky, J. A. (1983), 'Capitalism, ethics, and
classical Catholic social doctrine', *This World*, 6:
115–25.

Sauvage, G. M. (1907), review of *A Living Wage*,
by John A. Ryan, *Catholic University Bulletin*,
13: 470–75.

Stigler, G. (1952), *The Theory of Price*, rev. edn,
New York: Macmillan.

Waterman, A. M. C. (1982), 'Property rights in
John Locke and in Christian social teaching',
*Review of Social Economy*, 9: 97–115.

Woods, T. (2004), 'Forgotten facts of American labor
history', Mises.org, 22 November: http://www.
mises.org/fullstory.aspx?control=1685&id=74

Woods, T. E., Jr (2005a), *The Church and the Market:
A Catholic Defense of the Free Economy*, Lanham,
MD: Lexington.

Woods, T. E., Jr (2005b), *How the Catholic Church
Built Western Civilization*, Washington, DC:
Regnery.

## 6

# TAXATION AND THE SIZE OF THE STATE

*Philip Booth*

## Introduction

This chapter begins with a discussion of Catholic
teaching on the role of taxation. In the discussion
of Catholic teaching we concentrate on the
later teaching of the Church, starting with the
publication of *Rerum novarum* in 1891. There was,
of course, earlier authoritative comment by the
Church and her teachers on economic matters (see,
for example, Charles, 1998, vol. 1: 209, 361–71 for
some discussion of this early comment); also the
late Scholastics warned against excessive taxation.
The early Church's role in what could be described
as 'social witness' rather than social teaching in the
medieval period is important too: the Church, not
the state, was the dominant provider of welfare in
line with the principles of subsidiarity (see ibid.,
but also Bartholomew, 2004, for an account of the
remarkable achievements of the Church in welfare
provision in the UK). This earlier work and the
early examples of social witness are important,
but the post-1891 teaching of the Church made

this earlier analysis explicit in the wider public domain and so it is on the post-1891 period that we shall focus. The documents that have been used to express Catholic Church teaching since 1891 are easily available.

An understanding of taxation must be set in the context of the principle of private property and that of the universal destination of goods. There is not space for a detailed discussion of this issue here, but some brief comments are worth making. With regard to the principle of the universal destination of goods, the Catholic Church teaches that the fruits of God's creation are for all to be enjoyed. It does not follow from this, however, that all should have access to all goods equally or that redistribution and common ownership in a socialist political system should be the vehicle for facilitating the universal destination of goods. With this in mind, the Church also teaches that private property is an important way in which the universal destination of goods can be achieved. The principle of private property is not inviolable, but it accords with economic efficiency, family autonomy and free will: there is an excellent discussion of these issues in the recently published *Compendium of the Social Doctrine of the Church* (paras 171–84)[1] and also in Spieker (2005). Taxation, of course, violates private property. In the context of the Church's teaching on the universal destination of goods and on private property it can be seen that, while taxation may be permitted, excessive taxation is likely to be problematic. As such, the precise

---

[1] Referred to as Pontifical Council for Justice and Peace (2005).

level of taxation is clearly a matter for prudential judgement informed, at least in part, by economic reasoning. Therefore, the Church, in her teaching, has limited her statements to general principles and not made judgements about appropriate rates of taxation. That part of the laity involved in political debate and decision-making, however, will, of course, have to draw conclusions, informed by the Church's teaching and economic reasoning, on the appropriate level of taxation.

## Modern Catholic teaching on taxation and the role of the state: taxation for redistribution and welfare

### Rerum novarum
Pope Leo XIII's encyclical *Rerum novarum* was a landmark in that it began a stream of writing from the modern popes on economic problems and political choices in industrial and post-industrial society. It is often described as the 'workers' encyclical', and it was critical of many aspects of behaviour by the owners of capital and businesses. Interestingly, however, it provides no basis for arguments proposing a substantial tax burden or for the state to take upon itself wide-ranging functions akin to those it undertakes today in most developed countries. Furthermore, *Rerum novarum* provides strong a priori arguments against excessive taxation and frequently recommends other mechanisms for the achievement of specific economic objectives. For example, paragraph five states, 'Socialists, therefore, by endeavouring

to transfer the possessions of individuals to the community at large, strike at the interests of every wage earner, since they would deprive him of the liberty of disposing of his wages'. The state is to serve man, not the other way round: 'Man precedes the State, and possesses, prior to the formation of any State, the right of providing for the substance of his body' (RN 7). Paragraph 13 stresses the complete primacy of the family over the state and lays out the importance of the principle of inheritance to transmit productive property to children.

*Rerum novarum* sees no place for the pursuit of equality as an end in itself, nor for taxation for its own sake. Applying this to policy, this would appear to exclude systems of taxation that lead to greater equality but lead everyone, including the poor, to be poorer. In the words of *Rerum novarum*: 'The door would be thrown open to envy, to mutual invective, and to discord; the sources of wealth themselves would run dry, for no one would have any interest in exerting his talents or industry; and that ideal equality about which they [socialists] entertain pleasant dreams would be in reality the levelling down of all to a like condition of misery and degradation' (RN 15). Pope Leo then went on to express belief in the inviolability of private property[2] as the primary method of raising the condition of the poor, and suggested that inequality is far

---

[2] Pope Leo stated exceptions to that inviolability. Later encyclicals tended not to use the phrase 'inviolable' and, indeed, suggest that, though rights to property are of great importance, they are not inviolable. This later emphasis is in accord with the teachings of St Thomas Aquinas.

from disadvantageous to individuals or to the community. Pope Leo (for example, RN 22) lauds the principle of charity by which people should give to others that which they do not need for themselves. It is suggested that giving alms is not a duty of justice,[3] except in extreme cases, but of Christian charity – 'a duty not enforced by human law'. Action by voluntary groups and associations and by the Church herself are praised, and those who would replace voluntary action with a system of state relief are criticised.[4]

Pope Leo does not object to the principle of taxation, but even when proposing that taxation can be put to certain ends such as helping the poor it is suggested that the more in line with Christian principles are the general laws of a state, 'the less need will there be to seek for special means to relieve them [the poor]' (RN 32). Nevertheless, it is clear that providing citizens with a basic income (for food, clothing and shelter) is a potential role for taxation envisaged by Pope Leo. It might be added that *Rerum novarum* also implied certain forms of regulation of wages to achieve the objectives of assisting workers.

Excessive taxation and taxation of the poor was certainly not favoured by Pope Leo. The poor, it is suggested, can only escape their condition through the ownership of property (as many people as possible should become owners: RN 46)

---

[3] A duty of justice might imply intervention by the state.

[4] These sentiments also pervade Part II of Pope Benedict XVI's first encyclical, *Deus caritas est*, though they are expressed rather differently. *Deus caritas est* discusses how state action, however well directed and well intended, will always be incomplete. Welfare given from love and charity fulfils a deeper need.

– ownership should not be undermined by taxation as that would be to undermine the means to help the poor save.[5, 6]

## Quadragesimo anno

*Quadragesimo anno*, by Pope Pius XI, has been criticised by free-market economists[7] for taking a position sympathetic to the economic models proposed by fascists in the 1920s and early 1930s.[8] These involved cooperative economic arrangements between workers' organisations and employers' organisations, together with a suppression of competition. Nevertheless, a significant role for taxation in redistribution is neither envisaged nor proposed by Pope Pius. Much of the burden of

---

[5] It should be noted that the share of government spending in national income in the UK was about 10 per cent when *Rerum novarum* was written – about one fifth of today's level. This is also the case in almost all other European countries for which data exists (see Heath and Smith, 2006).

[6] The *Compendium of the Social Doctrine of the Church* has only a brief section explicitly on taxation – stating it is necessary for the provision of certain services and functions in the name of the common good. Although many of the warnings about the welfare state, discussed below, are referred to in other sections of the *Compendium*, there is no mention of the points discussed above in relation to arguments for limiting taxation. This would appear to be an omission. Also worth noting is that, in the back cover text of the English-language edition of the *Compendium*, it is stated, 'Through landmark encyclicals issued by popes since *Rerum novarum*, the Church has built up a wide-ranging body of teaching on justice, equality and human rights.' There is no mention of family and personal autonomy, freedom and property rights in this back cover text. And Church teaching on equality, at least in the economic sphere, is not what people might expect given its bracketing with 'justice' and 'human rights' in that sentence.

[7] See, for example, Rothbard (1960).

[8] It should be noted that this does not, in any way, imply that there was sympathy with other policies of fascists; the economic policies of fascist movements are not materially different from the corporatist policies pursued by, say, Heath's Conservative government in the early 1970s and by many Christian Democrat and Social Democrat governments in continental Europe. There is a good discussion of the nuances of this debate in Hinze (2005).

raising the condition of poor workers is allocated to corporations and to workers' and employers' organisations. Strong statements were made against taxation of the poor and the pursuit of equality for its own sake: 'Wherefore the wise Pontiff [Pope Leo] declared that it is grossly unjust for a State to exhaust private wealth through the weight of imposts and taxes' (QA 49). Strong statements are also made about the lack of resources of the poor, but charity is regarded as far more than the marginal activity that it has become today: 'the rich are bound by a very grave precept to practice almsgiving, beneficence, and munificence' (QA 50; see also QA 137, 'How completely deceived, therefore, are those rash reformers who ... in their pride reject the assistance of charity'). Ensuring that the poor can become property owners, and shareholders in the businesses for which they work, are regarded as important ways to raise the condition of the poor, help them to maintain a family and pass something to the following generation (see, for example, QA 61 and 65). Pope Pius does suggest that a wage sufficient for basic family needs (adjusted according to family circumstances) should be assured (QA 71). While the taxation system and the state are not mentioned explicitly for this purpose one assumes that the state should be a possible last resort in providing for basic needs if they are to be assured. Pope Pius was really appealing, however, for a reorganisation of the economic system along more corporatist lines: the practical implications of such a reorganisation would transcend our discussion of taxation.

## Vatican II and after

There is a change in tone in the Vatican II document *Gaudium et spes*. It notes (GS 63) that the economy is marked by 'increased intervention by the state', but differences in income and wealth are also noted and strongly criticised. References to the inviolability of private property are more heavily qualified than in the encyclicals referred to above (for example, GS 71). The issue of whether income differences should be alleviated by charity or through state taxation systems is also left much more ambiguous than in the encyclicals: 'Thus, under the leadership of justice and in the company of charity, created goods should be in abundance for all in like manner' (GS 69). Nevertheless, governments are urged to support the development of voluntary associations (from family to larger voluntary groups) and individuals are urged not to attribute excessive power to political authority nor to make demands upon it in their own interests (GS 74).[9] Remarkably, though, it suggests that 'the complex circumstances of our day make it necessary for public authority to intervene more often in social, economic and cultural matters' (GS 74).[10] These interventionist sentiments reflect the

---

[9] In a sense this prefigures public choice economics: it asks people to show moral restraint in the 'political marketplace' just as they should in the economic marketplace.

[10] This point reflects the intellectual trends of the time. It seems to be the case that it was only in the 1980s that intellectual opinion properly understood the implications of the 'calculation debate' of 50 years previously. The emphatic conclusion of that debate is that the more complex is economic life, the more important it is that individual economic agents have autonomy as they process and discover dispersed information so much more effectively than centralised decision-making units such as governments. Hayek uses, for the purpose of criticism, an almost identical quote to this one from *Gaudium et*

thinking of Pope John XXIII's encyclical *Mater et magistra*.

*Gaudium et spes* helps provide a context for the discussion of later encyclicals. There appears to be a shift of emphasis with fewer cautions against socialism and the undermining of family autonomy, combined with less emphasis on charity. It is a document written by committee, however, and which had to be agreed upon by a wide constituency. It is looser in its wording than the encyclicals are. It is appropriate, perhaps, to try to interpret *Gaudium et spes* in the light of Church documents that were produced in the following four decades.

*Sollicitudo rei socialis*[11] mainly deals with the plight of those in the poorest countries. The main issues brought up in that encyclical have been discussed in Chapter 4.[12] There are, however, other general messages in *Sollicitudo rei socialis* relevant to our analysis. It gives more concrete expression to many of the issues raised in *Gaudium et spes*. It was particularly critical of the gap between incomes of the developed and developing world and, oddly, suggests that the gap is widening.[13] Like the earlier encyclicals it is, nevertheless, against

---

*spes* at the beginning of Chapter IV of *The Road to Serfdom* (Hayek, 1944) – the quote is from Mussolini.

[11] Written by John Paul II in 1987.

[12] *Populorum progressio*, published two years after *Gaudium et spes*, communicated similar points and was also dealt with in Chapter 4.

[13] Of course, the gap between the developed and the developing world might be widening while the developing world becomes smaller! In other words, the income of the very poorest, often living in 'failed states', might not change but, as many poor states become better off and rich states continue to grow, the gap between the richest and the poorest grows wider while the number of poor people shrinks.

enforced equality as something that would destroy initiative and lead to a levelling down (SRS 15). It also recognises charity as fundamental to a genuine expression of solidarity (SRS 40). The concept of the 'preferential option for the poor' is introduced in paragraph 42. It is stressed that this relates to decisions of individual charity as well as to 'social decisions'. It is implied by the later discussion of property rights and trade reform (SRS 43–4) that the preferential option for the poor also relates to political decisions. It seems reasonable to conclude that Pope John Paul is suggesting that the normal presumptions of inviolability of property rights, the right for a worker to control use of his wages and so on can be suspended for the purposes of the state aiding the poor.

*Centesimus annus*, in many respects, echoes faithfully the sentiments of *Rerum novarum*. There are many warnings about the power and size of the state. Nevertheless, John Paul II continues to support redistribution to provide for basic needs, although, once again, the main responsibility for ensuring adequate incomes is placed on private-sector bodies – employers and unions (CA 15).

A clear expression of the problem of providing for contingent needs (such as help in times of disability, old age, unemployment, etc.) is also provided in *Centesimus annus*. Quoting *Rerum novarum*, and reaffirming its relevance today, John Paul II notes that the mass of the poor, particularly wage earners, have no resources to fall back on and should be specially cared for and protected by the government. This statement would appear to be difficult to justify in the modern developed world and was certainly not true in the UK even in the nineteenth century (see, for example, Bartholomew, 2004, but also the impressive range of original sources and evidence quoted by that author). If it is the only justification for the state providing for the contingent needs of low-wage earners, it is a poor one. More specifically, *Centesimus annus* calls upon the government to provide unemployment insurance (CA 15) and strongly implies that the government should be involved in efforts to provide training to employees to improve their productive capacity.

As is the nature of encyclicals, these sentiments are not backed up with economic theory or empirical evidence that suggests that the finance of training, or its provision, is best undertaken by government or that lower earners are not able, if they are not overtaxed, to provide welfare benefits for contingent needs. Also, these statements must be set in the context of a general comment on the welfare state which speaks for itself:

> In recent years the range of such intervention has vastly expanded, to the point of creating a new type of State, the so-called 'Welfare State'. This has happened in some countries in order to respond better to many needs and demands, by remedying forms of poverty and deprivation unworthy of the human person. However, excesses and abuses, especially in recent years, have provoked very harsh criticisms of the Welfare State, dubbed the 'Social Assistance State'. Malfunctions and defects in the Social Assistance State are the result of an inadequate understanding of the tasks proper to the State ... By intervening directly and depriving

society of its responsibility, the Social Assistance State leads to a loss of human energies and an inordinate increase in public agencies, which are dominated more by bureaucratic ways of thinking … and which are accompanied by an enormous increase in spending. (CA 48)

The paragraph goes on to explain how real needs are best answered by people who can provide fraternal love and support. Pontifical Council for Justice and Peace (2005) describes how solidarity without subsidiarity can '*degenerate* into a "Welfare State"' (CA 351, my emphasis).[14]

A right to various forms of insurance (health, sickness, old age and so on) is articulated in various post-Vatican II documents (see, for example, *Laborem exercens*), but, other than assistance being given to the unemployed, the state is not envisaged as the provider of such insurances. Indeed, in Pontifical Council for Justice and Peace (2005), quoting John Paul II, the onus is very much put on workers' associations to develop new ways of providing for income security against contingencies, as traditional models based on salaried workers in big business break down. The state is, nevertheless, regarded as 'the guarantor' of systems of social insurance (para. 355). But this role could take many forms without being intrusive and without

---

[14] Papal encyclicals choose words very carefully though they are, of course, translated from Latin. 'Degenerating' literally involves declining or deteriorating to a lower mental, moral or physical level, becoming debased, degraded or corrupt: it is a strong word to use. It should also be mentioned that the paragraph continues with cautions against 'subsidiarity without solidarity'. It is important to note, however, that solidarity does not necessarily imply political action: solidarity starts in the family, which is the smallest unit for welfare provision.

requiring significant levels of taxation (for example, providing a minimum basic income in times of need or upon the failure of private and mutual systems of social security, compelling membership of private systems, making payments into private systems on behalf of the poor or, perhaps most importantly, providing the legal framework in which private systems can operate).

*Centesimus annus* reiterates points made in many encyclicals that support should be given particularly to families to ensure that basic needs can be provided for. The family unit is regarded as including the elderly as well as children. Provision should be made so that women are not deterred from working within the home. Again, this has implications for the tax system – but perhaps more for the shape of the tax system rather than for the level of the tax burden. For example, tax allowances transferable between non-working and working members of the family may help achieve this particular objective (see below).

The right to an education is discussed in similar terms to the right to healthcare, to a basic income and so on. For example, in Pope Paul VI's encyclical *Gravissimum educationis*, published in 1965, it is stated (Section 1) that 'All men of every race, condition and age, since they enjoy the dignity of a human being, have an inalienable right to education'. This can be interpreted in a number of ways, and the duty to deliver education is put first on parents and the Church (see Sections 1 and 3). Nevertheless, in Section 3 it is made clear that, while the main role of the state is to protect the duties and rights of parents and teachers, providing those who cannot afford education with aid, financed by taxation, is also a duty of the state. In Section 6 it is made clear that such aid should facilitate parental choice and autonomy.[15]

Other Church documents confirm this interpretation. *Familiaris consortio*,[16] for example, suggests that the state should provide families with aid to meet their educational needs and that aid must be in proportion to the needs of the family. This would seem to suggest some form of means-tested assistance to help with the finance of education. The duty to provide education is clearly laid upon the family, the Church and other intermediate institutions. It is also worth noting that the Church goes as far as suggesting that it is an *injustice* for the state not to support attendance at non-state schools, that a state monopoly of education offends *justice* and that the state cannot *merely tolerate* private schools (Pontifical Council for Justice and Peace, 2005: para. 241). It is difficult to conclude other than that the Church is teaching that the state's role in *providing* education should be much more limited than it is in the UK today – even if the state were still to *finance* education.

Pope Benedict's *Caritas in veritate* did not address directly issues relating to the welfare state in the same wide-ranging way as *Centesimus annus*. The main purpose of *Caritas in veritate* was to stress that development had to be integral and moral, respecting life and the true nature of the

---

[15] In Anglo-Saxon Western countries (and also in much of western Europe with exceptions such as the Netherlands and Sweden) the state has provided funds for education by a method that explicitly reduces parental autonomy.
[16] Written by John Paul II, published in 1981.

human person. In paragraph 25, Pope Benedict laments the apparent reduction in the size of welfare states suggesting that there had been budgetary cuts in both emerging and established economies. The pathologies of the welfare state, pointed out as long ago as 1991 in *Centesimus annus*, did not seem to be recognised as the major problem by Pope Benedict. However, later in the encyclical, rather out of context, when suggesting how increases in foreign aid might be financed, *Caritas in veritate* suggests that developed nations should review: 'their internal social assistance and welfare policies, applying the principle of subsidiarity and creating better integrated welfare systems, with the active participation of private individuals and civil society. In this way, it is actually possible to improve social services and welfare programmes, and at the same time to save resources – by eliminating waste and rejecting fraudulent claims – which could then be allocated to international solidarity.' Perhaps the most important insights of this document, which from its construction clearly draws on the views of several authors, come in section III. Here it is stated: 'The Church's social doctrine holds that authentically human social relationships of friendship, solidarity and reciprocity can also be conducted within economic activity, and not only outside it or "after" it.' If we examine the structures that provided welfare before the welfare state, they exhibited these very characteristics of social relationships, solidarity and reciprocity – as well as commercial relationships. These institutions were embedded within both the market economy as well as in civil society. There would be much to be gained from the further development of these ideas in *Caritas in veritate* and their application to the welfare state.

## Summary
Catholic social teaching sees a legitimate, but limited, role for the state in the area of income redistribution. Charity is more virtuous than redistribution through taxation because it is based on love and not coercion. Equality is not a goal that should be pursued for its own sake. Mechanisms of improving the condition of the poor by giving them access to property (widely defined) are regarded as desirable. The principle of subsidiarity demands that government and coercive measures are a last resort. 'Subsidiarity means that the family, not the State, not large organizations, must be given responsibility in managing and developing its own economy' (Rio Declaration on the Family: para. 3.12).

A very important role is seen for various non-state institutions (unions, professions, employers' organisations, insurance and mutual societies and so on) in providing fraternal help based on commercial relationships as well as the principle of reciprocity and the virtue of solidarity. While the Church has proposed a role for the state in financing education, the state must nurture private provision. Contingent welfare in times of need (health and disability benefits, etc.) is another *potential* area of state intervention, but how such benefits are best provided and financed is left as a matter for personal, prudential judgement. The

Church also teaches that the *shape* of the tax system should not discourage family life.

## Modern Catholic Social Teaching and the role of the state: the provision of legal institutions

Church teaching on the provision of institutions is explicit and only brief consideration is necessary. There are institutions that are fundamental to the role of the state and the Church has always supported their provision by government. In the *Catechism* (Catholic Church, 1994) it states:

> The activity of a market economy cannot be conducted in an institutional, juridical or political vacuum. On the contrary, it presupposes sure guarantees of individual freedom and private property, as well as a stable currency and efficient public services. Hence the principal task of the state is to guarantee this security, so that those who work and produce can enjoy the fruits of their labours and thus feel encouraged to work efficiently and honestly … (para. 2431)[17]

Arguably these institutions that Church teaching suggests must be provided by the state are essential for the functioning of a market economy and the delivery of justice. They thus provide the framework in which a free economy operates.

Even though government intervention is encouraged in these matters the principle of subsidiarity still applies. Lower levels of government

---

[17] This is a direct quote in the *Catechism* from *Centesimus annus*, para. 48. The quote appears elsewhere in this text and its sentiments are referred to on other occasions. It is an important quote as it succinctly expresses both the role and limits of government in economic life.

are responsible before higher levels of government. Voluntary associations have the responsibility before any level of government. It is important to note that subsidiarity does not mean simply that higher levels of political authority do what cannot be done by lower levels of political authority.[18] Rather, subsidiarity is the process by which the state is used to help private and intermediate groups attain the latter's legitimate ends, never supplanting their initiative, only facilitating it.[19]

## Modern Catholic Social Teaching and the role of the state: the distinction between charity and taxation

In a number of places, it has been noted that the Church prefers voluntary action to coercive taxation. It is worth exploring the important distinction between taxation and charity further. Many people today discuss taxation in the same terms as charity, as if taxation were simply an extension of charitable giving. Words such as 'generous' and 'compassionate', which can relate only to voluntary sacrifice, are often used to describe the actions of government to achieve particular ends through coercive taxation. Church teaching, however, makes clear the difference between charity and action through political structures.

---

[18] The approach to subsidiarity in the European Union and between central and local government within the UK is entirely different. Higher levels of authority define the aims and fulfilment of those aims can be delegated to lower levels of authority: this is not true subsidiarity.

[19] This principle is so pervasive that it is difficult to give one reference. There is a discussion in several places in Charles (1998), for example in vol. II, pp. 97 and 98.

Those differences are many. They include the fact that charitable giving is a genuine act of love whereas taxation is coercive – there is no choice exercised by the taxpayer and therefore no 'generosity' or 'compassion' is possible. Taxation is impersonal in that it cannot be used to meet the concerns of the taxpayer and the payer of taxes cannot develop a personal relationship between donor and recipient. The ends to which taxes are put are determined through preferences expressed in the political system. The people expressing preferences as to how tax revenues are used may be placing the burden of paying the cost on other groups: acting in a self-interested manner. State redistribution through political structures is not an extension of charity but an alternative mechanism for the allocation of resources to that of the market and voluntary initiative.

These differences are well understood in Church teaching and it is therefore correct of Pope Leo to propose the use of coercive redistribution using political structures only after genuine acts of love, expressed through the charitable giving of money and time, have failed to make the necessary provision.

Pope Benedict XVI discusses some of these issues in *Deus caritas est*. He expresses the view that charity is a manifestation of love and a Christian duty that is inseparable from other aspects of the Church's mission. Charity involves an outpouring of love that combines material help with genuine personal concern. Pope Benedict confirms the message of *Centesimus annus* that a state that tried to provide for all material need would become a mere bureaucracy. He also notes that needs met by charities are not just material and that even in the most just state charity would be necessary – it meets needs in a way that is more fully human.

Charity can also be undermined by state action. This can happen in several ways. As the state undertakes functions that properly belong in the community or under the auspices of charity, its bureaucratic ways can prevent others helping those who are in need of charity. Furthermore state action crowds out charitable giving. If 50 pence of every pound earned is taken by the state (see below), it is harder for individuals to meet their own basic needs, to act for the good of themselves and their families and to contribute towards meeting the needs of others through charity. All this is not to deny a legitimate role for the state, but, in the Christian mind, that role should be subservient to solutions to need that involve the exercise of Christian love.

## Informing Catholic Social Teaching with economic theory: the burden of taxation

Having summarised some of the Church's teaching on taxation, this section examines the economics of taxation. Catholic social teaching looks to the social sciences for illumination on technical issues. The economics of taxation is one such discipline that can help inform the application of Catholic social teaching in particular circumstances. We do not include any analysis of the relative merits of the government *providing* services (health, education and so on). This is because, in theory at least, the provision of such services can be separated from their finance. We are concerned with the tax burden implied by the government financing various aspects of economic activity and financing income redistribution. The purpose of this section is to provide an understanding of the basic economic principles of taxation that can be used to help us make judgements about tax policy in a Christian context.

### Taxation, inefficiency and the work effort

The microeconomics of taxation suggests that tax leads to inefficiencies and disincentives to work. At high levels, taxation can impose costs on intended beneficiaries of the proceeds of taxation as well as on taxpayers.

Taxation on income drives a wedge between the product of a worker and his income and thus prevents a worker earning the full value of his product. A worker facing high tax rates may value the gross wage derived from an extra hour of work as worth the extra time spent working, but not undertake the extra work because the worker does not receive the full fruits of his labour. When considering the impact of taxes on efficiency one should include sales taxes too, as they are levied on products bought using a worker's net earnings.

Taxation at high rates also acts as an incentive to use labour that works outside the formal, taxed sector. Indeed, in some parts of the economy, work in the formal sector might be difficult to find once tax rates reach high levels. Heitger (2002), for example, shows that the high tax burden in the EU helps to explain the very high level of long-term unemployment. High tax rates can also reduce the incentives for training and education by reducing the net returns from such investment far below the gross returns.

There are situations where high tax rates can induce more work than a family would desire to undertake in the absence of tax.[20] High tax rates can therefore lead to a situation where more paid work than a family would desire in the absence of high rates of tax takes place. A current example of this phenomenon may be the increasing tendency for two parents to take on paid work because one parent cannot afford to stay at home as a result of the high taxes levied on the earnings of the primary earner.[21]

At high rates of tax the disincentives can become so severe, and people cut their work effort to such an extent, that overall tax revenue to the government is reduced if rates are increased further (or revenue is increased if rates are reduced). This is known as the 'Laffer curve effect'. It therefore makes no sense for the government to levy marginal tax rates on any group above this point, as nobody benefits.

---

[20] This is as a result of the so-called 'income effect'. The substitution effect, arising from a worker's net pay being below his gross pay, will always lead people to work less hard. The income effect leads people to work harder to maintain a given net income in the face of high tax rates. Both effects are welfare reducing and they can apply in different ways to different groups of people. High marginal tax and benefit withdrawal rates typically apply at the bottom of the income scale (see below). Thus somebody who cannot command a high wage may find that the substitution effect leads to him not working at all. On the other hand, a family with a moderate-to-high income may suffer a high average rate of tax that leads it to try to maintain its net income by working even harder.

[21] There are clearly other reasons for this trend, including the better education of women and also, in the UK, the high level of housing costs, caused largely by government regulation of the planning system.

It is clear from our discussion of Catholic social teaching that taxation merely to create equality, but where everybody suffers, cannot be justified. Intuitively, this effect can easily be seen once tax rates are 100 per cent. At this level, few people will undertake work, without being forced to work, because they would earn no money from it. The tax yield will therefore be zero (just as if the tax rate were zero). A reduction in taxes from 100 per cent to 90 per cent will therefore yield an increase in tax revenues. Similarly, a reduction in tax rates from 90 per cent to 80 per cent will increase the total tax yield to the benefit of taxpayers and non-taxpayers alike, even if it induces only a 12 per cent increase in hours worked.[22]

Estimates vary on how high tax rates have to be to lead to reductions in tax revenue from further increases in rates. Marginal tax rates on a person on average earnings in the EU vary between 40 per cent and 60 per cent (see Miles and Scott, 2002), though published figures frequently understate tax rates (see below). Those segments of the population that also face withdrawal of social security benefits as their income rises will face much higher marginal rates of tax and benefit withdrawal than those on average earnings. It is quite possible, therefore, that tax rates in many EU countries are at such levels that reductions in tax would lead to only small losses in revenue and might even raise revenue.

The Laffer curve also shows how redistribution to the poor can be undermined if the government

---

[22] This is, of course, declared hours worked – reductions in tax rates can raise yields simply by reducing the incentive to find ways (whether legal or illegal) of preventing earned income from being taxed.

uses tax to finance a wide range of government services. If the marginal tax rate on all groups in society is high because of government funding of services, further rises in the marginal tax rates on particular groups, to facilitate redistribution, may then induce a Laffer curve effect, reducing revenues. Thus, there is a tendency, when average tax rates are high, for the tax burden to be relatively even across all income groups in a country – because there is a limit to the tax burden that can successfully be imposed on only one group. Paradoxically, redistribution can be more effective when there are low general rates of tax.

Taxes on spending can affect efficiency in other ways. If some goods or activities are taxed and others are not, then consumers and producers will use goods that are not taxed to an extent that is inefficient. Most developed countries levy a sales tax[23] but have lower levels of this tax for transport, food and energy. This will encourage consumers to consume more energy, for example, than is efficient, because its relative price is lowered.

A further problem is that high taxes on labour can cause employers to substitute labour with capital, thus raising unemployment or lowering the take-home pay of workers.

These arguments mainly relate to the 'efficiency' debate. This should not be dismissed by Christians as some dry economic, materialistic concept. Broadly, inefficiency means that resources of greater value are used to produce a given level of output than need to be used. Given that all resources are scarce

---

[23] Value Added Tax (VAT) in the case of the UK and other EU countries.

and all needs will never be satiated, an inefficient use of resources leads to economic well-being being lower for a given value of inputs than if resources are used efficiently. The inefficient use of resources, in this respect, can include the inefficient use of environmental resources.[24] As man should act as a steward of nature's resources, their inefficient use is an issue that should be taken seriously. However, there are greater concerns given the ways in which inefficiencies might manifest themselves in practice as explained above. If the extra-legal sector expands at the expense of those lawfully employed this can undermine the whole ethos of the rule and authority of law within a country. Furthermore, artificial discouragement for people to improve themselves through training together with barriers to people being fully employed have wider human and social effects.

## The tax burden in practice

Thus, when looking at the tax burden in practice, we need to distinguish between two concepts: the marginal rate of tax on the next pound a worker earns and the average tax burden as a percentage of total income. A high marginal rate of tax is most likely to impair industry and effort in the group to which it applies, as suggested by Pope Leo, above. The average rate of tax shows the extent to which the government is financing activities that could be financed by subsidiary entities – including by families. It shows the extent to which the preferences of the state with regard to provision of

---

[24] In this respect it is particularly perverse that there is discrimination in almost all tax systems in favour of transport and domestic energy use.

education, health, pensions, insurances, such as for disability, and redistribution are being imposed on all, rather than families being able to make their own choices with regard to provision in these fields.

Average tax burdens today are very high throughout the developed world by historical standards, reflecting to a large degree the development of 'social assistance states' throughout the Western world (see Table 1). In fact, tax burdens do not tell the whole story. It is possible for one generation to finance consumption of government-provided goods, services and transfers at the expense of the next generation by borrowing. This borrowing can be explicit (when a government issues bonds to finance spending and future generations of taxpayers pay the interest and repay the capital) or it can be implicit (when the current generation promises itself pensions to be paid by future generations without funding those promises, for example).

The issue of government borrowing and inter-generational promises through state pension schemes is important and may be regarded as a crucial issue that Catholic social teaching should address. However, it will not be discussed further here. Nevertheless, it should be noted that the *long-term* tax burden of a given level of government activity is indicated by the level of government spending and not by the level of taxation – eventually, taxation will have to be raised to service government borrowing. As such, in Table 1, we show government spending in a number of countries.

Table 1 Average government spending in selected countries, 2008

| Country | Government spending as a proportion of GDP (%) |
|---|---|
| Sweden | 51.8 |
| France | 52.7 |
| Belgium | 50.1 |
| Germany | 43.8 |
| Italy | 48.7 |
| The Netherlands | 45.9 |
| United Kingdom | 47.5 |
| Japan | 37.1 |
| USA | 38.8 |
| Ireland | 42.0 |

Source: OECD (2010). The levels have increased since 2008 but 2008 probably provides a better picture of the underlying structural position as, since that time, the financial crash and subsequent recession will have led to increased spending. The exception is the US where underlying government spending has expanded rapidly in recent years so the quoted figure probably understates the true position.

Assuming that income from capital, labour and land are taxed in roughly equal proportions, these figures mean that, on average, in the EU, for every £100 of value produced by a worker, approximately the same amount is spent on the worker's behalf by government as by the worker's family.

The marginal tax rate represents the number of pence paid to the government from each extra pound of gross income earned. Some attempt to illustrate the very complex picture for the UK is given in Figure 3 (see below). The level of explicit taxes on income, the most frequently quoted marginal tax rate, is the smallest bar for each income group (this is zero at very low levels of income): this rate includes employees' National Insurance contributions and income tax. This does not, however, illustrate the full impact of tax. National

Insurance contributions are also paid by employers and, in a competitive labour market, the burden of this is borne by the employee.[25] The inclusion of employers' National Insurance contributions leads to marginal tax rates of between 30 and 45 per cent for all income groups, except the very lowest. Also frequently ignored is the impact of indirect taxes levied on spending from retained income.[26] This takes marginal rates to nearly 40 per cent or above for all income groups, except the very lowest. This estimate would seem reasonable, given the overall fiscal burden of 47.5 per cent quoted above, given that part of current spending is financed by borrowing. Figure 3, in fact, illustrates an important point for those who wish to try to achieve social justice by high levels of government spending. It is very difficult to substantially vary tax rates with income once the overall tax burden has reached a high level.

In the UK, 'child tax credits' are paid to families with children. These are, in effect, means-tested social security benefits. They are withdrawn as the income of a family rises. For a recipient of tax credits, the marginal tax and tax-credit withdrawal rates combined are 80 per cent between the lowest levels of income and average income (approximately £25,000).[27] While tax credits are not taxes as such,

---

[25] When calculating marginal tax rates the cost of this tax should also be added to gross wages as well as to the tax paid.

[26] These have been assumed to be 15 per cent of net income made up of VAT on half the expenditure base plus various excise duties. Council tax, stamp duty and inheritance tax are excluded even though they relate to the purchase, ownership and sale of assets purchased from net income, thus making the marginal rates in the figure a conservative estimate.

[27] This excludes the withdrawal of benefits such as housing benefit and council tax benefit. Tax credit can still be withdrawn at higher levels of income

and therefore not part of the tax burden, it is the rate of withdrawal of the credits combined with the rates of tax which determines the impact of decisions about whether to work and how much to work.

The tax system in the UK impacts on families in a particularly unfortunate way. Two examples are worth noting. If we take a family earning £25,000 with one earner and two children (for example, with the mother working in the home) the family would gain over £2,000 per annum of net income by having both family members going out to work with them each earning £12,500.[28] This arises because child tax credit is awarded on the basis of family income but income tax and National Insurance allowances are personalised. If the same couple split up and lived separately, the tax bill would be unaffected, but benefits would rise dramatically (by several thousand pounds). These illustrations are not dramatic examples of quirks; they are an integral part of the UK tax and benefits system (see Morgan, 2007).

These disincentives to self-sustaining family units and child-rearing within the home do not seem compatible with Catholic social teaching on tax and welfare matters. To put it bluntly, the major requirements for human flourishing in the economic sense are work and family and, in many Western countries, tax systems and the design of the welfare state militate strongly against both.

---

depending on precise family circumstances. The system is very complex.
[28]  In fact, this figure understates the difference by at least £1,000 as we have not included childcare tax credits or employers' National Insurance contributions.

It is possible to design tax and benefits systems that do not give incentives for income splitting and household disintegration, even with high levels of tax. There are three obvious methods. The first is to 'personalise' benefits. This would involve taking family income assessment out of the benefits system, thereby giving benefits to individuals who do no paid work but who live in a family unit with another earner: incentives for income and household splitting are thereby reduced. Alternatively, non-earning members of a household could be allowed to transfer their tax allowance to other members of a household who are earning. Thirdly, there could be work requirements attached to welfare benefits. This clearly takes us beyond the scope of this text, but it is an important issue in Catholic social teaching. Perhaps too much emphasis – certainly at the local level – is put on criticising government policy for not being sufficiently redistributionist whilst often, little is said about the way in which tax and welfare systems undermine work and family.

Figure 3 Marginal Tax Rates

199

## Conclusion

The levels of tax we experience in the social assistance states of the West are surely not consistent either with the principle of subsidiarity or with efficient economic outcomes.

As we have noted, deviation from principles such as the right of a worker to earn his product can be justified by Catholic social teaching if it helps to promote the 'preferential option for the poor'. The poor can, however, experience the most deleterious effects of high taxes. Redistribution cannot be effective unless the overall tax burden is reasonably low. The poor in the UK pay both high average and high marginal rates of tax. The poor are also less able to rearrange their affairs in ways that avoid high rates of tax, and they are often caught in the most complex aspects of tax systems. If the services provided using the proceeds of taxation are not of a good quality, it is the least well-off who are least able to find alternative provision.[29] Furthermore, long-term unemployment tends to be higher in countries with a higher tax burden. The poor can be particularly affected by high long-term unemployment and are also affected by a general reduction in economic growth caused by high levels of taxes – we should therefore not be surprised if the condition of the poor were worse in high-tax countries.

Evidence on this point is not unequivocal. One

---

[29] Perhaps this is most obvious with regard to schooling in the UK, where better-off families can purchase houses in the catchment areas of good schools (see Leech and Campos, 2003) and very well-off families can buy private education. Less well-off families have their net income reduced by taxation and have no means to escape inadequate state education.

can certainly reject the hypothesis that the poor are necessarily better off in high-tax countries, however. Comparing high-tax Sweden with the lower-tax USA is instructive, for example (see Woods, 2005). At the turn of the 21st century, not only were median incomes in the USA 50 per cent greater than those in Sweden, the median income of US blacks (the lowest income group in the USA) was greater than median income across the whole of Sweden. Similarly, the income of the poorest 20 per cent of US citizens was higher than that for the average German citizen.

In summary, it could be pointed out that work, family and saving are extremely important for human flourishing in the economic sense. The first two of these are very clearly discussed in Catholic social teaching though not always from the economic dimension. Saving is also important in many societies because it allows for independence in old age, in the event of misfortune and so on.[30] Modern-day welfare states very strongly discriminate against work, family formation and saving. This should be a matter of great concern.

## Informing Catholic Social Teaching with economic theory: public goods and externalities

There are certain 'public goods' that economists often argue are more efficiently provided by the state than by the private sector. Public goods are goods that other individuals cannot be prevented

---

[30] There are some cultural contexts where saving might be less important such as where extensive and strong family networks exist. Saving may also be implicit through insurance and mutual society arrangements.

from consuming if they are provided for one individual.[31] Public goods will not necessarily be efficiently provided in the private sector because consumers have an incentive not to reveal their preferences for them so that they can 'free ride' on the provision made by others. It can be argued that the provision of public goods by the government does not undermine the principle of subsidiarity because their provision is *assisting* families and communities in achieving its legitimate objectives though it is clear that if they are provided they should be provided at the lowest level of government.

Just because there may be a theoretical case, it does not follow that public goods can be effectively provided in the public sector in practice.[32] As long as the constituency that benefits from a public good can be identified (for example, if it resides in a particular geographical area) public goods can be provided through subscription mechanisms, clubs and neighbourhood groups: this would, of course, accord even more effectively with the principle of subsidiarity and perhaps allow community bonds to be built in a way that it is difficult when such goods are simply provided by the state.[33] Nevertheless, there is a case for at least considering some form of intervention to promote the provision of public goods as such provision might enable individuals, the family and the community to flourish in ways

---

[31] The classic example is street lighting – if one person in a neighbourhood puts up a street light, it will provide light for others in the neighbourhood.

[32] Coase (1974), for example, showed how lighthouses, another classic public good, were much more effectively provided in the UK guided by private initiative than they were provided by the state in other countries.

[33] Volunteer fire services in the USA and the lifeboat service in the UK illustrate this principle well.

which would not be possible in the absence of such public goods. In other words, the promotion of the common good might be inhibited. One example would be where the absence of some form of police force in public areas led to violent attacks and other forms of crime perpetrated against persons.

Taxation can also improve economic efficiency where it is used to 'correct' for 'externalities'. For example, if certain economic activities (such as driving a car) impose costs on others, car use will exceed the efficient level because the car user does not bear all the costs. Certain activities may provide external benefits – it is sometimes suggested, for example, that primary education confers wider benefits on society. If this is the case, subsidising such activities, where the subsidy is financed through taxation, may lead to a more efficient use of economic resources.

Every economic activity confers some external benefits and costs and it is impossible for these to be calculated and for appropriate taxes and subsidies to be imposed to correct for externalities. Public choice economics (see below) also helps us to understand the limitations of the state both in providing public goods and in using taxes and subsidies to 'correct' externalities. Furthermore it should be said that Catholic social teaching does not have much to say about efficiency arguments alone when it comes to making judgements about the appropriate role of the state in economic life: these are very much matters for prudential judgement.

A reasonable and pragmatic approach, compatible with the principle of subsidiarity and economic theory, would suggest that, where possible, markets or sophisticated social orders should be allowed to evolve to deal with problems created by externalities. Voluntary action should then be free to address problems where market solutions do not evolve.[34] If both these solutions are inadequate, taxes levied to deal with externalities should be explicit and used only where the externality is considerable. In some cases, such taxes can be regarded as a price for the use of shared resources and can be levied as charges rather than taxes.[35] Taxation or charges levied for these purposes, as a 'price for the consumption of shared resources', are effectively used to adjust the costs of private activity for the social costs associated with the activity. As such they are not necessarily a violation of property rights, nor do they necessarily impair economic efficiency.

## Informing Catholic Social Teaching with economic theory: public choice economics

Public choice economics developed in a formal sense from the early 1960s. It is a discipline that should be at the forefront of the thinking of those seeking to develop Catholic social teaching for the simple reason that it examines the results of

---

[34] The provision of Church schools, with subsidised places for the poor, is an obvious example of voluntary action in the case of primary education.

[35] The best example here would be road pricing. A car user imposes congestion costs on other road users. It is the absence of a market in road space which creates the under-pricing of road use. If possible, markets in road space should be facilitated. If not, a statutory authority (which should be the lowest level of statutory authority that will be effective for this function) should levy a charge for road use. Technically, this is not a tax but a 'charge'. Nevertheless, the revenue can be used to reduce other taxes, which impair efficiency. See Glaister and Graham (2004) for a thorough analysis of the application of road pricing to the UK.

applying the assumption of the imperfectibility of man in political life. This manifests itself in this discipline through the assumption that those in the political sphere may frequently pursue their own interests rather than the general public interest.[36] A very important aspect of human nature that we should take into account also is that those acting on behalf of government are not omniscient. As such, we should not assume that problems arising within the free economy can be corrected by government.

The most important premise of public choice economics is straightforward. It is that we should not assume that people will behave in one way in the political arena and behave in a different way in the economic arena. In the economic arena we generally recognise that agents act in their own self-interest and that they have imperfect knowledge, thus leading to certain problems that governments may try to address. In the political sphere, however, agents will have these characteristics too: they will have a tendency to act in their own best interests and they will act with imperfect knowledge. That is not to say that all agents in the political sphere will behave only in their own best interests: altruism is possible in both the political and economic arenas. Nevertheless, it is prudent to adopt a working assumption that the pursuit of self-interest in the political sphere is likely.

There are a number of implications from combining the adoption of the assumption of the self-interested participant in the political process

---

[36] It should not be thought that self-interest is the same as selfishness or a disregard of the needs of others (see Chapter 1).

with our understanding of various administrative aspects of the political process.[37] The most important of these for our purposes are as follows:

- Electors have little interest in being perfectly informed about political issues because the probability of an individual's vote impacting on the result of an election is close to zero.

- Where the benefits of government regulation or subsidy are concentrated among particular voter groups, such voter groups have an incentive to lobby for regulation and subsidy – particularly if the cost is widely dispersed.

- Politicians will, other things being equal, respond to the preferences of the 'median voter'.

- Politicians may act in their own best interests when designing and supervising regulatory agencies.

- Bureaucrats cannot 'correct' the failure of markets to find efficient outcomes or socially desirable outcomes, even if they wished to do so, because they lack the information to know what the outcome of the market process would have been, had the 'failure' not existed.

- Bureaucrats will act in their own best interests, taking courses of action that will lead to promotion and advancement, including increasing the size and power of their regulatory bureau.

- Because of this, there are information asymmetries between regulatory bureaus

---

37 See Tullock et al. (2000), reprinted, with revisions, in the USA as Tullock et al. (2002), for a clear and full discussion of these issues.

and those to whom they are ultimately accountable (electors) – thus electors are at a relative disadvantage when assessing the merits of proposed regulations and other political decisions.

In many areas of political life it is possible to see how these problems manifest themselves. The EU Common Agricultural Policy is an example of a policy that confers concentrated benefits on farmers and dispersed costs on people throughout the world. Local Education Authorities and central government bureaucracy, which account for about one third of all UK education spending, seem to many to be risk-averse organisations that not only frequently do not act in the best interest of parents, but which cannot know the diverse objectives and aspirations of parents and thus cannot, even if they should have the desire to do so, act in the best interests of parents.

Public choice economics does not lead to specific and strong conclusions. Rather, it leads in the direction of some important cautions about the role of government, as well as towards the view that some forms of institutions are likely to give rise to better results than others. The main caution can be outlined as follows:

One [area of policy into which public choice economics has been integrated] is simply a lack of enthusiasm for government as a solution to problems. The view that government is the automatic perfect solution to innumerable problems no longer exists. Not very long ago, the simple proof that the economy did not function perfectly was regarded as an adequate reason for governmental action. Today, we start from the knowledge that the government also does not function perfectly and then make a selection between two imperfect devices ... (Tullock et al. 2002: 11–12)

It seems that this fits in very well with the general thrust of Catholic social teaching on the role of government and, more specifically, with the principle of subsidiarity. As has been discussed above, there is a general scepticism in Catholic social teaching about the ability of a 'big state' to resolve economic and social problems. Public choice economics provides us with a rigorous framework that should strengthen such scepticism. The framework is based on assumptions that accord with a Christian view of human nature. In Catholic social teaching, there is a general presumption in favour of private property, the market economy and individual and family autonomy. There is also, however, an obligation to pay special attention to the plight of the poor. Public choice economics suggests that, even where the market produces an outcome that may seem unsatisfactory for the poor, intervention – including intervention using taxation and redistribution – may not produce a better outcome, as a political and bureaucratic process being used to allocate resources may favour the poor even less than the use of the market.[38]

---

[38] Education is a good example. Education in the UK is controlled through the political process. Better-off parents can improve their children's education through the purchase of private education, through moving house to the catchment area of a better school, or through lobbying either the school or

There is an important moral lesson from public choice economics too. Frequently, as has been noted above, taxation and government spending are regarded as a seamless extension of charitable activity. Community and society are treated as synonymous with the state and the government. Public choice economics shows how government action replaces resource allocation through individual economic decisions by resource allocation through majority political decisions.[39] Both the market and the political process will be affected by self-interest. There is no reason to suppose that self-interest will be pre-eminent in the economic sphere but not in the political sphere. The majority will, or the will of the political or bureaucratic bodies that take and implement government resource allocation decisions, is not, of course, destined to fulfil God's will. Indeed, it may behave in a way that is fundamentally opposed to God's will.[40] When government initiative supplants

---

the local political authority to improve the service: none of these options may be available to the poor, particularly if they are not self-confident and articulate. The absence of a market means that the right of exit and freedom of choice are also not available to poor parents to help them improve education services for their children. Whereas the poor buy similar-quality television sets to the rich, they have dramatically worse educational outcomes.

[39] Via the political and bureaucratic structures set up for the purpose.

[40] An obvious example would be the provision of abortion funded by government health services, but there are many other examples. I have not come across mainstream Catholic teaching on whether it is legitimate to withhold taxes used to finance ends that are objectively evil: given the extent of state spending and the nature of the services on which taxpayers' money is spent, this is an area that should be given urgent attention. There should be a distinction, of course, between ends that are not immoral in themselves (for example, the conduct of war) but of which individual Catholics may disapprove and ends that Catholics regard as always objectively evil – such as abortion.

and displaces individual initiative, individuals have their realm of moral choices reduced and may be required to finance choices that are immoral.

## Conclusions: taxation and the role of the state

Our understanding of economic theory confirms the central importance of the principle of subsidiarity and private property while not contradicting the legitimacy of some role for the state in the provision of public goods and in income redistribution. In particular, there may be particular instances where charity is insufficient to provide the minimum necessary for human flourishing. Some level of taxation can therefore be justified in the name of the common good – not just to ensure that the government provides the legal and governance framework in which free economic activity can flourish. Government must ensure, however, that all have the right to economic initiative and that taxation to finance redistribution and the mechanisms of redistribution themselves do not undermine this right.

It is difficult to be specific about the proportion of GDP that involvement by government in legitimate areas might entail. Reducing the role of the state in the UK, to financier of last resort for welfare and education provision, however, combined with some income redistribution, would probably reduce spending to less than half of what is currently spent in the UK on such items (see Congdon in Booth (2006) for some estimates and Booth (ed.) (2011) for a discussion of how government spending could be reduced radically whilst retaining support for the poor). As has been noted, when *Rerum novarum* was published, government spending was around one fifth of current levels as a proportion of a much smaller national income.

The current tax system in the UK is not compatible either with the provision of appropriate incentives or with the maintenance of family independence. It seems clear that Catholic social teaching supports giving the poor the means to purchase education and health provision, although this should not necessarily mean universal free access and certainly not state provision of these services.

A flat-rate tax with a relatively high allowance would enable the objectives of taxation to be met while not destroying the reward for economic initiative. The granting of additional tax allowances for children and transferable allowances for married couples and cases where families look after elderly relatives would allow the phasing out of many cash benefits and remove the discrimination in the tax and benefit system against families living under one roof (again, see Booth (ed.) 2011).

Taxes might be appropriate on certain economic activities that cause harm to those not party to the activity. Such taxes, or charges, need not violate property rights or reduce economic efficiency. Public choice economics might suggest, however, that alternative ways of dealing with such problems should be found, if possible by trying to widen the scope and role of private ownership (perhaps involving private ownership in common) of shared resources: this is compatible with the principle of subsidiarity.

More generally, the Church is aware of the

limitations of political structures, something that is studied in detail in public choice economics. Certainly, the idea that political structures, so long as they are democratically elected, should have no restraints on their power in the economic realm is explicitly rejected: 'Experience shows that the denial of subsidiarity, or its limitation in the name of an alleged democratization or equality of all members of society, limits and sometimes even destroys the spirit of freedom and initiative' (Pontifical Council for Justice and Peace, 2005: para. 187).

Indeed, state action is regarded as the exception and not the norm and certainly not an ideal for which we should aim: 'state action in the economic sphere should also be withdrawn when the special circumstances that necessitate it end' (ibid.: para. 188). On the issues discussed in this chapter there is much scope for prudential judgement. Catholic social teaching, however, informed by economic theory, provides little succour for those who believe that government spending (and hence, in the long-term, taxes) should be raised further from its current level of between 45 and 60 per cent of income in most of the EU.

## References

Bartholomew, J. (2004), *The Welfare State We're In*, London: Politico's.

Booth, P. M. (ed.) (2006), *Towards a Liberal Utopia*, London: Continuum in association with the Institute of Economic Affairs.

Booth, P. M. (ed.) (2011), *Sharper Axes, Lower Taxes, Big Steps to a Smaller State*, Hobart Paperback no. 38, London: Institute of Economic Affairs.

Catholic Church (1994), *Catechism of the Catholic Church*, London: Geoffrey Chapman.

Charles, R. (1998), *Christian Social Witness and Teaching: The Catholic Tradition from Genesis to Centesimus Annus*, Leominster: Gracewing.

Coase, R. H. (1974), 'The lighthouse in economics', *Journal of Law and Economics*, 17: 357–76.

Glaister, S. and D. J. Graham (2004), *Pricing our Roads: Vision and Reality*, Research Monograph 59, London: Institute of Economic Affairs.

Hayek, F. A. (1944), *The Road to Serfdom*, London: Routledge and Kegan Paul.

Heath, A. and D. B. Smith (2006), *At a Price! The True Cost of Public Spending*, London: Politeia.

Heitger, B. (2002), 'The impact of taxation on unemployment in OECD countries', *Cato Journal*, 22(22): 333–54.

Hinze, C. F. (2005), '*Commentary on Quagragesimo anno (After Forty Years)*', in K. R. Himes (ed.), *Modern Catholic Social Teaching: Commentaries and Interpretations*, Washington, DC: Georgetown University Press.

Leech, D. and E. Campos (2003), 'Is comprehensive education really free?: a case-study of the effects of secondary school admissions policies on house prices in one local area', *Journal of the Royal Statistical Society*, Series A, 166(1): 135–54.

Miles, D. and A. Scott (2002), *Macroeconomics: Understanding the wealth of nations*, Chichester: Wiley.

Morgan, P. (2007), *The War Between the State and the Family: How Government Divides and Impoverishes*, Hobart Paper 159, London: Institute of Economic Affairs.

OECD (2010), *OECD Factbook 2010, Economic, Environmental and Social Statistics*, Paris, France: OECD.

Pontifical Council for Justice and Peace (2005), *Compendium of the Social Doctrine of the Church*, London: Burns & Oates.

Rothbard, M. N. (1960), *Readings on Ethics and Capitalism*, Unpublished memo to the Volker Fund, USA.

Spieker, M. (2005), 'The universal destination of goods: the ethics of property in the theory of a Christian society', *Journal of Markets and Morality*, 8(2): 333–54.

Tullock, G., A. Seldon and G. L. Brady (2000), *Government: Whose Obedient Servant? A Primer in Public Choice*, IEA Readings 51, London: Institute of Economic Affairs.

Tullock, G., A. Seldon and G. L. Brady (2002), *Government Failure: A primer in public choice*, Washington, DC: Cato Institute.

Woods, T. E., Jr (2005), *The Church and the Market: A Catholic Defense of the Free Economy*, Maryland: Lexington Books.

# BUSINESS, THE CONSUMER AND CULTURE IN CHRISTIAN LIFE

Part Two

BUSINESS, THE GOVERNMENT,
THE FINANCIAL CRISIS AND THE LAW

# 7

# FREE MARKETS AND THE CULTURE OF CONSUMPTION

*Andrew Yuengert*

*'In his riches man lacks wisdom;*
*he is like the beasts that are destroyed'*
Psalms 49:13

## Introduction

The Catholic tradition's warnings about wealth
are based on two principles, each confirmed by
millennia of sad experience. The first principle is
that material goods do not guarantee happiness;
they are not by nature bad, of course, but they do
not give meaning to life, and great wealth often
leads to great emptiness. The second principle is
that wealthy people often forget the first principle.
They firmly attach themselves to this world, and
detach themselves from God and the treasures of
heaven.

One of the distinctive features of modern times
is the large number of people who are exposed
to the spiritual dangers of material riches. The
development and spread of free markets have
generated tremendous increases in material

prosperity, and wider access to that prosperity. Along with all this new wealth, we have seen the rise of consumerism – large numbers of people acting as if goods alone will make them happy, and organising their lives primarily around the pursuit of more and newer things. No one can begrudge the multitude (to which most of us belong, after all) their release from grinding material poverty, made possible by free markets. At the same time, it is disheartening to see people released from poverty by markets, only to embrace the consumerist lifestyle.

It should not be surprising to anyone in the Judaeo-Christian tradition that many squander the abundance of modern industrial society on an empty consumer lifestyle. The Jewish and Christian scriptures predict as much, and this chapter offers no new insight into human sinfulness and folly. Instead, I address a more modern concern: do free markets play a direct role in the rise of consumerism, apart from their indirect role in making widespread access to consumption possible? A closely related question is: what does consumerism imply for the regulation of free markets? This essay seeks answers to these questions in Catholic social teaching, particularly in the encyclicals of John Paul II.

Theories of consumerism and free markets fall along a continuum. At one end is the libertarian position (von Mises 1998; Rothbard 1971; Kirzner 2002). Libertarians, out of respect for individual liberty, privilege the desires and preferences on which consumers act in markets. Markets give people what they want; if they want material consumption, markets give it to them; if they want moderation, markets will also give that to them. From this perspective, any problems of consumerism are problems of culture, not of markets. Moreover, since markets are not the problem, restrictions on markets are not the solution.

The other extreme is illustrated by the attitudes of the anti-market left and conservatives in the Southern agrarian tradition (Schindler 2003; Berry 1990; O'Neill 1998). Both these groups are suspicious of markets: the spread of the market, with its arm's-length exchanges and rationalistic logic, erodes the fellow-feeling necessary for community and culture to flourish. In this account, markets directly cause consumerism, by undermining the conditions for true community. Any cultural initiative to address consumerism must therefore modify the market substantially, replacing its impersonal exchange with something more personal. The bonds of culture cannot withstand the solvent of the market.

Catholic social teaching adopts neither of the extremes outlined above. On the one hand, it recognises that markets effectively meet consumer preferences, which are backed by money, but it is not shy about criticising the content of those preferences, or about expressing reservations about the role of advertisers in distorting consumer preferences. On the other hand, the Catholic tradition recognises that there are important human goods which cannot be produced in markets, and which require protection from markets, but it stops short of drawing a necessary connection between markets and the decay of culture. John Paul II is especially confident in the ability of a renewed culture to resist any threat to its foundations from markets.

Catholic social teaching on consumerism and markets can be summarised in six points. The first three points address its nature; the second three address its causes and consequences. Firstly, consumerism is the expression of a materialistic, secular world-view, part of a system of belief that exalts the things of this world without reference to eternal, spiritual realities. Secondly, although consumerism is new in the sense that it is the expression of a modern world-view, it is at the same time a chapter in an old drama – that of original sin. Concupiscence makes us vulnerable to consumerism and the world-view that supports it. Thirdly, consumerism is a real problem, a real threat to happiness in developed economies. The critique of consumerism cannot be dismissed as a cranky, elite rejection of new things, based on a false nostalgia for simpler, more virtuous times.

The last three points address the consequences of consumerism for culture and markets. Firstly, consumerism is primarily a problem of culture. The modern materialistic world-view can offer no source of meaning other than material consumption, and no other forum in which to pursue meaning other than markets. Secondly, although markets do not generate consumerism, there are important goods that can be produced only outside markets: any cultural renewal that makes consumerism less widespread will entail restrictions on the extent of markets. Finally, government restrictions on markets may play a role in addressing consumerism, but only in support of a renewed culture – not as a substitute for culture. Respect for the principle of subsidiarity (sorely lacking among most legislators and bureaucrats) reduces the sphere of government action on this issue.

Catholic social teaching is unwilling to entrust all of life to markets, but neither does it despair that a healthy culture might harness market exchange towards the promotion of happiness. Culture is primary in papal teachings on consumerism; John Paul II in particular places the hope for combating materialistic consumerism in the renewal of culture (*Sollicitudo rei socialis*, 36).

## Papal encyclicals on consumerism

The first significant treatment of the dangers of consumerism is Paul VI's 1967 encyclical *Populorum progressio*. At that time there were a host of newly established countries, freshly freed from colonial rule. Although these countries were poor, some economists and others were optimistic that they would soon become prosperous through statist, protectionist economic policies. Although these policies have since been discredited, at the time many assumed that they would work, and Paul VI thought it necessary to put economic development into a moral context.

The encyclical reaffirms the age-old warning that material abundance can lead individuals to forget that goods are not the ultimate purpose of human existence. Wealth is only instrumentally good – good insofar as we use it to meet the most important human needs. This list of needs includes life, of course, but also the goods of society and culture: family and community, the pursuit of truth and beauty, the worship of God and love of neighbour. It is an unfortunate fact of human existence that, when life is easy and goods are abundant, men often lose sight of the full range of human goods as they unreflectively pursue more material goods.

Thus, material want is not the only evil to be avoided: one can have too many things as well as too few, if one forgets the purpose of things: 'Every kind of progress is a two-edged sword. It is necessary if man is to grow as a human being; yet it can also enslave him, if he comes to regard it as the supreme good and cannot look beyond it' (PP 19). It is a great tragedy when a society frees itself from a great material evil – subsistence poverty – only to embrace a moral evil – consumerism (PP 21). Paul VI encourages developing nations to strive to become, not just richer, but better places.

In the first encyclical of his pontificate, *Redemptor hominis*, John Paul II addresses the phenomenon of consumerism again, although he does not treat it in depth until later encyclicals. Technological progress and material prosperity have improved the material lot of many, but

> … there is a real perceptible danger that, while man's dominion over the world of things is making enormous advances, he should lose the essential threads of his dominion and in various ways let his humanity be subjected to the world and become himself something subject to manipulation in many ways … (RH 16)

A modern dynamic is at work here: the human person is somehow diminished by his own technical, economic progress (*Gaudium et spes*, 4). He becomes less an acting person, who reasons about his good and pursues it in the world, and more a person who is *acted upon*, ruled by passions, and subject to outside manipulation of his desires.

John Paul II describes a grim contrast, between the material evil of abject poverty in the developing world (poverty that is an affront to human dignity) and the surfeit of goods in the 'consumer civilisation' of the developed world (consumption that diminishes those who buy into its materialistic premises). According to John Paul II, the world situation is the parable of the rich man and Lazarus writ large (RH 16). Caught up in his feasting, the rich man of the scriptures does not see the important human good outside his door – a man in need of basic material goods.[1]

In *Sollicitudo rei socialis*, John Paul II both celebrated the twentieth anniversary of *Populorum*

---

[1] In *Redemptor hominis* John Paul II asserts in passing that terrible poverty is somehow a necessary condition of material abundance in the developed world, and not simply a condition that calls for renewed efforts by the First World to help the Third World develop (RH 16). This claim is based on the same economic theories of dependency and exploitation that gave rise to the failed development strategies of the sixties. As they have fallen out of favour in the theory of economic development, they have disappeared from papal encyclicals. In *Sollicitudo rei socialis* (published in 1987), in his discussion of consumerism, John Paul II makes the contrast without asserting a necessary connection, and in *Centesimus annus* in 1991 he does not make the contrast at all in his long treatment of consumerism. The obligation of the First World to help the Third, even at some significant material cost, is a grave one (as the parable of Lazarus attests); those who are rich in this world's goods bear a heavy responsibility towards those who have nothing. This moral responsibility need not be based on theories of neocolonial dependency and exploitation, however: that is, it should not be assumed that underdeveloped countries are poor because developed countries are rich.

*progressio* and developed Paul VI's teaching on consumerism more fully. In the section entitled 'Authentic Human Development', he begins by noting that the 'naïve mechanistic optimism' that inspired the development schemes and political programmes of the 1960s had been replaced by 'a well-founded anxiety for the fate of humanity' (SRS 27). This anxiety has many causes, but chief among them is the discovery that economic growth does not necessarily lead to moral improvement:

> ... the 'economic' concept itself, linked to the word development, has entered into crisis. In fact there is a better understanding today that the mere accumulation of goods and services, even for the benefit of the majority, is not enough for the realization of human happiness. (SRS 28)

Although man has at his disposal more productive technology and economic systems capable of making full use of that technology, more than ever he needs 'a moral understanding and ... an orientation toward the true good of the human race' to put material abundance into moral perspective (SRS 28).

At this point John Paul II repeats the comparison of *Redemptor hominis*, between the 'miseries of underdevelopment, themselves unacceptable' and 'superdevelopment, equally inadmissible' (SRS 28).

> This superdevelopment, which consists in an excessive availability of every kind of material goods for the benefit of certain social groups, easily makes people slaves of 'possession' and of immediate gratification, with no other horizon than the multiplication or continual replacement of the things already owned with others still better.

This is the so-called civilization of 'consumption' or 'consumerism,' which involves so much 'throwing away' and 'waste.' (SRS 28)

In this passage, John Paul II makes three points. Firstly, an abundance of goods makes people vulnerable to consumerism, or slavery to possessions. The seeming plenitude of choice in prosperous economies can mask restrictions on the person's inner freedom. Secondly, consumerism is essentially an inability to see beyond material goods: human beings have no broader 'horizon' against which to see material goods in perspective. Thirdly, there is a restlessness in consumerism: it generates a constant search for new products, and an excessive 'throwing away'.[2]

Although consumerism generates in many a 'crass materialism', its most important effect is a 'radical dissatisfaction', according to the Pope. The dissatisfaction with material goods is radical because it has a perverse effect. Instead of moderating consumption when it fails to satisfy, the slave to consumption seeks out more goods, even as 'deeper aspirations remain unsatisfied and perhaps even stifled' (SRS 28).

Echoing Paul VI, John Paul II takes pains to note that material goods are not bad in themselves, and that the desire to have more is not in itself sinful: 'having' and 'being' are not mutually exclusive: 'The evil does not consist in "having" as such, but

---

[2] I must express some scepticism about the criticism that modern societies throw too many perfectly serviceable products away. When a person buys a new car, the old one is sold on a used car lot. The existence of yard sales and the spectacular success of eBay attest to the strong desire not to throw things away. Consumer societies may be too eager for 'the latest thing', but rarely do they throw the old things away while they are still useful to someone.

in possessing without regard for the *quality* and the *ordered hierarchy* of the goods one has' (SRS 28). The value of goods is measured against man's vocation. Human dignity and purpose are the appropriate 'horizon' against which to put goods in perspective.

It must be noted that John Paul II paints here an exalted vision of the potential of material goods to promote human happiness. The human need for basic food and shelter by no means exhausts the usefulness of material goods. Just as human beings are meant for more than subsistence, the goods of this world can contribute to man's good beyond keeping him alive. New products can open up 'new horizons' for man, contribute to his full development (SRS 29). The true value of material goods, however, depends crucially on man's willingness to place those goods at the service of his true dignity. John Paul II characteristically locates this dignity in the creation of man, male and female, and in the dominion granted to them over the material world.

The dominion granted to Adam and Eve was not absolute, however. The original sin of Adam distorts the relationship between man and the material world (SRS 29). Consumerism is therefore another chapter in the ongoing drama of original sin and redemption:

> It is logical to conclude, at least on the part of those who believe in the word of God, that today's 'development' is to be seen as a moment in the story which began at creation, a story which is constantly endangered by reason of infidelity to the Creator's will, and especially by the temptation to idolatry. (SRS 30)

The person who piles up goods for their own sake, thinking they are the key to happiness, rejects God's dominion over his life, and denies his own nature as a human being called to communion with God. Human development consists in 'subordinating the possession, dominion and use to man's divine likeness and to his vocation to immortality' (SRS 29). It is one of the paradoxes of sin that, granted the immense bounty of the earth to develop through work and ingenuity, human beings make an idol of material goods, and reject the happiness intended for them by the One who grants the bounty.

In *Sollicitudo rei socialis*, John Paul II ends his meditation on the nature of consumerism, not with hand-wringing over its dangers, but with a call to substitute for it a truer vision of the nature of the human vocation, and the legitimate role of economic development in that vocation. The task of promoting true development is made arduous by original sin, but our duty to promote man's true happiness is not diminished by the difficulty of the task set before us (SRS 30).

The four years between the publication of *Sollicitudo rei socialis* in 1987 and *Centesimus annus* in 1991 saw the fall of communism and the discrediting of the totalitarian project in Europe. In *Centesimus annus* John Paul II took the opportunity to reflect on the errors of socialism and on the requirements of true freedom in democratic, market-oriented societies. It is here that he discusses most fully the problem of consumerism and the role of the market.

The error of socialism, and the source of its

downfall in Europe, was not in its failure to 'deliver the goods':

> …the fundamental error of socialism is anthropological in nature. Socialism considers the individual person simply as an element, a molecule within the social organism, so that the good of the individual is completely subordinated to the functioning of the socioeconomic mechanism. Socialism likewise maintains that the good of the individual can be realized without reference to his free choice. (CA 13)

It was not the lack of goods which doomed communism: the low productivity of communist economies was a symptom of the real problem – the lack of true human freedom in the political and economic spheres. To blame the fall of communism on a lack of goods is to make the same mistake as the communists – to assume that human well-being depends on material consumption alone (CA 19). One of the goals of *Centesimus annus* is to combat this materialistic error – to encourage Christians to foster in free societies social institutions that will orient those societies towards true human development.

*Centesimus annus* begins its treatment of consumerism in the same way *Sollicitudo rei socialis* does, by contrasting poor subsistence societies with more prosperous ones. In a subsistence economy there is a limited range of options for production – a minimum of food and shelter are all the economy produces (CA 36). In developed economies, consumers choose from a much wider range of goods. How this choice is made reveals a society's values: 'A given culture reveals its overall understanding of life through the choices it makes in production and consumption' (CA 36).

What 'understanding of life' do Western cultures reveal through the choices they make? According to the Pope, the production and consumption patterns of modern culture reveal rampant materialistic consumerism:

> It is not wrong to want to live better; what is wrong is a style of life which is assumed to be better when it is directed toward 'having' rather than 'being,' and which wants to have more, not in order to be more but in order to spend life in enjoyment as an end in itself. (CA 36)

The Pope offers three pieces of dramatic evidence of the underlying consumerism in modern culture. The first piece of evidence is the prevalence of drug use and pornography in modern societies, which reveals a radically distorted view of happiness:

> Widespread drug use is a sign of a serious malfunction in the social system; it also implies a materialistic and, in a certain sense, destructive 'reading' of human needs. In this way the innovative capacity of a free economy is brought to a one-sided and inadequate conclusion. Drugs, as well as pornography and other forms of consumerism which exploit the frailty of the weak, tend to fill the resulting spiritual void. (CA 36)

The twin vices of pornography and drug abuse (one might include a third today, that of 'gaming') are extreme expressions of consumerism. Where the modern world glorifies expanded freedom of choice for consumers, John Paul II sees a lack of freedom; drug and pornography addicts are frail and 'exploited', both by producers and by their own disordered orientation towards goods.

A second phenomenon that reveals an underlying consumerism in society is the abuse of nature. In the same way that material goods are only good for man when they are put into proper perspective, the use of the natural environment to produce those goods must also be appraised in light of man's divine vocation:

> Man thinks that he can make arbitrary use of the earth, subjecting it without restraint to his will, as though the earth did not have its own prerequisites and a prior God-given purpose, which indeed man can develop but must not betray. (CA 37)

One need not be a tree hugger, or embrace the Kyoto protocols, to see the sense in this. To misuse the gifts of nature, to use them as if man may do whatever he wishes with creatures and matter, is to thwart the benevolent purpose of the gift and, ultimately, to betray the Giver.[3]

The third piece of evidence that modern culture is in thrall to a materialistic mindset is the most telling. Central to the Pope's treatment of 'human ecology' is a discussion of the ills of the family. The decline of stable marriage, and a materialistic attitude towards the decision to have children, is the clearest evidence that people are putting material goods ahead of their most important purposes as human beings.

> But it often happens that people are discouraged from creating the proper conditions for human

---

[3]  It must be noted that markets play an important role in the solution to environmental problems. The establishment of clearly defined property rights often forces individuals to take into account the environmental effects of their actions.

reproduction and are led to consider themselves and their lives as a series of sensations to be experienced rather than as a work to be accomplished. The result is a lack of freedom, which causes a person to reject a commitment to enter into a stable relationship with another person and to bring children into the world, or which leads people to consider children as one of the many 'things' which an individual can have or not have, according to taste, and which compete with other possibilities. (CA 39)

Although the Pope goes on to condemn systematic anti-childbearing policies, here he notes that there appears to be an anti-childbearing mindset even in the free nations. Note that he characterises the decision not to marry and not to have children as a 'lack of freedom': many in the grip of consumerism are *not free* to marry, *not free* to embrace the married state. Both individuals and societies suffer as a result.

Whatever the arguments about the causes of consumerism or the solutions for it, Catholic social teaching clearly teaches that it is a gravely disordered lifestyle, and a severe problem in modern society. People who give overriding prominence to material possessions are often so attached to material consumption that they neglect commitments to God, family and community that are critical to their own happiness and the health of society. Anyone who takes Catholic social teaching seriously cannot dismiss concerns about consumerism as mere differences in taste. The critique of consumerism is more than a fastidious, ascetic distaste for sports utility vehicles, fast food and cheap gadgets.

## Consumerism and public policy

In light of the gravity of the problem, what solutions does Catholic social teaching suggest? To understand the solution, we must first locate the source of the problem. As noted in the introduction, two accounts bracket the possibilities. The first is that a materialistic, individualistic culture is the source of consumerism, and that markets merely reveal the problems of culture. The second is that market exchange, by its nature individualistic and anonymous, destroys culture, leaving individuals vulnerable to consumerism.

A close reading of the encyclical tradition favours the first account. Although the popes do not deny that economic change can radically alter the cultural landscape – think of the Industrial Revolution – one does not find in their writings any conviction that the logic of market exchange is necessarily corrosive of culture. There are simply too many plausible alternative explanations: there is ample evidence for sources of cultural decay in the decline of religion and the philosophical dead-end of materialistic relativism, and the widespread material abundance made possible by free markets puts more people at risk of consumerism than ever before.

John Paul II is particularly adamant that the source of consumerism is the culture itself. Two excerpts from *Centesimus annus* confirm this point:

> A given culture reveals its overall understanding of life through the choices it makes in production and consumption. It is here that *the phenomenon of consumerism* arises … (CA 36)

234

These criticisms are directed not so much against an economic system as against an ethical and cultural system. The economy in fact is only one aspect and one dimension of the whole of human activity. If economic life is absolutised, if the production and consumption of goods becomes the centre of social life and society's only value, not subject to any other value, the reason is to be found not so much in the economic system itself as in the fact that the entire socio-cultural system, by ignoring the ethical and religious dimension, has been weakened, and ends by limiting itself to the production of goods and services alone. (CA 39)

In the first quotation, John Paul II asserts that the culture *chooses* consumerism – it 'reveals its overall understanding of life' through production and consumption. In the second quotation, he asserts that it is the logic of secular culture, not the logic of markets, which drives consumerism. A world-view that cannot see beyond this world – beyond man's animal nature to his spiritual and transcendent nature – will be unable to find meaning in anything other than material consumption. In such a world-view, the market becomes by reluctant default 'the centre of social life and society's only value'.

It is tempting at this point in the analysis to draw a libertarian conclusion; Christians have a responsibility to try to put the culture right, and leave market institutions alone: put consumer preferences right, and producers will then meet the new, improved, consumer desires. This reading of the Catholic social tradition is premature, though, for two reasons. Firstly, John Paul II's set of market institutions does not include marketing or advertising: in the Pope's scheme these are instruments of culture, of mass communication and media, and they are an important proximate cause of consumerism. This means that both consumers and producers bear a responsibility for consumer culture. Secondly, a reformed culture will not place the market at 'the centre of social life', but will embed and circumscribe markets, putting them at the service of true human flourishing.

The Catholic tradition does not buy into an extreme account of consumer sovereignty in markets; nor does it treat advertising and marketing as mere exercises in discovering what consumers want. It certainly respects the ability of markets to respond to human needs, insofar as they are backed by purchasing power, as shown in the following passage:

> Certainly the mechanisms of the market offer secure advantages ... above all they give central place to the person's desires and preferences, which, in a contract, meet the desires and preferences of another person. (CA 40)[4]

As effective as markets are in responding to human desires, marketers and advertisers, when they appeal to immediate sense experience and instinct, can distort the desires of consumers. John Paul II hints at the problem in *Sollicitudo rei socialis*, where he attributes consumerism to 'the flood of publicity and the ceaseless and tempting offers of products' (SRS 28). In John Paul II's analysis, marketers and advertisers are part of the cultural

---

[4] See also CA 34.

sphere, and they can affect consumer preferences for better or for worse:

> If ... a direct appeal is made to human instincts – while ignoring in various ways the reality of the person as intelligent and free – then consumer attitudes and lifestyles can be created which are objectively improper and often damaging to the person's physical and spiritual health. (CA 36)

Because the problem of consumerism is not simply a problem of consumers wanting the wrong things or too many things, independent of producers, both producers and consumers must be part of the cultural response to consumerism:

> *Thus a great deal of educational and cultural work* is urgently needed, including the education of consumers in the responsible use of their power of choice, the formation of a strong sense of responsibility among producers and among people in the mass media in particular, as well as the necessary intervention by public authorities. (CA 36)

Of course, consumers must learn to put their purchasing and savings choices at the service of their true vocation as children of God. Nevertheless, producers and others in the 'mass media' have a responsibility to develop and sell products that are good for people. Advertising and sales are not neutral activities; they help to build (or destroy) culture.

In the above quotation, a third party is in need of 'educational and cultural work': the 'public authorities'. This brings us to the question of the role of state regulation in correcting the tendencies towards consumerism in modern cultures. Although the culture is the primary source of consumerism, and must therefore be the source of alternative world-views, the state has some role to play in safeguarding the community from consumerism and its effects.

*Centesimus annus* outlines the role of the state at length; in this chapter we are concerned only with its role in promoting a non-consumerist culture. Central to the government's role in this area is the fact that certain human goods cannot be produced in markets, although feeble imitations of these goods are for sale. To understand the role for the state outlined here, we must return to John Paul II's discussion of modern culture's failure to resist consumerism.

A healthy culture generates in the person a love for ultimate goods – the virtues, truth, beauty, goodness. It is not founded on the person's autonomous choice of these goods; it orients him towards them. To this extent, culture is founded on those vital things that we do not choose. We inherit these things from family, community and religion. Because modern materialism offers no wellsprings of meaning – no ultimate goods – it does not orient the individual towards any goods beyond those chosen by the individual himself; therefore, it allows the market to dominate cultural life. In the event that a more humanistic culture emerges from the current societal chaos, one of its effects will be to push the market out of some of the areas of social life it currently dominates, or at least to regulate its effects. It may also lead to reforms of advertising and marketing practices. The state has a role to play in supporting these cultural initiatives: 'It is the task of the State to provide for the defence and preservation of common goods such as the natural and human environments, which cannot be safeguarded simply by market forces' (CA 40). Healthy cultures will not rely on markets for all their needs; indeed, they cannot rely on them for every human need.

It is here that conservatives of every stripe get nervous. Is the admission that the state has a role to play a warrant for any arbitrary regulation of markets in the name of 'human ecology' and 'spiritual good'?

The current over-regulation of society by government should not force us to renounce a legitimate role for the state in helping a resurgent culture to keep market-generated prosperity in human perspective. For example, a society infused with a renewed spirit of religion may call for public expressions of that consensus, in Sabbath laws restricting business activity on Sundays and holidays. It may also insist on restrictions on the ways in which advertisers use sex to sell products.

What is most important in all this is that the state does not get ahead of the culture, or attempt to replace it. The most important check on government activity in this area is the Catholic principle of subsidiarity (see also the chapters by O'Brien and Gregg in Part Three):

> A community of a higher order should not interfere in the internal life of a community of a lower order, depriving the latter of its functions, but rather should support it in case of need and help to coordinate its activity with activities of the rest of society, always with a view to the common good. (CA 48)

The institutions of culture are the subsidiary communities of society: families, churches, businesses, non-profits and countless professional and community associations. A government which takes upon itself to create and safeguard the culture misunderstands the principle of subsidiarity and, consequently, the nature of culture. Culture is not the business of government; government is neither the arbiter nor the creator of culture.

Life is lived in the wide, rich social space between the individual and the government (CA 49). It is here that the hard work of cultural renewal must take place, and from which any initiatives for government action in support of cultural renewal must come. Modern governments are philosophically ill-suited to this supporting role. Many government activists are suspicious of these subsidiary communities – family and church, in particular – because they are not as comprehensive as the state, or are obstacles to utopian, rationalist programmes of social improvement. This statist philosophy of government is a misreading of society, and disregards the potential of subsidiary communities to renew culture. Active resistance to the attempts of subsidiary communities to affect the culture, under the guise of separation of Church and state or hostility to the family's role in the raising of children, is a serious impediment to the renewal of culture.

The most fundamental community of society is the family, and any renewal of society must begin with a renewal of family life. The *Compendium of the Social Doctrine of the Church* makes this point forcefully: 'the family is presented, in the Creator's plan, as "the primary place of humanization for the person and society" and "the cradle of life and love"' (Pontifical Council for Justice and Peace, 2005: 209). Any resistance to consumerism must begin with the family, supported by church and community. The state must safeguard the natural family in concrete ways, and allow the subsidiary communities, including the churches, a role in public life. It cannot simultaneously renew culture and suppress the institutions of a healthy culture.

## Conclusion

Catholic social teaching has always taken culture seriously. It rejects the Marxist critique that culture is simply an elaborate justification for economic power. Similarly, it refuses to make culture a creature of the state, dependent for its existence and vibrancy on state initiative. Culture is prior to both economics and politics. It provides the virtues necessary for market production and exchange, and the common goods that give purpose to politics emerge from culture. It is the culture, and not the forum or the marketplace, which ought to orient us towards those things that make life worth living. After all, the Church lives in the culture, even though it is not the only cultural institution.

Because culture is so primary in Catholic thought, it naturally looks to culture for the roots of consumerism. The ascendancy of a materialistic, secularist world-view leaves the culture unable to find meaning in the things of the spirit, and thus culture turns to markets and material goods for meaning. A materialistic culture, widespread access to consumption in free-market economies and fallen human nature combine to create ideal conditions for consumerism.

A weak culture assigns a greater role to material goods and to the markets in which they are exchanged. This is not the fault of markets, but a renewed culture may look at markets differently, because the goods of markets will be seen in perspective – not as sources of ultimate meaning, to which the goods of family and society are sacrificed, but as supplemental means by which to attain the greater goods of life. The work of cultural renewal will affect politics, through demands to protect, or at least to respect, the institutions that strengthen culture.

The popes would have us get to work on culture – on our families, our churches, our communities. A healthy culture provides the energy by which we can order the tremendous material abundance of modern economies towards true human development. Without this order, we will continue to live diminished lives of the saddest sort – those of people who have every material blessing, but are still desperately unhappy. We risk more than unhappiness, according to the Scripture verse at the beginning of this essay; the more we become like beasts, driven by unreflective instinct to seek material comfort for its own sake, the more we risk being destroyed by those very instincts. Freedom undisciplined by wisdom leads to inner slavery, and can lead a society towards political tyranny.

# References

Berry, W. (1990), *What Are People For?*, New York: Northpoint Press.

Kirzner, I. (2002), 'Advertising', in E. Heath (ed.), *Morality and the Market: Ethics and Virtue in the Conduct of Business*, Boston, MA: McGraw-Hill.

O'Neill, J. (1998), *The Market: Ethics, Knowledge, and Politics*, New York: Routledge.

Pontifical Council for Justice and Peace (2005), *Compendium of the Social Doctrine of the Church*, London: Burns & Oates.

Rothbard, M. (1971), *Power and Market*, Menlo Park: Institute for Humane Studies.

Schindler, D. L. (2003), '"Homelessness" and market liberalism: toward an economic culture of gift and gratitude', in D. Bandow and D. L. Schindler (eds), *Wealth, Poverty, and Human Destiny*, Wilmington, DE: ISI Books.

Von Mises, L. (1998), *Human Action: A Treatise on Economics*, New York: Ludwig von Mises Institute.

# 8

# BUSINESS AND THE COMMON GOOD

*Robert G. Kennedy*

## Introduction

The social doctrine of the Catholic Church is not new. It is as old as the Church herself and flows directly from the conviction that human persons, as images of the Trinity, are social creatures, impelled by their nature to live and flourish only in communities. As a branch of moral theology, the social doctrine has developed over a period of nearly two thousand years in response to a deepening understanding of the practical implications of the Gospel as well as to a variety of changes in the cultural, political and economic dimensions of social life.[1]

Until the modern era, reflections on the economic dimension of the social question were relatively

---

[1] See Pontifical Council of Justice and Peace (2005: 72–4). The *Compendium* is the first authoritative and comprehensive exposition of the social doctrine of the Catholic Church. Where almost all official documents dealing with social questions in the past have been occasional, i.e. provoked by a specific problem or set of questions, the *Compendium* sets out to summarise the tradition as a whole. A number of private summaries have been prepared over the years, some of them quite well done, but the *Compendium* has an authoritative character that other treatments cannot claim.

primitive. The Church's main preoccupation was with a spectrum of political issues: the proper relationship of Church and state, the nature and limits of authority to govern, religious freedom, and so on. It was not until the sixteenth century, with the explosion in trade and wealth brought about by the European voyages of discovery, that theologians turned their attention to an analysis of the dramatic changes in the economic arena. Still later, near the end of the nineteenth century, the challenge of socialism provoked Pope Leo XIII to address contemporary economic issues in an encyclical letter.[2] Some of his successors, notably Pius XI, John XXIII and John Paul II, similarly wrote about economic questions in prominent encyclical letters of their own.

The thrust of the encyclicals, however, tended to be a defence of some elements of the moral tradition of the Church (e.g. the right to private property, the right to just wages, the integrity of the family) against socialism and other forms of statism, coupled with urgent expressions of concern about social justice. In their turn, the encyclicals inspired generations of theologians, religious and lay persons to become engaged in efforts to

---

[2] This encyclical, *Rerum novarum* (1891), has real historical significance in that its publication marked the first time that a pope addressed contemporary economic issues in such an authoritative document. Many people mistakenly regard the letter as the starting point for the Catholic social tradition, at least in its modern form. Leo himself, however, had already written no fewer than six encyclicals on issues in the arena of politics and governance before the appearance of *Rerum novarum*, including one on the problems of socialism. Furthermore, to exaggerate the distinctiveness of the encyclical is also to overlook the pains that Leo took to emphasise that his teaching was a continuation of, not a departure from, the Catholic tradition of moral theology.

implement some of the principles they articulated. Still, it is probably fair to say that, while the social encyclicals were especially concerned with the dangers of socialism, advocates of social justice came to be more concerned in practice with critiques of free-market economies.

In either case, what has been missing is a sustained and comprehensive consideration of the role of private enterprise in a modern society.[3] At best, some of the encyclicals have given attention to certain aspects of business and acknowledged in general that it has an important role to play in the community.[4] At worst, many advocates of social justice have regarded business with suspicion in principle and ironically turned to socialist analysis in an effort to craft a better society.[5] There has

---

[3] In the ancient world, indeed in Western civilisation up to the nineteenth century, commerce and trade were often regarded with suspicion and disdain by the nobility and the Church. Respectable wealth came from the land and entailed a variety of customary responsibilities. The new wealth that came from commerce and trade was thought often to be the result of deception and dishonesty. This attitude of suspicion has diminished a bit over the past two centuries as business activities have become such a large part of modern economies, but it has not entirely been dispelled. One important area for development for the Catholic social tradition, therefore, has to do with the marketplace.

[4] Prominent in this regard are Pius XI, *Quadragesimo anno* (1931), and John Paul II, *Centesimus annus* (1991). Though much less well known, the occasional speeches and radio messages of Pius XII and John Paul II often gave attention to specific questions concerning business.

[5] Note that while the social doctrine of the Church is a product, strictly speaking, of the Magisterium (i.e. the Pope and the bishops in union with him), there are countless additional witnesses to the Church's concern with social questions. These witnesses include individual bishops, clerics, theologians and faithful laity, many of whom have made it part of their life's work to translate the principles of the social doctrine into practice. Not every witness, however, is an authoritative representative of Catholic thought. In particular, the bias against business and the marketplace that has become a common feature of advocates for social justice should not be regarded as a formal element of Catholic doctrine.

been, however, no systematic theory of business to rival the theory of law and governance that the Catholic social tradition has elsewhere developed. The elements of such a theory are present in the tradition but they have not been effectively drawn together. The purpose of this chapter is to address one part of this larger project, namely to explore the relationship of business to the common good of civil society in light of the principles of the Catholic social tradition.

## Catholic social thought and the good society

Businesses of every sort exist only in the context of a larger social body, a civil society. At the same time, every business, even a publicly owned corporation, is composed of individual persons who conceive of the organisation, assemble the resources to make it possible, make decisions about strategy and operations, and execute those decisions. The organisation does not interact with an impersonal environment; persons representing the business interact with other persons external to the organisation. As a consequence, the nature of a business becomes clear only when it is examined in the context of the persons who bring it to life and in the context of the society in which it lives that life.

What, then, makes a society good? The Catholic social tradition conceives of the ideal human society as an integrated whole, a network of relationships between individuals, their families and a wide variety of other associations (Pontifical Council for Justice and Peace, 2005: 185). Society arises as a natural result of the individual's pursuit of personal fulfilment and its function, its only reason for being, is to facilitate that fulfilment. Good societies can take many shapes since there are a great many avenues for human fulfilment but all good societies have some common traits.[6] Bad societies – the tradition has no doubt that there are indeed bad societies – all fail in critical ways to support authentic human development.

One of the marks of a good society is respect for the primacy of the person. Catholic doctrine insists that human persons each have a transcendent destiny, which is to share in God's life for time without end.[7] No society is an end in itself; each is instrumental and exists to serve the ultimate end of the persons who are its constituent members (ibid.: 132). Societies and social structures betray this principle when they frustrate the destiny of some of their members for the sake of the perceived well-being of others. Prominent examples of such flawed societies are the communist and fascist governments of the twentieth century, in which the state claimed

---

[6]  In the Catholic view, no society short of the Kingdom of Heaven can be a perfect society. This conviction, which is not unique to Catholicism, has sometimes served as an excuse to avoid giving attention to the genuine ills and injustices of a particular community and to focus energy instead on private piety. While acknowledging that all human lives, and therefore all human communities, are blemished by sin, the Church nevertheless insists that an essential part of its mission is to work for the reform of society. Even something that cannot be made perfect can still be made better. By the same token, the fact that every society is flawed does not support the conclusion that no societies are better than others or that none is more readily improved than others. In the end, Christians have a clear duty to work constantly for the reform of the societies in which they live. See Pontifical Council for Justice and Peace, 2005: 52–66.

[7]  This conviction is captured by the Second Vatican Council, which said that 'man is the only creature on earth that God has wanted for its own sake'. See *Gaudium et spes*, 24. See also Pontifical Council for Justice and Peace, 2005: 47.

primacy and acted to subordinate the most critical human rights of its citizens (to life and liberty, to property, to freedom of religion, and so on).

Another mark of a good society is variety and plurality in relationships and associations among its members. While human beings have an ultimate end in common – God – there is a broad spectrum of genuine human needs that can be addressed in a virtually infinite number of ways.[8] For example, people have a range of material needs related to life and health. We have to eat and drink, find shelter and clothing, receive medical care, and so forth. We also have needs for knowledge, beauty, play and friendship, to name a few. A good society offers possibilities for satisfying a very wide range of authentic human needs and it typically does this by encouraging and supporting families as well as a great many clubs, businesses, charities and specialised associations of all sorts. Some of these organisations may be very small and local, while others may be quite large and national or international in their scope. Each of the organisations is in some way a manifestation of the energy and creativity of individuals and a means for their self-expression.

According to the Catholic tradition, the family is the fundamental and irreplaceable association at the

---

[8] We have a 'need' for any good thing that genuinely contributes to our development and well-being as persons. Needs are not merely those things without which we die. Needs may be very general (we all need to eat but we can satisfy this need in a great many ways) or very specific (we need a particular medication here and now). Frequently needs must be distinguished from wants. Sometimes we really need less of something than we want. Sometimes we want something that actually adds nothing to our development or well-being.

core of a good society. Its stability and flourishing must be encouraged as an essential foundation for the health of the community. In addition, the good society must have formal government but also a number of non-governmental associations that pursue aspects of human welfare, such as church-related and other charitable organisations, universities and cultural associations, and so forth. It must also have a variety of associations engaged in market activities, for example businesses that aim at producing a profit and creating wealth by addressing human needs. Thus the good society will include the family and the state as well as intermediate bodies engaged in both market and non-market activities. Seriously defective societies seek to suppress one or another of these categories of associations, usually the intermediate bodies.

The myriad associations that flourish in a good society inevitably give it a hierarchical character. The idea of hierarchy is in disfavour today but that is because it is usually taken to refer to a situation in which an authoritarian figure (or group) dominates the rest of society, suppressing legitimate liberties and self-expression. This is an unfortunate caricature of hierarchy and quite different from that which the tradition recognises. In the tradition, every ordered society – and no good society can be disordered – is hierarchical, and appropriately so. On the one hand, order requires coordination, which in turn demands some principle of authority for resolving disagreements. A well-ordered society in this respect will have levels of authority, increasingly broad in application, that exist to resolve these disagreements when compromise and concession fail. On the other hand, a society with a great many associations, some local and highly focused in their activities, others regional or national and comprehensive in their interests, naturally manifests a different sort of hierarchy. Here, for example, a local golf club might reasonably defer to a regional or national association in regard to the rules of the game in order to preserve a uniformity that serves everyone well.

It is certainly the case that persons in positions of broader application and greater power can and do abuse their authority. The Catholic tradition is well aware of this and so insists that the bedrock principle guiding the exercise of authority in any community or society is subsidiarity (ibid.: 185–8). Underlying this principle is the conviction that a good society demands the flourishing of this wide variety of associations. As a consequence, every superior authority has a twofold duty. Firstly, it must provide assistance as needed to subordinate associations to enable them to perform their functions as effectively as possible. Secondly, it must always exercise restraint in its use of power so that the legitimate activities of these subordinate associations are never destroyed or absorbed. If the principle of subsidiarity is properly observed, the good society will be an organic whole in which small associations multiply and flourish, quite distinct from a centralised organisation in which subordinate units are merely extensions of the dominant power.

## The person and the common good

The nature of the contribution that a good business makes to society depends upon what the human person is understood to be. Given the primacy of the person in the Catholic social tradition, it is necessary to be clear about what the tradition teaches on this question.

At the very foundation of Catholic doctrine on the person is the conviction that each and every person is an image of God, created for his own sake and therefore possessed of a value (dignity) as an end in itself. While persons, or their activities, may also function as instruments for the achievement of other goals, they are never merely instruments. Instruments always have contingent value. They are valued for their capacity to achieve goals and may be discarded once they lose this capacity. Even though persons may sometimes be useless as instruments, they nevertheless always have value as reflections of the divine.

As mentioned above, human persons also have a destiny that transcends material creation and physical life. This destiny contributes to the intrinsic value of each person but also implies that persons are never completely fulfilled by created goods or even by other creatures. While created goods are necessary to sustain physical life and contribute in important ways to human happiness (we are *embodied* spirits, after all), they are not enough. The deepest human desires and fulfilments transcend the material world and, by implication, no one should concentrate so strongly on obtaining created goods so as to close off the possibility of obtaining the transcendent good.

All creation is a reflection of the Creator but human persons are unique images because they possess intellect and will, their two most Godlike characteristics. As a consequence, an essential part of human well-being consists in knowing the truth and choosing well. This is really the foundation for the principle of subsidiarity, for a superior authority frustrates human flourishing if it suppresses freedom of action in individuals. By the same token, such an authority does violence to individuals, in a way, if it deceives them or distorts and conceals the truth they ought to know.

Because they can know the truth and choose freely, human persons can be independent actors and are fulfilled in part by the productive activities in which they engage. The Catholic tradition insists that each person is called by God to work, to be a collaborator in the unfolding of creation. This fact of vocation has implications for both businesses and the state, for each has a responsibility, at minimum, not to interfere unreasonably in the efforts of individuals to obtain good work and to respond to their vocations.

Furthermore, properly human work and indeed the whole effort of an individual in pursuit of fulfilment are understood to be collaborative because human persons are social by nature. In this they are once again reflections of God since the Trinity is a community itself. The conviction that human persons are social and not atomistic individuals brings the Catholic tradition into sharp contrast with some modern political and economic theories. At the same time, the conviction that individuals matter enormously and that the function of the state is to facilitate the flourishing of these individuals brings the tradition into conflict with another set of political and economic theories. The result is a body of doctrine that, on the one hand, defends the primacy of the person and the right to private property and, on the other hand, emphasises the importance of the common good and solidarity.

Finally, the larger Catholic tradition acknowledges that the human being is a fallen creature, a creature whose natural capacities have been maimed by his sinfulness, a creature in need of salvation, and in the end a creature who has been saved by God made man. This reality accounts for the unavoidable defects in human societies, human associations and social systems, but it also provides another reason for respecting the dignity of individuals, who were each worthy of God's saving acts.

Based on this understanding of the human person, the Catholic social tradition has something to say about the world of creation. In the first place, the material world is the proper sphere of human operation and human dominion. The world, in all its complexity and richness, is the object of human work and creativity. Its resources, living and non-living, are to be cultivated for the sake of general human well-being, and never to be put to wasteful uses. Moreover, the Christian God is a God of abundance, not a God of scarcity. The material resources of the created world are more than sufficient to meet the needs of the human population, though it may well require ingenuity, work, restraint and solidarity actually to provide the necessary resources to each person.[9]

## Common goods and the common good

The nature of the human person as a social being who must seek his fulfilment in community with others places a set of demands on society (ibid.: 164–5). As a consequence of what people are, every civil community must have certain characteristics if it is to serve effectively as a context in which individuals can develop and flourish. While it is not primarily in the larger civil arena that individuals pursue their proper ends – families and the various intermediate bodies are more likely to be the actual communities in which people flourish – it is still true that this arena provides the foundation on which all other communities depend. The name we give to this set of characteristics is the 'common good', but in truth this is only one common good among many.

---

[9] While this may seem at first to conflict with a fundamental principle of economics – which assumes scarcity rather than abundance – the apparent conflict is not difficult to resolve. In the first place, economics concerns itself with the allocation and distribution of things that are scarce in particular instances, and more or less ignores things that are abundant. Scarcity and abundance are relative terms, comparing the available quantity of a thing with the amount desired. When more is desired than is available, the thing is scarce; when more is available than is desired, the thing is abundant. Economics has little or nothing to tell us about the absolute quantity available of any resource or about whether that quantity will in the future be sufficient or insufficient to meet human needs. While acknowledging that physical resources are finite in some way, Catholics nevertheless believe that, in an absolute sense, creation is not deficient nor is the Creator miserly. The earth provides enough for every human person to have a reasonable share. In a fallen world, however, scarcity of one sort or another is the common experience at the practical level. It is here that economics can suitably inform theology. See Pontifical Council for Justice and Peace, 2005: 323–9.

A common good by definition is one that is, or may be, shared (owned, used, enjoyed or pursued) by a number of people (we might say that a private good, by contrast, is one that is not or cannot be shared with other members of a group). Since human persons are naturally social beings, and their genuine fulfilment inevitably involves a community of some sort, common goods are always important.

Goods, or a good, may be described in a number of ways.[10] Both private goods and common goods, for example, may be *actual* or *potential*. Actual goods are those that, at a given point in time, really are owned, used or enjoyed. Potential goods are those that, while not presently owned, used or enjoyed, are seen as real possibilities: they are goals. Potential goods serve to motivate goal-directed action, and potential common goods motivate collaborative action. Indeed, underlying any genuinely collaborative action (as opposed to an aggregate of individual actions aimed at the same goal such as a gold rush) there must be at least one potential common good.

Common goods may also be *instrumental* or *final*. An instrumental good is one that is valued for its capacity to help us obtain something else that we want, while a final good is the ultimate object of our actions.[11] Potential common goods (i.e. goals)

---

[10] It can be a mistake to speak of *the* common good, as if there were one good (or collection of goods) that composed the common good. The Catholic social tradition does speak of *the* Common Good as a sort of shorthand for the common good of a civil community. This is a legitimate usage but it should not obscure for us the fact that there are many other important common goods.

[11] Money is the model of an instrumental good. We value it only because it

are valued by the individuals who pursue them in collaboration with others because they are always understood to promote private goods. Players work together in a team because each wants to be part of a winning effort or at least each wants to share in the camaraderie of the group. Employees work towards the success of a business for similar reasons but also so that they can participate in the financial rewards.

On a larger scale, peace, order and justice in a society are valued because they promote individual flourishing, not because they have an intrinsic value apart from their utility in supporting human well-being. Individuals may make extraordinary sacrifices to bring such common goods into being and to protect them, but it is because they understand and rightly value the private goods that follow.[12]

The common good of a society has a distinctive character. Since societies are intended to endure over time and through a succession of generations, their characteristic common good does not consist in a goal to be achieved once and for all. While there may be something potential about this common good, it is not a goal that, were it to be achieved, would mean the end of the society. Moreover, as the

---

can be exchanged for other things we want.

[12] Totalitarian states make the serious mistake of regarding such common goods as absolutely final, and so in the end become willing to sacrifice all manner of private goods for their sake. Even in wiser societies, caution must always be exercised in crafting and applying positive laws so that the conditions that must exist in a society to promote the flourishing of its members are adequately protected while at the same time private goods are not threatened. To be sure, in any society, some private goods are incompatible with sustaining these public conditions and so may be legitimately curtailed – but a prudent balance must nevertheless be maintained.

function of the society is to support the flourishing and fulfilment of its members, its common good is instrumental. That is to say, it is not a final good valued in and for itself (as basic goods are, for example), but it is something valued, supported and protected by the members of the society for what it permits them to do and to be.

More precisely, the common good of a society is *constructive*, which means that it is a set of conditions that makes possible the individual flourishing of each and every member of the community.[13] To the extent that some necessary conditions are not present in a society, or that the well-being of some members is not addressed, the common good has not been achieved. We recognise as a practical matter that in a fallen world the set of goods and conditions that constitutes this common good is never fully achieved and so remains a goal for the members of the community. Even if it were to be achieved, the continued maintenance and support that it would require would still make it a goal of ongoing collaboration.

Potential common goods not only shape the collaboration of members of an organisation, they also define organisations and communities. In particular, the potential common goods that define business organisations make them quite different from other kinds of communities.

A specialised association, as the name implies,

---

[13] See Pope John XXIII, *Mater et magistra*, 65, for a classic definition of the common good of political communities: '[The common good] embraces the sum total of those conditions of social living whereby men are enabled more fully and more readily to achieve their own perfection.' As a practical matter, this set of goods includes such elements as peace, justice, universal education, participation in culture and public life, and so on.

is ordered not to the integral fulfilment of its members, but rather towards attaining some human good or limited set of goods.[14] A business organisation is a specialised association, but so is an army, an orchestra, a charitable organisation, a bowling club, a university, a criminal syndicate, and virtually an indefinite number and variety of human organisations.

Our understanding of the relationship between a specialised community and a political community needs further refinement. Until relatively recently (perhaps in some places as late as the nineteenth century) specialised associations played only a small role in human life.[15] In the twentieth century, however, that role expanded greatly, in terms both of the size of specialised associations and of their numbers. In developed societies today, virtually everyone is dependent upon specialised

---

[14] The *Compendium* and some elements of the Catholic social tradition seem to prefer the term 'intermediate' to refer to 'associations', 'bodies', 'entities' or 'groups' that exist and function between the family and the state. This term of art suggests, in English at least, an organisation that acts as an intermediary between the domestic society and the civil society. Some intermediate groups do function in that way but the majority simply focus on, or one might say 'specialise in', a specific set of human goods. Furthermore, the tradition has tended not to give much attention to businesses as intermediate groups though they certainly belong in this category. As a result, the term 'specialised associations' seems to me to be more inclusive and so a better one.

[15] The triumph of the nation-state in Europe after the seventeenth century diminished the role of what had been a rich web of specialised associations (villages, churches, guilds, and so on). In this earlier period, people tended to shape their personal identities from their membership in these associations and therefore saw themselves as integral and important parts of small wholes. After the seventeenth century, many people tended to see themselves as small parts of large wholes (which were the nations). It is easy to exaggerate the significance of this change, however, since it is also the case that these earlier specialised associations never achieved the size and extent of so many contemporary organisations.

associations, directly or indirectly.[16]

Specialised associations differ from political communities and families in several important respects. First of all, there is the difference in purpose. A specialised association is always organised in order to pursue some particular good or set of goods, at least for those who collaborate in the association and often for others as well. Where the society or family functions to sustain a set of conditions within which persons may mature and seek their own fulfilment, a specialised association is directed to the creation of actual goods that its members can possess or enjoy.

Secondly, the nature of specialised associations makes their potential common goods (i.e. the goals of the organisation) more important for their day-to-day functioning than would be the case in other communities. In business, for example, specific kinds of collaboration are required because of the organisation's goals. In order to elicit this collaboration, the goals must be clearly understood and they must be compelling. The success of the organisation will require a certain kind of active contribution from each member, where the common good of a society can often be supported by the choices of citizens *not* to engage in behaviours that undermine this common good.

Thirdly, specialised associations have a clear relationship to the societies in which they exist

---

[16] Which is not, however, to say that we lead lives that are socially richer. In many cases, while we may do what we do in the context of an organisation of some sort, we do these things not as members of a true human community but as strangers in a crowd. Robert D. Putnam (2000) has described the curious decline of community at a time of the increased importance of organisations.

and function. It is sometimes assumed that, to be legitimate, specialised associations must serve the common good of the society in all that they do. This, however, is a misunderstanding.

The common good of a society is oriented to the flourishing of all its members. This flourishing, however, entails the flourishing of the organisations and associations formed by members of the society to seek and obtain private goods (ibid.: 168). These associations derive their legitimacy from the authentic human goods they seek, not from their contribution to the general common good. Indeed, the general common good must create the circumstances in which these organisations can function.

As a result, in a good society, these organisations should have considerable freedom in identifying and pursuing goods, which, to the extent that they serve to focus and motivate collaboration, will genuinely be common goods for that organisation. To be morally legitimate these common goods must be true human goods (and not merely apparent goods, such as revenge or pornography) and they must be pursued by morally sound means (so a criminal organisation might pursue real goods but do so by immoral means). Of course, the pursuit of these goods cannot undermine the constructive common good of the larger human community. Insofar as the goods pursued really are human goods, however, it is not necessary that the goods of a specialised association intentionally and directly support the common good of the larger community. They may quite legitimately do nothing more than facilitate the attainment of private goods by those associated with the organisation.[17]

These private goods may include the direct satisfaction of a variety of human needs, as well as opportunities for good work. Also included, and not least in importance, is the creation of wealth.

## The contribution of business to the common good

Something new has emerged in the modern world: a sophisticated commercial system that makes possible the creation and distribution of products and services on an unprecedented scale. The significance of this development, and the possibilities inherent in it both for promoting and for undermining human well-being, have not been correctly or sufficiently recognised within the Catholic social tradition. While some official statements, notably the 1991 encyclical by Pope John Paul II, *Centesimus annus*, acknowledge in broad strokes the potential of the new system, most discussions, whether official or unofficial, represent a primitive view of modern economic realities. This is one area in which the tradition urgently needs updating.

---

[17] That is, while the common goods of smaller communities must ordinarily be subordinated to the common good of the larger community within which they exist, it is not the case that the common goods of smaller communities must always be directed to serve the common good of the larger community. To put it another way, the actions of smaller communities or associations must not be such as to undermine the common good of the larger communities of which they are a part, although their actions need not always aim deliberately to enhance that common good in particular ways in order to be morally sound. Business organisations, therefore, need not use their resources to address social problems in order to be morally worthy associations. They are morally worthy if they pursue authentic goods in ways that properly respect other private goods and the common good of the larger community.

Even though a business need not make a direct contribution to the common good of the civic community in order to be good and legitimate, business as a system in fact does make such contributions. The system organises and integrates a number of separate elements for the sake of the common good. These elements include:

- a business culture in which individual businesses, from small to large, create an environment in which certain procedures and values are shared for the sake of more effective collaboration and even competition.[18]
- a stable financial infrastructure, which depends upon sound fiscal and monetary policies and international cooperation.
- a system of laws and regulations concerning business operations that are stable, economically sound and ordered to the common good.
- the effective application of technology, especially in the areas of communication and transportation, that serves to facilitate business operations.

The history of the development of modern business need not concern us here. It is sufficient to say that the invention and spread of the limited liability corporation made possible the creation of the large organisations required for the production

---

[18] Despite some dramatic exceptions, contemporary business relationships and operations are facilitated by a culture in which certain attitudes and practices are taken for granted. These include respect for market mechanisms, an attitude of service, and commitments in practice to transparency and good record keeping, honouring promises, and so on. By way of illustration, as formerly communist countries worked to re-enter a global marketplace in the 1990s, one of the things businesspeople were particularly keen to learn from the West was the set of habits required to compete and be taken seriously.

of many modern products and services.[19] These organisations could survive their founders and the principle of limited liability encouraged investors to take risks. The early successes of these organisations gave some indication of the possibilities (and the perils) that lay ahead. Over time we came to realise that exploiting the potential of this new way of doing business would also require the cooperation of government in setting in place sound financial policies as well as sensible laws and regulations. It was also important, in some areas, for government to take a hand in shaping the institutional framework, and sometimes facilitating the provision of infrastructure, in which new technologies would facilitate business operations. The appropriate role of government here is arguable but it can include facilitating the development of railway networks, roads and motorways, and air travel, as well as aspects of the Internet and modern telecommunications.

Much of the government interest in the development of the modern business system was motivated, or at least justified in public discussion, by a concern for the common good of the community. Like any powerful tool, this system can be abused and turned against the common good. This fact should not be ignored but neither should we make business the natural enemy of society and overlook the real good it is capable of doing. When

---

[19] Many of the foundations of modern life would be impossible without large business organisations. From railways, automobiles and aircraft to telecommunications, computers and modern medicine, much of what we take for granted cannot be produced entirely by small companies. The limited liability corporation made practical the assembly of financial resources required by these large businesses.

it functions well, the modern system of business contributes to that common good in two principal ways.

First, the system of business greatly augments the wealth-producing capacity of the community. In the Christian tradition, wealth is not understood simply as money but rather as an abundance of the material goods required for a good human life (see Kennedy, 2006). To create wealth is to apply human labour and ingenuity to the resources of creation in order to produce the goods that satisfy human needs. To have an abundance of these goods is to be prosperous and in the most important sense prosperity is a sought-after condition of communities and societies, not merely of individuals (Pontifical Council for Justice and Peace, 2005: 323–9). The wealth-producing capacity of a society, therefore, is its ability to bring into being the abundance or prosperity necessary to sustain the good life for each of its members.[20]

Business may do this in two ways. Firstly, it often seeks ways to organise human work more effectively, which at its best makes work more

---

[20] One might argue that this abundance of goods is impossible to achieve because human wants are unlimited; as soon as one desire is satisfied another one can arise. A truly good life for an individual, however, is not the satisfaction of every desire but rather the reasonable satisfaction of the desires of a virtuous person. Since the deepest human desires, the ones that are properly unlimited, are spiritual and intellectual, not material, it remains possible in principle to generate an abundance of goods. That even 'wealthy' societies fail to do this may say more about the reasonableness of their desires than about the capacity of the society to create prosperity. Furthermore, as a practical matter unlimited goods would require unlimited productive labour. While a good life requires some good work, it also requires leisure properly understood. Therefore, in a prosperous society material goods are available in abundance, making a good life possible, but desires are moderated by virtue as well, making unlimited goods unnecessary.

productive without necessarily demanding more time and energy from the worker.[21] Secondly, business in many societies has the task of converting common resources (whether natural like oil or virtual like bandwidth) into useful products and services.[22] Developed economies generally recognise that business manages this conversion better than the public sector and therefore contributes more to the common good by doing so. Thus in more highly developed economies a great many activities are privatised that once were conducted by a branch of government.

Business does not have a monopoly, so to speak, on productive human labour. Wealth can be created by any segment of society but business by its nature focuses on wealth-creating activities. While well-managed businesses aim at particular goods for their members and customers, they also augment the capacity of a society to create general prosperity, which is indeed an element of the common good.

The second broad contribution that the system of business makes is related to the first. Business organises work and resources to generate not only *more* products and services to address the material needs of members of the community but also better

---

[21] Needless to say, businesses are not immune to the disorganisation and inefficiency that are found in other sectors. Incentives to deal with these problems are, however, more strongly present in business settings than in most non-profit or government organisations. Very few people, if any, recommend that businesses study government agencies or university faculties to find models of efficiency and effectiveness.

[22] That is, societies convey to businesses in some fashion the right to extract or exploit a resource owned by the community. In doing so, the society may benefit from a fee paid to acquire the rights as well as from the relatively efficient conversion of the resource into something that serves human welfare.

and more sophisticated ones.[23] This is exemplified by the healthcare industry in which so much progress has been made over the last few generations. From extraordinary new technologies to creative surgical techniques to breakthrough medications, the industry has made routine what was once thought impossible. Similar things have happened in communications, transportation and information management. Though some are commissioned by the public sector, most of these innovations are actually produced by private business, which also does a great deal of fundamental research.

All this is a significant contribution to the general common good, but from the perspective of the Catholic social tradition it does carry with it a certain risk. This is the danger of losing sight of what genuinely contributes to human well-being and instead employing our enhanced technological capacities merely to respond to wants. Medical technology, for example, can be turned to frivolous cosmetic surgery or communications technology can produce and distribute ever-increasing amounts of pornography. Neither business nor engineering has internal compasses that can direct practice unerringly to good ends (ibid.: 360, 376). Instead, they both depend upon external ethical guidance, which can be supplied by the social tradition, among other sources.

By the same token, the Catholic social tradition is at risk of becoming impractical and esoteric unless it is informed by practical disciplines such as business, economics, engineering and politics. The

---

[23] On the desirability of this, see *Centesimus annus*, 36.

tradition does indeed have something to teach these disciplines but it also has some important lessons to learn. We turn to that now.

## What the Catholic social tradition has to learn from business and economics

The ultimate measure of the success of a business is neither its margin of profit nor the market price of its shares. Its true success lies in the human needs that its activities satisfy, including the needs of workers, customers, investors and others. This is a moral criterion but then business, and the economic arena in general, is not simply a technical exercise; it should also be truly moral. The Catholic social tradition reminds us of this (ibid.: 338–40). The tradition and its advocates, however, are often less mindful that there are crucially important lessons to be learned from the social sciences and the professions, such as management (ibid.: 378).[24] Indeed, to be morally good in the fullest sense an activity or a practice must not only be oriented to genuine goods, it must also employ morally sound means to achieve these goods. And a morally sound means must be both effective and efficient.[25]

---

[24] It should be noted that while, at some level, the Church acknowledges the need to learn from the social sciences and other disciplines, this has often not translated into a real appropriation of what these disciplines have to teach. Too frequently a passion on the part of advocates for better economic outcomes has resulted in commitments to policies that are unwise, even if well intentioned. The problem is compounded when such a policy preference is later understood to be a necessary entailment of the Church's social teaching.

[25] Cardinal Ratzinger (later Pope Benedict XVI) made a similar observation many years ago: 'A morality that believes itself able to dispense with the technical knowledge of economic laws is not morality but moralism. As such it is the antithesis of morality. A scientific approach that believes itself capable of managing without an ethos misunderstands the reality of man. Therefore

Consider, for example, the doctrine of the just wage (ibid.: 302). The idea that a worker ought to be paid fairly for his work is at least biblical in origin.[26] During much of the Middle Ages wages for labourers were established not so much by agreement between employer and employee as by law or custom. Until the modern era prices were comparatively stable and labourers rarely suffered from inflation. In the modern era, however, as fairly rapid inflation became a fact of life and as developed countries moved away from customary forms of labour to industrial employment, the question of just wages became more acute. It was no longer quite enough to encourage employers to pay a just wage when such a wage was being set by a market of sorts.[27] The doctrine of the Church evolved somewhat to demand that the wages paid to a full-time worker be sufficient to permit that worker, and his family, to live a minimally decent life, taking into account the time and place. Simply relying on the market was not enough since a market mechanism alone could result in wages below a subsistence level.

One response to this problem which was

---

it is not scientific. Today we need a maximum of specialised economic understanding but also a maximum of ethos so that specialised economic understanding may enter the service of the right goals.' See Ratzinger (1986).

[26] See Leviticus 19:3, Deuteronomy 24:14–15, Judges 5:4.

[27] While acknowledging the legitimate freedom of persons to negotiate the terms of contracts, there was some initial suspicion among Catholic thinkers of negotiated wages and wage contracts. Some theologians argued that wage contracts were immoral, but this view was definitively rejected by Pius XI in his encyclical *Quadragesimo anno*, 64. Nevertheless, the Church has always insisted that negotiation by itself does not make a wage just and that other, non-negotiable, factors must be considered: see Calvez and Perrin (1961: 282–5).

championed by many advocates of the social tradition early in the twentieth century was a legislated minimum wage. This policy recalled the medieval practice of legally determined wages and in principle offered some protection to workers who were vulnerable in the absence of unions. Nevertheless, despite the fact that minimum wage legislation had (and has) the energetic support of a number of priests and bishops, it remains merely one policy option that follows from the general principle that workers ought to be paid fairly. As a policy option, not a moral principle, it ought to be examined for its effectiveness and its consequences in the times and places in which it might be imposed (see Chapter 5). There is considerable evidence to suggest that minimum wage legislation increases unemployment while not accomplishing as much as it was once thought to do to ensure that workers are paid enough. If that is the case then perhaps alternative policies ought to be considered. At the very least, we should keep in mind that the social tradition is ordinarily not committed to policies and practices at this level. Advocates should be prepared to revise their preferences in the light of sound economic evaluation while at the same time remaining firmly committed to the relevant moral principles.

Numerous other examples could be cited concerning such topics as corporate taxation, executive compensation, marketing and accounting practices, and so on. There are three important broad areas concerning business and the common good, however, in which we might say that economics and business practice can inform the social tradition.

The first of these has to do with the importance of wealth creation in a society (ibid.: 332, 334). The tradition acknowledges that wealth may be created, not merely distributed, and recognises that the true and ultimate source of wealth is human ingenuity and the capacity for work (see CA 32). Still, the tradition has not fully appropriated the significance of this idea. It remains more concerned with the distribution of wealth and income than with its creation. It is similarly concerned with the danger posed by a materialism that springs from prosperity. One answer to both concerns (which are indeed real enough) is to urge people in developed countries, by law or by persuasion, to adopt simpler lives and to share more of what they have. Both may have some benefits (especially if not coerced) but policies that expand the sum of wealth to be shared may be wiser and more effective. This could be especially true if coupled with cultural models, perhaps inspired by Christian teaching and preaching, that discourage excessive consumption through personal moral restraint and encourage people to bend their energies to obtain genuine human goods rather than empty consumption.

The second area is related to this. No one disputes that there are indeed problems of poverty and deprivation that urgently need attention. In parts of the world there are people who need help – food, shelter, healthcare – immediately. There is no time to wait for the development of these countries, as there is an urgent need for relief: material resources for their relief must be brought to bear, transferred, without delay (see the chapter on foreign aid by Booth for a discussion of development aid, which is different in character from this form of relief). Not every situation, however, is so urgent. In many cases the resolution of immediate problems needs to be accompanied by an appreciation of the importance of economic initiative and responsibility.

Once again, the tradition recognises this but does not always explore the full implications (ibid.: 187). Human persons, as images of God, are endowed with intelligence and freedom. An important element of their flourishing as persons is the exercise of these capacities, including their exercise in the economic arena. This means that people have a need to solve problems, to make choices, to be creative, and to express themselves, especially through their work. An implication of this on one level is that the full dignity of the person is not respected when welfare replaces work (assuming an individual is able to work). Far better for the person that he or she exercise all the capacities that are the gift of God rather than be a passive recipient of what others share.

This has implications, too, for policies quite removed from concerns about poverty. There is considerable evidence from business practice, for example, that procedures are more effective and more efficient when the creativity of employees is released and when they have a significant degree of freedom in which to do their work. Government policies that unnecessarily constrain business practices or that stifle creativity, to say nothing of management practices that do the same, are wasteful, or worse. They smother the human spirit and ignore the fact that the economic segment of life produces more than merely material goods: it also shapes the soul of participants. The Church understands this, again at some level, but a tight focus on distribution of resources in practice tends to obscure some of the deeper and more human goods meant to be served by an economy or a business (ibid.: 189–91).

One last consequence of the creativity and freedom of individuals, one that modern economics has come to appreciate far more strongly than the social tradition, is change in technology, in work and in economic relationships. A society in which creativity and freedom are suppressed, whether by design or by circumstance, is also a society in which much is stable. This is probably a convertible proposition: a stable society is one in which creativity and freedom are not adequately enjoyed by the population (and in which the common good is defective to that extent). A healthy society is dynamic and characterised by Schumpeter's 'creative destruction'. This does not mean that the economy in such a society needs to be brutal but perhaps that what is to be preferred is a sort of dynamic equilibrium rather than economic stasis. In contrast, some elements of the social tradition of the Church have had a wistful longing for economic relationships that belong to an earlier era and which would not be possible today without sacrificing some of the benefits of modern civilisation.[28]

A third area in which the Church could learn from economics, and perhaps the most direct area,

---

[28] One thinks in this regard of the economic nostalgia of Chesterton and Belloc, or of the romantic attachment that the Church often has to agriculture as a way of life.

has to do with what we might call the economic realities of a fallen world. The world in which we live is not the Kingdom of Heaven: it is populated by men and women who are not only sinners but whose perceptions and inclinations are damaged by original sin. Economic relationships and behaviours are shaped by this reality. While it is certainly true that the economy must, in the end, be at the service of man, it also functions the way it does because of who man is.

From Kant we have inherited the idea that genuinely moral actions cannot at the same time be self-serving. In other words, the moral act cannot and should not benefit the person acting. On this analysis, most business activities are non-moral at best and immoral at worst since they aim at obtaining benefits for employees and shareholders through service to customers and communities. Catholic moral theology, however, has never adopted this view. It does not see a conflict, in principle, between moral behaviour and self-interested behaviour (though such a conflict can certainly exist in particular cases). On the other hand, neither does it fully subscribe to Adam Smith's notion of a tradesman indifferent to the welfare of his customers. Moral business people, in the Catholic view, attend to the well-being of their customers and understand that their own well-being, both spiritual and material, is intimately connected with the excellence of their work.

Economics, for the most part, would not dispute this analysis but it has a greater appreciation of the degree to which even good people fall short of seeing and pursuing the good in every case.

This leads to an appreciation of the importance of incentives.

In a world populated by saints, people would make economic choices that reflected a sound understanding of and a deep commitment to what is truly good, for themselves and for everyone affected by their actions. In the world in which we really live, we often make choices that are not so much self-interested as selfish. We prefer the good for ourselves even when our actions deny the good to others, and we often prefer our private goods to the common good.

As a practical matter, then, leaders in an organisation or a community must provide some additional motivating factors to assist people to work for the good of others and for the common good. This entails providing incentives that channel behaviour in more appropriate directions. One difficulty with the practical side of the social tradition is that it too often relies on persons to act with the most saintly motives and too often is frustrated when they fail to do so. Sometimes this frustration results in a desire to provide legislated incentives of a different sort.

It would be far better for advocates of the tradition to understand more deeply the ways in which people, in the aggregate, respond to economic pressures and opportunities in order to craft more effective and respectful incentives.

Finally, the social tradition needs to overcome its apprehensions and hesitations about markets. Again, at an abstract level, the tradition recognises that markets play an important role in society (ibid.: 347–50; see also CA 42). There remains in practice, however, a very considerable conviction that markets are inevitably abusive and that freedom in the marketplace is to be avoided, that profitability is morally suspect, and so on.[29] In fact, as we can learn from economics, it is not so much free markets which are abusive as defective markets, such as those in which monopolies persist or competitors are prohibited from entering or where information is deficient.[30] Nevertheless, markets do respect human dignity and do reward human creativity, initiative and virtue (e.g. fairness, industry, self-discipline, and so on) while at the same time efficiently providing for human needs. The social tradition needs to acquire an appreciation of the value of markets and wean itself from its long infatuation with planned economies.

## Conclusion

The Catholic social tradition is an integral element of the Church's teaching on moral matters. Its concern with the societies in which people live and work and pursue holiness is a legitimate part of its mission to continue the work of Christ. One

---

[29] See Ratzinger (1986: 201–2). Consider, too, the criticisms commonly levelled against companies in the energy or pharmaceutical industries when they profit from high prices in their markets.

[30] To be sure, even free markets, properly understood, can result in harms to participants when unscrupulous people cheat. Their cheating is not really a failure of the market and over time market mechanisms will introduce corrections. On the whole the market will function but in specific cases individuals may be harmed in the meantime. One can support free markets and at the same time acknowledge the necessity of external authorities to impose rules for the common good and correct for bad behaviour. But bad behaviour also occurs in regulatory authorities, of course, sometimes without self-correcting incentives. We therefore have to choose between different imperfect mechanisms. Who regulates the regulator?

major thrust of this tradition is a project to describe the nature of a good society and help people in particular places and particular times to bring that good society into being. Within this tradition the practice of business has a place. Good businesses address genuine human needs directly and form communities of work in which investors and employees can use their resources, their talents and their energies to support human well-being. Good businesses also make vital contributions to the common good of the societies in which they operate by creating wealth, by providing opportunities for good work and by making efficient use of the resources of the community.

The Church can play an important role in carrying forward its own mission and in making societies better by helping people to understand how business contributes to individual well-being and to the common good. To do this more effectively in practice, the Church needs to learn from disciplines like economics about the obstacles to and the practical means for supporting healthy businesses.

## References

Calvez, J-Y. and J. Perrin (1961), *The Church and Social Justice*, Chicago, IL: Regnery.

Kennedy, R. G. (2006), 'Wealth creation within the Catholic social tradition', in H. Alford et al. (eds), *Rediscovering Abundance*, Notre Dame, IN: University of Notre Dame Press, pp. 57–86.

Pontifical Council for Justice and Peace (2005), *Compendium of the Social Doctrine of the Church*, London: Burns & Oates.

Putnam, R. D. (2000), *Bowling Alone: The Collapse and Revival of American Community*, New York: Simon & Schuster.

Ratzinger, J. (1986), 'Church and economy: responsibility for the future of the world economy', *Communio*, 13: 199–204.

# 9

# THE ENTREPRENEUR IN THE LIFE OF THE CHURCH AND SOCIETY

*Anthony Percy*

## Introduction

There can be no doubt that the Church definitely has a bias against consumerism. In his encyclical letter on the Fatherhood of God – *Dives in misericordia* ('Rich in mercy') – the late Pope John Paul II noted that 'side by side with wealthy and surfeited people and societies, living in plenty and ruled by consumerism and pleasure, the same human family contains individuals and groups *that are suffering from hunger*' (DM 11).[1]

The Catholic Church has long had a deep concern for the poor. In fact, as Rodney Stark has discovered, one of the reasons why the Catholic Church had great success in evangelising the world in the first few centuries of its existence was its love and care for the poor. Survival rates among Catholics, for instance, after famines and plagues in the ancient world, were higher than among other groups in society. Catholics put into practice the *Mandatum novum.* They loved one another, cared

---

[1] All citations of the encyclicals of Pope John Paul II are from Miller (2001).

for one another and thus had greater survival rates (see Stark, 1997: 74–5). Loving one another had practical consequences.

But it doesn't quite follow that railing against consumerism and having a preferential option for the poor means that you are against business, businessmen, entrepreneurs or money. After all, it is wealth which alleviates poverty. And poverty is what we want to remove. Wealth creation, therefore, should be promoted as a significant contributor to the good of the human person and the common good. Wealth is a means to an end.

Besides, and perhaps surprisingly so, the Word of God is quite clear about this. Consumerism is not fuelled by money itself. Rather, it is the love of money which causes the problem. According to St Paul's first letter to Timothy, 'the *love of money* is the root of all evils' (1 Timothy 6:10). It is a warning whether you happen to be an entrepreneur or not.

## The entrepreneur

Needless to say, having an interest in money (a commercial focus) and in making money is an important ingredient in what makes an entrepreneur tick. Along with this interest, an entrepreneur is extremely creative, and alert to information and new possibilities in the marketplace. He or she will be good at bringing both people and the factors of production together for a project, and will not be overawed by the risk – usually large – of undertaking such a project. Finally, and importantly, the Christian entrepreneur should carry out his work conscious of the common good.

## The entrepreneur and the Word of God

The Word of God deals with God's saving action among us and it has a preoccupation, as regards social justice issues, with caring for widows and orphans. One would not expect, therefore, to find the latest investment or share advice in the sacred text. Still, all is not darkness with respect to the entrepreneur. We do find, particularly in the Wisdom literature, small rays of light with respect to his activity: 'These are the things you should not be ashamed of ... of making small and larger profits, or gaining from commercial transactions' (Sirach 42:1, 5).

Besides affirming commercial exchange and the profits that flow from it, this pithy text alerts us to the fact that each generation of businessmen and businesswomen does face a particular challenge: people are generally suspicious of anyone who makes money from commerce. Why else would the biblical author counsel the reader to avoid feelings of shame?

The New Testament, too, alludes to the value of the entrepreneur. The parable of the talents (see Matthew 25:14–30) encourages diligence in the use of our God-given gifts. We are to avoid all forms of fear so that we are fruitful. To be sure, the parable has an eschatological flavour about it. But this should not stop us from recognising that the Lord, in telling the parable, made use of a measure of wealth – a talent. Other parables include two that run side by side in the Gospels:

> The kingdom of heaven is like treasure hidden in a field, which a man found and covered up; then

in his joy he goes and sells all that he has and buys that field.

Again, the kingdom of heaven is like a merchant in search of fine pearls, who, on finding one pearl of great value, went and sold all that he had and bought it. (Matthew 13:44–6)

These parables are evidently about the offer of eternal life – it is worth doing everything to gain it. But, as Bernard Lonergan has pointed out, they use the *principle of sublation* (Lonergan, 1972: 241). That is, the parable does indeed introduce something new and distinct (i.e. eternal life), but it does not interfere with or destroy the work of the businessman and merchant. On the contrary, the parable needs and preserves their work and activity and brings them to a fuller realisation. Thus there is an *implicit* approval of entrepreneurial activity in the scriptures.

## The entrepreneur in the Fathers of the Church

Much the same can be said of the writings of the Church Fathers. On many occasions they approve of entrepreneurial work – implicitly. For instance, Basil the Great (329–79) approves of the work of merchants within the paradigm of the Creator's garden:

[T]he sea is good in the eyes of God … because it brings together the most distant parts of the earth, and facilitates the inter-communication of mariners. By this means it gives us the boon of general information, supplies the merchant with his wealth, and easily provides for the necessities of life, allowing the rich to export their superfluities, and blessing the poor with the supply of what they lack.[2]

The merchant, his work and his wealth are praised within a general theology of the creation. At the same time the poor benefit from such activity. The work of the merchant is thus of great service to humanity – particularly in its alleviation of poverty.

John Cassian (360–435) describes – quite remarkably – some 'infant' Christians who were searching for perfection and found it among a group of Christians whose only activity, it appears, was business. They were businessmen by weight of necessity and used their intelligence for survival. In some way, they must be considered the forerunners of the Dutch:

> And so we came by a very lengthy voyage to a town of Egypt named Thennesus, whose inhabitants are so surrounded either by the sea or by salt lakes that they *devote themselves to business alone* and get their wealth and substance by *naval commerce* as the land fails them, so that indeed when they want to build houses, there is no soil sufficient for this, unless it is brought by boat from a distance.[3]

## The entrepreneur and the virtue of magnificence

From a preliminary perusal of the tradition, then, it would appear that those involved in business

---

[2] St Basil the Great, 'Nine homilies on the Hexaemeron', Homily IV (Upon the gathering together of the waters), in Schaff and Wace (1999: 75) (one finds similar thoughts in the writings of Chrysostom and Jerome).
[3] John Cassian, 'Description of the town of Thennesus', ibid.: 415.

were not regarded as ogres. Rather, there seems to be a healthy appreciation – albeit an implicit one – of their activity.

St Thomas Aquinas (1225–74) adds weight to this claim in his treatment of the virtue of magnificence.[4] He lived at a time when a market economy was beginning to emerge (Charles, 1998: 197f). His analysis – remarkably – anticipates modern corporate finance theory with its emphasis on the relationship between risk and return, which was developed some seven centuries later.

According to Thomas, to carry out a 'magnificent work' requires both form and matter: largesse of soul (form) and largesse of outlay (matter). Thomas says, rather strikingly and incisively, that people would never carry out such works if they had not first *moderated their love for money*. If they truly loved money, then, according to St Thomas, they would never assume such a grand undertaking with its consequent risks. They would, presumably, be content to protect their sum by banking the money and obtaining the interest. It is precisely the ability to moderate one's love for money which leads an entrepreneur to engage in large and risky projects. Clearly, St Thomas thought there was virtue in the type of work and activity that we call 'entrepreneurial'.

## Social doctrine and the entrepreneur

If circumstances and changes within society led St Thomas to consider more thoughtfully the importance of works of magnificence in the field

---

[4] See *Summa Theologica*, 2, 2, Q. 134 (especially Article 3).

of business and economics, then the Industrial Revolution in the eighteenth and nineteenth centuries definitely forced the Catholic Church, as well as many other institutions, to rethink – seriously – relationships in the social order. This was particularly true of the relationship between capital and labour. Pope Leo XIII was to focus his thoughts on this precise relationship in what became the Catholic Church's first and most famous social encyclical. It was called *Rerum novarum* and means 'Of new things'.

Society had been predominantly agrarian up until the eighteenth century, but changes late in that century meant that it was shifting towards being an industrial society. Men no longer worked from home; technology and inventions contributed to vast changes in the quality and quantity of production; the means of production settled in the hands of a few; capital, not labour, was being considered as the main resource; wealth was increasingly focused in the hands of those in control of capital; inevitably tension developed between the new class of industrialists and a new – poorer – class of workers.

In 1891 Leo XIII, with the encouragement of many of the world's bishops, was to respond to this massive shift in society with his famous and groundbreaking encyclical. It was some time in coming, but according to the late Pope John Paul II has provided the Church with a lasting paradigm for Catholic social thought (*Centesimus annus*, 5).

Two issues preoccupied Leo's thoughts. Firstly, he defended the rights of workers to a just and fair wage. Secondly, he provided compelling arguments against socialism. The socialists reacted to the Industrial Revolution by promoting the socialisation of the means of production. They thought this was the best chance they had of fighting the inequalities between the emerging working class and the new class of wealthy industrialists.

The issue of socialisation is of interest to entrepreneurs, since Pope Leo defended vigorously the right to private property. He saw this right as flowing from human nature itself and wisely judged that if this right were taken away, human beings would lose all interest in their welfare. They could no longer call anything their own. His reasoning, to this day, is compelling.

Forty years later, Pope Pius XI wrote another social encyclical to coincide with the anniversary of *Rerum novarum*. It was called *Quadragesimo anno* and means 'Forty years' (or strictly speaking, 'In the fortieth year'). The year was 1931 and the world was in a mess.

> In 1931 Pius faced a very different situation. World War I had shattered liberal confidence. Parliamentary democracy seemed almost helpless in the face of the mass movements of fascism and communism. And the economy of the Western world lay in the ruins of a worldwide depression. (O'Brien and Shannon, 2000: 40)

Addressing the problems, Pius's encyclical was on the restructuring of the social order. While Leo had developed marvellously the right to *private property* in the social order, Pius moved to a defence of *private action* in the social order. This itself was a clear development in Catholic social thought, occasioned by culture and political factors.

The right to private action and initiative was threatened in a world filled with Nazi predators and communistic wolves. Moreover, the depression and its resultant despair opened the door to a particular political temptation: that of abolishing private initiative and the replacing of it with the installation of the welfare state.

Pius XI resisted the temptation forcefully. He reaffirmed, and developed for generations yet to come, the *principle of subsidiarity*. Subsidiarity derives its meaning from the Latin word *subsidium*. It means 'to help'. Thus the state is there to help and *not replace* the role and work of private citizens. The state is there to provide the *conditions* under which private enterprise can flourish. In this way the state serves and does not suffocate both private initiative and the common good.

And so, within 40 years two critical developments took place in the social teaching of the Church with respect to the entrepreneur and his work. Firstly, the right to private property and private action was vigorously defended and affirmed. In the face of a rapidly changing world, and in response to the challenge of socialism and other 'isms', the Church taught clearly that no one should have their right to private property denied. Likewise, their right to private initiative must be considered sacrosanct. The good of the person and society depended on this being the case. Secondly, the Church clearly articulated what we now call the 'two arms' or 'two wings' of her social teaching – the *principle of solidarity* and the *principle of subsidiarity*. The Church could not stand idle at a time when the rights and dignity of workers were threatened.

She defended the right to a just wage[5] and the right to private property to ensure the material well-being of humanity, and these were the bases of the principle of solidarity. John Paul II would deepen the Church's understanding of solidarity in his three social encyclicals.[6]

Equally important was the principle of subsidiarity. How could poverty be eliminated if there was not freedom of action in the social and economic sphere? Who would create wealth? The enunciation of this principle proved to be more than prophetic with the collapse of the Berlin Wall in 1989. That wall was a symbol of stupidity, closed-mindedness, state enslavement and suffocation. It led to mass poverty. It took years of immense suffering in communistic societies for people to realise the truth of Pius's words in 1931.

## The wisdom of Pope Pius XII

Between the years 1950 and 1956 Pope Pius XII made a significant contribution to the development of Catholic social doctrine with respect to business, banking and the entrepreneur.[7] His teachings on these matters come to us not in encyclical form, but rather in the form of radio addresses and talks to specialised groups of people.

What distinguishes Pius's addresses from the writings of both Popes Leo XIII and Pius XI is

---

[5] Whether a just wage should be one decided by agreement, with the state removing impediments to free negotiation, or have other characteristics too has been debated through the ages: see Chapter 5.

[6] *Laborem exercens, Sollicitudo rei socialis* and *Centesimus annus.*

[7] For a full treatment of Pius's teaching and the relevant references, see Percy (2004).

their *concreteness*.[8] He moves beyond principles and speaks very specifically about particular types of business and entrepreneurial activity. To my knowledge, he is the first Roman pontiff to use the word 'entrepreneur'. This is important since many commentators have suggested that it was Pope John Paul II in his encyclical letter *Centesimus annus* (1991) who shifted the Church's thinking to a more favourable assessment of the workings of business and the market economy. Some even see it as a radical shift in papal social thought.

In the brief material that I present below, and indeed from what I have said about the encyclical letters *Rerum novarum* and *Quadragesimo anno*, one can see that this latter claim is a touch wide of the mark. It is true that an encyclical letter carries more weight than a papal audience or papal address. For that reason, people tend to take more notice of an encyclical. Still, both an encyclical letter and a papal address form part of the ordinary teaching Magisterium of the popes and of the Church and because of this both should be duly acknowledged. As we shall see, Pope John Paul II did indeed affirm a society of *free work, enterprise and participation* in his encyclical letter of 1991. Entrepreneurs and those working for free societies must have jumped for joy on reading the Pope's thoughts.

---

[8] Like his predecessors – Leo XIII and Pius XI – Pius forcefully articulates the principles of private property and private initiative. He also introduces the principle of the *universal destination of material goods*. The material riches of the world are an endowment made by the Creator to every human being – and not just those who happen to lay their hands on them first. Nevertheless the principle of private property is not in conflict with that of the universal destination of goods: the latter principle does not mean that all people have a right to all goods.

But we should not overlook the wisdom of Pius XII some 40 years prior. His addresses on the dignity of business and entrepreneurial activity are like the treasure hidden in the field that Jesus spoke about in chapter fourteen of Matthew's gospel. Upon reading these addresses, no budding entrepreneur would want to do anything other than sell what he had and enter the world of money and thus serve the needs of others.

Let me cite two of Pius's addresses.[9] A section of his address to an International Congress on Credit Questions on 24 October 1951 is worth quoting at length. His address has a similar flavour to that of St Thomas Aquinas in his treatment of the virtue of magnificence. The message is forceful: money should not be hoarded but is there to be used for the greater good of society; risks should be taken, fear set aside. I have highlighted some key points in italics:

> How much capital is lost through waste and luxury, through selfish and dull enjoyment, or *accumulates and lies dormant without being turned to profit!* There will always be egoists and self-seekers; there will always be misers and those who are *short-sightedly* timid. Their number could be considerably reduced if one could interest those who have money in *using their funds wisely and profitably, be they great or small*. It is largely due to this *lack of interest that money lies dormant*. You can remedy this to a great extent by making ordinary depositors collaborators, either as bond or share-holders, *in undertakings whose launching and*

---

[9]  See note 7 above for a fuller treatment of Pius's teaching and the references it contains.

*thriving would be of great benefit to the community*, such as industrial activities, agricultural production, public works, or the construction of houses for workers, educational or cultural institutions, welfare or social service. (Pius XII, 1951: 121)

And then, in what must surely be regarded as an extraordinary address with respect to its affirmation of the entrepreneur, Pius XII in his address of 20 January 1956 to the First National Congress of Small Industry had these things to say. Again, emphasis added is mine:

Among the motives that justified the holding of your convention, you have given the first place to '*a vindication of the indispensable functions of the private entrepreneur.*' The latter exhibits in an eminent degree the *spirit of free enterprise* to which we owe the *remarkable progress* that has been made especially during the past fifty years, and notably in the *field of industry*. (Pius XII, 1956: 50)

## The Church is a 'joy and hope'

Pius XII died in 1958 and was replaced by Pope John XXIII. Between the years 1962 and 1965 the Second Vatican Council took place in Rome. It was a Church council with many of the world's bishops in attendance. Unlike previous Church councils, however, the Second Vatican Council faced no specific doctrinal or disciplinary issues. Rather, John XXIII called the Council to deepen the Church's understanding of herself and of her age-old truths. He was concerned that the 'treasure' or deposit of faith was not reaching the hearts of her people. In a rapidly changing world, moreover, he was deeply concerned as to how the Church could best communicate these truths and so reach the 'inner sanctum' of the faithful.

In this sense it is probably more accurate to say that the Council was a 'spiritual' rather than a 'pastoral' council. It issued sixteen documents on various ecclesial matters. Two documents took centre stage. One of the them was entitled *Lumen gentium* – the Church is a 'light to the nations'. The other received the Latin title *Gaudium et spes* – the Church is a 'joy and hope to the world'.

While *Lumen gentium* dealt with the very nature of the Church herself, *Gaudium et spes* directed its attention to the relationship between the Church and the modern world. A small section in this document discusses the entrepreneur and his activity. Again, it is an affirmation of private initiative, although the term now employed for this is *spirit of enterprise*. The Council taught:

> [T]herefore we must encourage technical progress and *the spirit of enterprise*, we must foster the eagerness for creativity and improvement, and we must promote adaptation of production methods and all serious efforts of people engaged in production – in other words of all elements which contribute to economic progress. The ultimate and basic purpose of economic production does not consist merely in the increase of goods produced, nor in profit nor prestige; it is directed to the *service of man*, of man, that is, in his totality taking account of his material needs and the requirements of his intellectual, moral, spiritual, and religious life. (GS 64)[10]

---

[10] Citations of Vatican II documents are from Flannery (1992).

This passage is interesting, not only for its employment of the term *spirit of enterprise* but also for its rejection of what I would call 'economism'. Economism is the ideology of making economics or money the standard around which we judge all reality. Having an interest in money is important. So is the study of economic theory. It is important to put fear aside, so that a spirit of enterprise embeds itself deeply in a society and its culture. Also, the rejection of goods and profit as the 'ultimate and basic purpose' of enterprise is not to say that the price mechanism and the profit signal are not fundamental in directing enterprise towards promoting the common good. The authors of the Vatican II documents would not regard it as their role to make a definitive judgement on this. The extent to which the price mechanism and the profit signal are best fitted to direct enterprise in the service of man is a matter for economists and political economists to debate.

But all this should be subordinate to the *service of man*. And man, as the Church likes to remind us, is not just a 'consumer'. Man is also a 'creator' – of sorts. That is, he has a profound spiritual centre. He is gifted with a powerful intellect and the ability to reason things through. He can remember things and so foster the virtue of hope. His spiritual centre – according to the Word of God – is his heart, and so he has an immense capacity to love and forgive. Putting these marvellous attributes together, we come to the conclusion that, like no other creature on earth, man can transcend material things. In fact, he can transcend himself and thus reach out to touch the divine.

Man, then, cannot be analysed solely from an economic perspective, important as that may be. The laws of demand and supply are important. So, too, is the relationship between risk and return. But these realities do not capture the total reality of what it is to be human. Man is part of the material world and subject to laws of the human sciences, but not a slave to them. He in fact transcends them because he is made in the image and likeness of God and called to a destiny beyond this earthly life. The divine law imparts its authority, too. This is what the Church means by putting technological, productive, economic and financial advances at the service of man.

## The Pope from Galilee – John Paul II

In the year 1978 the Catholic Church experienced the end of the pontificate of Pope Paul VI, the rise and fall of the pontificate of Pope John Paul I (he lasted just thirty-three days) and the election of the first non-Italian Pope for over four hundred years. The new Pope was the first Polish Pope elected in the history of the Church and he would reign on the throne of Peter for almost twenty-seven years. The sorrow of losing Paul VI and John Paul I gave way to the joy of expectation. The new Pope was just 58 years of age. He was vigorous and healthy in appearance and exuded the confidence of a rock star. His charisma was simply extraordinary. Through his pastoral visits and writings he reminded the Church and the world that the Magisterium of the Church is not primarily juridical, but *prophetic*. This is particularly true of his social teaching and with regard to the entrepreneur.

He issued three social encyclicals. This brings to eight the number of social encyclicals since 1891. The first of John Paul's social encyclicals was issued in 1981 and was called *Laborem exercens* – 'On human labour'. It was the first encyclical devoted exclusively to the nature and meaning of *human work*. The second social encyclical was published in 1987 and was called *Sollicitudo rei socialis* – 'On social concerns'. The third of the Pope's social encyclicals is *Centesimus annus*, meaning 'The hundredth year'. This encyclical letter, published in 1991, was timed for the 100th anniversary of *Rerum novarum*.

*Laborem exercens* is significant for three things. First, the Pope establishes that work has an objective character. He means by this two things. On the one hand, in our work we take something, act upon it and produce something new or significantly altered from its original state. We are responsible for the new 'status' or 'nature' of the transformed matter. This is important for us as human beings. We naturally like to make a difference and you cannot do so if you do not work. Hence unemployment is not only a scourge for its obvious material deprivation, but also for the loss of dignity that people feel when their natural gifts are not put to good use.

Work has another objective meaning flowing from the biblical text. In the Book of Genesis, Adam is commanded to work. John Paul II sees human work as a 'mirror' of God's work. When human beings work they are reminding others of God's creating work. In a frenetic society, this second aspect of objective work is well worth reflecting upon. God wants to speak to us as we work and particularly as we observe others work. Work is not just an objective transformation of things, but it is an action that is in accord with God's creative action. For this reason, work is like a sacrament. People should be led to God when they see and experience others working. We don't often think like this, but John Paul II encourages us to do so.

Next, John Paul II articulated in *Laborem exercens* the subjective meaning of work. That is, when we work we are not just transforming matter, but we are – most importantly – transforming ourselves. We are called to perfection – to bring our humanity to its fulfilment – and work plays a large role in achieving this.

> Man has to subdue the earth and dominate it, because as the 'image of God' he is a person, that is to say a subjective being capable of acting in a planned and rational way, capable of deciding about himself, and with a tendency to self-realisation. *As a person, man is therefore the subject of work.* As a person he works. He performs various actions belonging to the work process. Independently of their objective content, these actions must all serve to realise his humanity, to fulfil the calling to be a person that is his by reason of his very humanity. (LE 6)

It is this subjective meaning of work which allows John Paul to develop what he calls the *personalist argument*. It argues for the priority of labour over capital. *Capita* originally referred to the heads of cattle, but had come to mean the natural resources of the earth and the means of production that would transform them. This argument was, we recall, part of the battle that Leo XIII had entered into some 80 years before. John Paul II puts a name to this deeply rooted gospel principle. Human beings – whether they be managers or workers (to use traditional terms that are not entirely necessary these days) – are far more important than capital.

This subjective meaning of work is, of course, intimately related to the objective meaning of work. All work begins in the human person, proceeds to transform matter in one form or another, and then produces a finished product or service with a view to aiding human persons. So work *begins* with us and it is *for* us. In addition, the way we do our work will influence whether we do really perfect ourselves – whether we honour the subjective meaning of work. Put bluntly, sloppy, slapdash work won't perfect us and neither will it get the job done! We will fail in our divine calling to perfect ourselves and we will fail in producing something for the good of humanity. The objective and subjective meanings of work, therefore, are intimately tied to each other.

The third significant contribution of the encyclical lies in the fact that it tries to articulate a spirituality of work. The Benedictines had done so years before – emphasising work, worship and reading as part of one's daily routine. So, too, had the founder of Opus Dei in the twentieth century. St Josemaria Escriva, a Spanish priest, taught that work has a triple dimension: we are called to sanctify our work, sanctify ourselves and thereby sanctify others in and through our work.

It was not uncommon, therefore, for various

groups and persons in the life and history of the Church to attempt to develop a spirituality of work and thus highlight its meaning. But the waters were uncharted for popes. John Paul II, in *Laborem exercens*, decided to broach the topic and in doing so elevated the lay vocation. Vatican II had taught that all the baptised are called to be saints, and John Paul II was suggesting that work forms an intricate part of the call to sanctity.

Unfortunately, however, much of what he had to say about a spirituality of work was lost in the English translation of the official Latin text. For in the Latin text the Pope contrasted work as *opus* with work as *labour*. As human beings we experience work as something necessary and fatiguing. God's work, however, is neither necessary nor tiring. Rather, his work is an *opus* – it is free, without any form of compulsion or exhaustion. It is a consequence of his inner life with the Son and the Spirit and it is a result of his love for humanity.

Human beings are called not only to offer their necessary and exhausting tasks to the Creator and Father of all. In this they can imitate Christ's work of redemption on the cross. Work has a redemptive meaning and Christians are called to discover it and teach it. But also, with the aid of divine grace, they are called to acknowledge and experience their work as an *opus*. We are called to see our work as a participation in God's totally free and gratuitous love. In this we imitate our God and so make him present throughout the world. We participate in God's creative work and thus begin to understand that work is and can be an expression of love.

*Centesimus annus* was the third of John Paul's

social encyclicals. It contains six chapters. The first recalls Leo's famous encyclical. The second and third deal with the current changes in society, especially the collapse of communism in 1989, while chapter four revisits the Church's position on private property and material goods. It is this chapter which raises the profile of entrepreneurial work. Chapter five presents an excellent summary of the relationship between the state and the Church and chapter six returns to a favourite theme of the pontificate and is headed 'Man is the Way of the Church'.

Besides chapter four, the following passage from chapter two, entitled 'Toward the "new things" of today', is of the utmost importance. It is critical, not just for a correct understanding of why the Church sees merit in entrepreneurial work, but also for insight into how Pope John Paul II has deepened the Church's social doctrine. From the passage it becomes clear why socialism must be rejected. Not only does it devalue the principle of private property, but it also denies the freedom of the human person. That is, the reason socialists scorn private property is because of their inadequate and reductionist understanding of the human person. Upon reading this most enlightening papal text, we recognise the Pope's own personalist philosophy; his experience of living under a socialistic and atheistic regime; and the wisdom of 100 years of Catholic social teaching.

> [T]he fundamental error of socialism is *anthropological in nature*. Socialism considers the individual person simply as an element, a molecule within the *social organism*, so that the good of

299

the individual is completely subordinated to the functioning of the socio-economic mechanism. Socialism likewise maintains that the good of the individual can be realized without reference to his *free choice*, to the unique and exclusive responsibility which he exercises in the face of good or evil. *Man is thus reduced* to a series of social relationships, and the concept of the person as the *autonomous subject of moral decision disappears*, the very subject whose decisions build the social order. From this *mistaken conception of the person* there arise both a distortion of law, which defines the sphere of the exercise of freedom, and an opposition to private property. A person who is deprived of something he can call 'his own,' and of the possibility of earning a living through his own initiative, comes to depend on the social machine and on those who control it. This makes it much *more difficult for him to recognize his dignity as a person*, and hinders progress towards the building up of an authentic human community. (CA 13)

Importantly, and this cannot be overstated, the essential error of socialism is a *defective* and *deceptive anthropology*. The error of socialism lies not only in its *overplay* of the state, but also in its *underplay* of the human person. This insight we owe to John Paul II and it is well worth treasuring and remembering as we begin the 21st century.

With this passage in mind, it becomes clear that John Paul II will affirm the entrepreneur and – to some degree – free markets and free societies, not just because they produce more wealth and thus alleviate material poverty. Rather, he affirms them because they come closer to recognising the profound truth of the human person made in the image and likeness of God. In this sense, it becomes clear to any serious student of the Pope's writings that John Paul is entirely consistent in his thought and philosophy. For, more than any other pope in history, he wants to recognise, proclaim and defend the dignity of the human person made in the image and likeness of God. This he has done in each of his fourteen encyclicals, but it is especially true in *Redemptor hominis, Veritatis splendor* and *Evangelium vitae*. He has done this also in *Centesimus annus*, as the above citation demonstrates admirably.

Let us now move to the fourth chapter of the encyclical and in doing so complete our argument. Unfortunately, many of the papal insights into the relationship between the factors of production cannot be commented upon here. We restrict ourselves to the following passage. Entrepreneurs will not be left in two minds. The Church deeply appreciates their work and efforts.

> A person who *produces something* other than for his own use generally does so in order that others may use it after they have paid a just price, mutually agreed upon through free bargaining. It is precisely the *ability to foresee* both the needs of others and the *combinations of productive factors* most adapted to satisfying those needs that constitutes another important *source of wealth* in modern society. Besides, many goods cannot be adequately produced through the work of an isolated individual; they require the cooperation of many people in working towards a common goal. *Organizing* such a productive effort, *planning* its

duration in time, making sure that it corresponds in a positive way to the demands which it must satisfy, and taking the necessary *risks* – all this too is a source of wealth in today's society. In this way, the role of disciplined and *creative human work* and, as an essential part of that work, initiative and *entrepreneurial* ability becomes increasingly evident and decisive. (CA 32)

## Conclusion

Catholic social thought has been in existence since the time of Christ. Indeed, since revelation began. But it is in the last 100 years or so, beginning with Pope Leo XIII, that the Church's social teaching has undergone a marvellous and breathtaking development. Both changes in society and insights from the popes have occasioned this development.

Wisdom would dictate that we be somewhat cautious in making an assessment of these recent developments. Thomas Stransky, in his preface to Pierre Blet's revealing work on Pius XII, cites Walter Raleigh and then Chou En-lai:

Any writer of modern history who treads too closely on the heels of events may get his or her teeth knocked out. And one ponders the calm reply of Chou En-lai when a European intellectual had asked the premier of China what he thought of the eighteenth-century French Revolution: 'It's too early to tell.' (Blet, 1999: xi)

We do not want to be hasty. None of us likes getting our teeth knocked out. But the weight of evidence in the last 100 years of Catholic social thought strongly suggests that entrepreneurs can take their place in the life of Church and of society without any fear whatsoever. Their task is a noble one – building their own humanity and constructing the common good.

The path travelled in these last few years of the Church's history is, to say the least, impressive. It begins with a robust defence of *private property* and a devastating critique of socialism by Leo XIII. Then Pius XI moves to defend and highlight the importance of *private action* in the social sphere. Pius XII, that much maligned pope, steps into the social ring as a heavyweight and has no qualms in naming the entrepreneur as crucial to social advancement. Vatican II praises the *spirit of enterprise*, while Pope John Paul II proves the true prophet by alerting us to the spiritual meaning and significance of work in general and entrepreneurial work in particular. We are well placed as we begin this new century.

## References

Blet, P. (1999), *Pius XII and the Second World War: According to the Archives of the Vatican*, (trans. Lawrence J. Johnson), New York: Paulist Press.

Charles, R. (1998), *Christian Social Witness and Teaching: The Catholic Tradition from Genesis to Centesimus Annus*, Leominster: Gracewing.

Flannery, A., OP (ed.) (1992), *Vatican Council II: The Conciliar and Post Conciliar Documents*, new revised (study) edn, New York: Costello Publishing Company.

Lonergan, B. (1972), *Method in Theology*, New York: Herder and Herder.

Miller, M. J. (ed.) (2001), *The Encyclicals of John Paul II*, Huntington: Our Sunday Visitor Publishing Division.

O'Brien, D. and T. Shannon (eds) (2000), *Catholic Social Thought: The Documentary Heritage*, Maryknoll, NY: Orbis Books.

Percy, A. (2004), 'Private initiative, entrepreneurship, and business in the teaching of Pius XII', *Journal of Markets and Morality*, 7(1): 7–25.

Pius XII (1951), 'Function of bankers', *Catholic Mind*, LII(1094): 121–2.

Pius XII (1956), 'The small business manager', *The Pope Speaks*, 3(1): 49–52.

Schaff, P. and H. Wace (eds) (1999), *Sulpitius Severus, Vincent of Lerins, John Cassian*, 14 vols, vol. 11: *Nicene and Post-Nicene Fathers*, second series, Peabody: Hendrickson Publishers.

Schaff, P. and H. Wace (eds) (1999), *Basil: Letters and Select Works*, 14 vols, vol. 8: *Nicene and Post-Nicene Fathers*, second series, Peabody: Hendrickson Publishers.

Stark, R. (1997), *The Rise of Christianity: How the Obscure, Marginal Jesus Movement Became the Dominant Religious Force in the Western World in a Few Centuries*, San Francisco, CA: HarperCollins.

# 10
# THE ENVIRONMENT, THE COMMON GOOD AND THE ECONOMIC WAY OF THINKING [1]

*Philip Booth*

## Solidarity and subsidiarity

There is much discussion in other chapters of this book about the terms 'solidarity' and 'subsidiarity'. Here, we will simply highlight particular aspects of that debate which are important for our discussion of the environment.

Christians, and especially Catholics, frequently use the phrases 'solidarity' and 'subsidiarity' to describe the extent to which a free-market economic policy should be balanced by government intervention. Sometimes these concepts, which are discussed widely in Catholic social teaching, are regarded as being in competition – as if the application of one should be balanced by the other in any thinking about public policy. But when these concepts are properly understood, it is only in extreme cases that their application can lead to the necessity to balance one against the other, thus

---

[1] Much of an earlier version of this chapter appeared in Spencer and Chaplin (eds) (2009): reprinted with permission.

trading off, say, a decrease in subsidiarity for an increase in solidarity.

One way of thinking about solidarity is to consider it to be the duty of the political authorities to pursue what is sometimes called a 'preferential option for the poor'[2] through government intervention, redistribution and so on. The argument would continue that such intervention should be limited because of the principle of subsidiarity which requires that government intervention should take place at the lowest level of government and, preferably, that autonomy should remain with voluntary groups and the family.

This way of thinking tends to lead to a moderate left or a moderate conservative view of politics. According to this view, the state should redistribute income and wealth but protect private property. It should also devolve responsibility to lower levels of government where possible, thus giving the family autonomy in fields such as healthcare, education and so on. This produces an outturn rather like some of the Christian Democratic states of the European Union. However, from the point of view of political economy, such an equilibrium is not stable. The reality of the fallen nature of man can lead to the accumulation of increasing responsibilities within an increasingly centralised state, unless we actively try to restrain it.[3]

In fact, we need to think of both the concepts of subsidiarity and solidarity in a richer context. If we do so, it leads to conclusions about the appropriate

---

[2]  This term has been used frequently in Catholic social teaching in the last 40 years (see below).

[3]  See the literature on public choice economics, such as Tullock et al. (2000).

role of government in economic life that are less obviously clear but more sustainable – it also helps us to better understand how we might make recommendations about environmental policy.

If one reads Church statements that use the word solidarity, it is clear that only one aspect of the concept relates to the pursuit of ends through the means of the political system – in other words government action to help the poor, the homeless and so on.[4]

So, what do we mean by 'solidarity' and from where does the phrase arise? Properly understood, solidarity is an attitude and virtue. It relates, firstly, to how we view our neighbours. It is an attitude that is then translated into good works through our actions as employers, within our families and extended families, through professional associations, community groups, schools, parishes and so on. Finally, in Catholic social teaching, there is action through the political sphere – where the state has a role, though not the primary role, of overseeing the exercise of human rights in the economic sector (*Centesimus annus*, 48). Action through the political sphere is coercive and thus circumscribes the freedom and creativity of those trying to address social problems. The idea of solidarity has been used throughout Catholic

---

[4] See, for example, the discussion of *Laborem exercens* by Lamoureux in Himes (ed.) (2005) and the encyclical *Sollicitudo rei socialis*. Indeed, it is important to note that even the phrase 'preferential option for the poor' was introduced specifically in the context of charity in *Octogesima adveniens* (Pope Paul VI, 1971) and that the discussion of the concept by Pope John Paul II, in for example *Sollicitudo rei socialis*, is wide ranging – including both action of a charitable and political character. Poverty also relates to our spiritual and moral inadequacies, not just to material poverty.

social teaching but John Paul II's encyclicals have a particular emphasis on the theme. The principle is rooted in the biblical values of awareness of the needs of others and of our common humanity as children of God, as well as in our obligations to those in need which are clearly stated in both the Old and New Testaments. As a virtue, solidarity is grounded in rational free choice and is about choosing the good of our neighbour wherever we encounter him. In this context, it can be seen how relatively unimportant the political dimension is intended to be. This is emphasised, for example, in Pope Benedict's 2009 Peace Day message when he said: 'it is timely to recall in particular the "preferential love for the poor" in the light of the primacy of charity, which is attested throughout Christian tradition, beginning with that of the early Church'.[5]

In turn, the application of the principle of subsidiarity does not generally involve a crude balancing act with solidarity. Amongst other things, it aids us in developing the philosophy by which we should judge *how* to implement public policy in the economic sphere. The principle of subsidiarity demands that government and coercive measures in the economic sphere are a *last* resort. As the *Catechism* (1994, para. 1885) puts it, 'The principle of subsidiarity is opposed to all forms of collectivism. It sets limits to state intervention.' The application of the principle demands that government *helps* or *assists* lower levels of community – and especially families – in

---

[5]   See: http://www.vatican.va/holy_father/benedict_xvi/messages/peace/documents/hf_ben-xvi_mes_20081208_xlii-world-day-peace_en.html

achieving their legitimate objectives.[6] In the words of the Rio Declaration on the Family: 'Subsidiarity means that the family, not the State, not large organizations, must be given responsibility in managing and developing its own economy'.

We have seen the principle of subsidiarity enshrined in the EU – especially in the Treaty of Maastricht. In EU governance, subsidiarity means that lower levels of government are responsible before higher levels of government for implementing EU policy. However, in its proper context, subsidiarity means that there should be intervention in economic life only where it is deemed necessary; it also means that voluntary associations have responsibility to meet economic ends before any level of government. But, crucially, subsidiarity is the process by which the state *helps* private and intermediate groups attain *their* legitimate ends, never supplanting their initiative, only facilitating it. This is very important and quite distinct from the interpretation of subsidiarity within the EU. A good example of the application of this principle would be in education where the Church has often proposed a role for the state in financing education, but always stated that this finance should be provided in such a way that parents' wishes are never supplanted and that private – including Church-provided – education is not discriminated against. Another example where the principle could be applied is in the field of environmental policy: the subject of this chapter.

The principle of subsidiarity, like the principle

---

[6] See, for example, *Centesimus annus* and *Quadragesimo anno* written by Pope John Paul II and Pope Pius XI respectively.

of solidarity, is not just plucked out of thin air. It has long been a key part of Catholic social teaching, if not always explicit. It arises from the idea that the individual has free will and is of infinite value to God. The individual is by nature social and the community is more than just the sum of the parts. However, political structures exist to aid the individual and the community – and in doing so promote the common good. The state should be subservient to individuals, families and communities – not the other way round. This is drawn from the Church's understanding of the nature of man, and his special place in creation, an understanding that is shared by all Christians.

Of course, debates between Christians on the appropriate scope of the market and the domain of the state in economic life are legitimate. There are occasions where we are asked to balance the principles of solidarity and subsidiarity (see Pontifical Council for Justice and Peace, 2005, para. 351, hereafter referred to as the *Compendium*). Application of the principle of solidarity sometimes implies action by the state, just as the application of the principle of subsidiarity calls for that action to be limited and designed in a particular way. But neither the Catholic Church nor scripture exhibit a bias in favour of the general use of socialised, political mechanisms to achieve objectives such as the protection of the environment that Christian communities and others hold dear.

In the words of the *Compendium*: 'Experience shows that the denial of subsidiarity, or its limitation in the name of an alleged democratization or equality of all members of society, limits and sometimes even destroys the spirit of freedom and initiative... state action in the economic sphere should also be withdrawn when the special circumstances that necessitate it end' (Compendium, paragraphs 187 and 188). There is, of course, legitimate debate to be had on what those special circumstances are and when they have ended and perhaps this is especially so in the area of environmental policy.

Such legitimate debate should focus on the promotion of human dignity and the 'common good' – the sum total of conditions necessary for human flourishing. It is not the purpose of the statutory authorities, through regulation, to deal with all moral failing. However, it can be argued (see Townsend in Spencer and Chaplin, 2009) that the state can respond to sins of omission where such sins of omission do undermine human dignity and the common good and state action may help rectify the problem. The state should also uphold private property rights and so on in order that the common good can be promoted. Thus, at least in principle, there is a Christian justification for certain laws that might come under the heading of 'environmental protection', though sometimes it may be better to rely on voluntary action or alternatives that extend the realm of private property rights. In all its actions, the state should bear in mind the principle of subsidiarity. The state should assist the community in achieving appropriate objectives in the field of environmental protection – the community should not be subservient to the state.

## Catholic Social Teaching and the environment

We will now move on to discuss how Catholic social teaching might guide us in developing public policy applied to environmental problems. There should be a natural affinity amongst Christians for economic frameworks that are effective in preserving the environment – after all, the environment is part of God's creation. Notions of 'stewardship' come easily to mind when Christians consider this subject, though this does not necessarily help us determine the legitimate role of public policy. As it happens, however, it does seem that the modern economic way of thinking about environmental problems is quite compatible with a Christian approach that applies the ideas of 'subsidiarity' and 'solidarity'. This framework though has implications for policy that are quite different from those implied in the statements of many Christian groups on environmental matters.

Whilst the subject of the environment has not had the same attention in Catholic social teaching as, say, the problems of poverty and under-development, clear statements have been made regarding the responsibility of all Christians towards the created environment. In *Octogesima adveniens,* an Apostolic Letter published in 1971, the exploitation of nature was raised as a problem. Also, a letter from the bishops, assembled at a synod in Rome, published in the same year,[7] suggested that it was not possible for all countries to have the same kind of development that had been pursued by the then rich nations. Himes in

---

[7] *Justitia in mundo*

312

Himes (ed.) (2005) suggests that the bishops, in that letter, were referring particularly to natural resource exploitation.

More particularly, there have also been statements in Catholic teaching about the environmental responsibilities of businesses and consumers. A business must 'contribute to the common good also by protecting the environment' (Compendium, 340 – a message emphasised in *Centesimus annus*). Businesses are told that they must see that their environmental impact is factored into their costs (Compendium, 470). Consumers are warned about creating lifestyles that involve pillaging the natural environment from future generations (Compendium, 360 and CA 37) and are called to temperance and restraint (Compendium, 486). As well as consumers and businesses having a responsibility, states are also asked to draw up juridical frameworks to ensure that the natural environment is protected (Compendium, 468).

Pope Benedict showed particular concern for environmental issues. He commented on environmental issues in *Caritas in veritate*, stressing the responsibility of all people: 'Today the subject of development is also closely related to the duties arising from *our relationship to the natural environment*. The environment is God's gift to everyone, and in our use of it we have a responsibility towards the poor, towards future generations and towards humanity as a whole' (CV 48). In that document it was pointed out that a reduction in environmental impact may come through technical progress or through restraints on consumption and it was also stated that environmental costs should be borne by those who incur them and not by others (CV 50). An important theme of the encyclical tied issues to do with economic development to the importance of adhering to Christian truth. In that spirit, the Pope emphasised the importance of ensuring that the human person was treated properly as it is as a result of respect for human nature that respect for the environment arises (CV 51).

Perhaps four themes come clearly out of Pope Benedict's teaching and that of Catholic social teaching more generally:

- Christians should have a deep concern for the environment.
- We should not be ideologically attached to the protection of the environment for its own sake.
- We should not despair about environmental degredation.
- We cannot divorce respect for the environment from other Christian obligations and truths – concern for the environment cannot be dissociated from a correct 'human ecology'. The environment, human development and moral truth cannot be separated – if we abuse the human person, we cannot be caring for creation and if we abuse other aspects of creation we are not paying due respect to the human person.

In the remainder of this chapter, the focus will be on the public policy issues related to the political economy of environmental protection. As such, this fourth point is not taken forward here – but its importance in Pope Benedict's thinking should not be neglected.

There are a variety of economic approaches to dealing with environmental problems and below an approach is discussed which is compatible with the general tradition of Catholic social teaching and with specific teaching on environmental issues.

## Solidarity and subsidiarity and the environment

As has been noted, Catholic Church teaching on the environment is carefully crafted and is not intended to lead people to accept a reductionist interpretation whereby all laws and regulations that restrict business activity and consumption to the apparent benefit of the environment are to be welcomed. In this field, as in others, statements of a specific policy nature in key teaching documents of the Catholic Church are generally sparse.

In the first place, in an expression of solidarity, we are called to conversion as consumers and producers – we should be careful and act with restraint and moderation in our consumption patterns. Indeed, Christians should act with restraint and moderation in all areas of their lives – a point which again illustrates the unity of our approach to the environment with our approach to living in general. Also, to promote the common good, the state should develop an appropriate juridical framework that ensures the appropriate protection of the environment, which may well involve calling businesses and consumers to account, *in one way or another,* for the impact of their actions on the environment. It does not follow that this should involve direct regulation to restrict business activities – Christians are free to disagree about such matters. It will be argued below that extending the realm of private property, so ensuring that those who consume environmental resources are held to account in their production and consumption decisions, is the most important approach. This does not, of course, rule out more specific intervention in some circumstances. However, the primary goal should be for public policy to provide the framework within which individuals, families and communities can deal with environmental problems in ways that are appropriate given their circumstances.

## Private property and environmental protection

Private property has long been regarded by the Church as the essential building block of a sustainable society.[8] It is interesting, therefore, that economists regard environmental problems as symptoms of poorly defined or incompletely defined property rights. For example, if the property rights to my house include a right to a view, then my neighbour is not able to build a block of flats that obstructs my view without first purchasing that right from me. On the other hand, if I have no property right to a view and the legal system prevents me from obtaining one, then it is much more difficult to resolve this environmental problem satisfactorily.

In practice, strong private property rights provide effective incentives to preserve the environment. An interesting real-life case study is

---

[8]   There was a particularly robust defence of private property in *Rerum novarum.*

given in Bate (2001). He shows how a voluntary group (the Anglers' Conservation Association – ACA), acting in solidarity and using the Courts, ensures that people do not pollute rivers that they do not own. The ACA were able to assert their property rights and prevent individuals, firms and often government bodies from polluting and destroying rivers.

Perhaps more pertinent, given the concern about environmental problems in the under-developed world, is an example from Nigeria. As is noted below, forest destruction in Africa is a serious problem. A detailed report in the *New York Times*[9] provides an extraordinary story of how trees in the Niger valley gradually came to be regarded as the property of local farmers. Instead of illegally logging for firewood, farmers had an incentive, once they became owners, to nurture the trees and sell their produce. In turn, the significantly increased forest density helped to keep the soil more fertile.[10]

The effective establishment and enforcement of private property is an essential aspect of the principle of subsidiarity. The existence of private property does not mean that there will not be abuses of the environment, but abuses can most effectively be resolved, whether by negotiation or by government action, once ownership of environmental resources is well defined. The institution of property rights and the application

---

[9] 11 February 2007: (http://www.nytimes.com/2007/02/11/world/africa/11niger.html?pagewanted=3&_r=1&ei=5087&em&en=d93708af7caaf675&ex=1171342800)

[10] A further example of property rights solutions to environmental problems is discussed in the context of fishing below.

of the principle of subsidiarity, which are basic features of market economies, also ensure that all resources are used more efficiently in economic processes, including environmental resources. Conservation is built into the system of incentives when resources are owned because their use has to be paid for. A well functioning market system, together with the price mechanism, promotes conservation of existing resources and the development of alternatives to finite resources in the face of scarcity of those existing resources.

In response, it might be argued that the institution of private property would allow people to destroy those parts of the natural environment which they owned, even if this had no direct effect on other persons, and that this is incompatible with the notion of persons being stewards of creation. However, it should be noted that there is no Christian imperative to simply *preserve* the environment in its current state. As is stated in the *Compendium* (299), 'God entrusted to man the task of exercising dominion over the earth, subduing it and cultivating it.' Moreover, the extension of private ownership would seem to provide strong incentives to cultivate and use environmental goods productively and sustainably because the value of land, rivers and other environmental resources at any given time will depend on their sustained productivity into the indefinite future. Indeed, countries where governments uphold property rights effectively have much better environmental protection than those that do not.

One interesting example in this respect is that of

forest destruction.[11] Forest burning simultaneously involves the production of greenhouse gases and the destruction of what is known as a carbon sink – as well as having local impacts on towns and villages close to forests. There is growing evidence that a general environment of economic development and strong property rights is effective in limiting deforestation. United Nations figures,[12] suggest that the global rate of net deforestation, has fallen from nine million hectares per year to seven million hectares per year, comparing the last decade of the twentieth century with the first few years of the twenty-first century (despite an increase in world population). More pertinently, nearly all the net loss is now confined to South America and Africa: the USA, Europe and Asia are now reforesting on balance. There is also a very strong correlation between economic growth and reforestation. No nation with an annual GDP per capita of more than $4,600 per annum had net forest loss in the period 2000–2005. Of course, there is also a strong correlation between effective property rights protection and national income. Thus it seems that strong property rights protection, national income growth and a nurturing of the local environment can go hand-in-hand.[13]

It should not be thought that any particular

---

[11] Of course, forest destruction is not intrinsically inappropriate. Throughout human history, forests have been developed and destroyed.

[12] See Hayward and Kaleita (2007).

[13] Many other indicators suggest a positive relationship between the quality of the environment and national income – most notably indicators of air quality. This is likely to be partly because the quality of the environment is a 'luxury good' of which people wish to consume more as they get richer, but also because, as noted, strong property rights go hand-in-hand with both effective environmental protection and economic development.

imposed solution to problems such as forest preservation and the use of environmental resources will be effective. It is also important to note that 'private ownership' is not synonymous with purely 'personal' or 'individual' ownership. There are very many forms of private collective claims on property (often described as several property). These can include properties owned by communities of monks or situations where individuals own buildings that are on land that is owned by a freeholder. The freeholder of the land then has an incentive to impose restrictions on the activities of individual owners of the buildings that benefit the environment enjoyed by the group of owners as a whole. Arguably, the concept of several property, and the freely negotiated restrictions on use to which it leads, has much to offer environmental preservation in both developed and developing countries (see, for example, Pennington, 2002 and Boudreaux and Aligica, 2007). It is important not to become trapped in a mentality that assumes that property or environmental resources must be owned either by the state or by individuals (or companies). It is quite compatible with the principle of subsidiarity for a voluntary or local community to own property or resources and determine their own rules and systems for the use of that property. Indeed, the work of recent Nobel Prize winner Elinor Ostrom[14] examines this particular issue and stresses the importance of the resource-owning community being able to adapt their own rules to changed circumstances.

[14] See, for example, Ostrom (2008).

In summary, there is a rich vein of modern economic thinking that examines environmental problems as property ownership and management problems. This economic thinking is developing solutions that are simultaneously compatible with the promotion of the common good and the principle of subsidiarity. The latter requires action at the lowest level – including voluntary action by individuals and communities themselves – and requires that the action by government assists the lower order communities. The state, therefore, undertakes its legitimate function when it helps enforce systems of property rights that allow individuals and families to pursue their objectives without costs being imposed upon them by the actions of others. More generally, economic advancement should not cause us to despair about environmental problems. The greatest abuse of the local environment frequently occurs in poor countries – especially where property rights are not protected.

## International environmental problems

More challenging, however, are environmental problems that cross national boundaries. Here, there are many situations where the effective definition and trading of private property rights has not arisen for one reason or another and these provide particularly good examples of environmental degradation or even catastrophe. One such example is fishing rights in European Union waters such as the North Sea. Nobody owns the North Sea and, though the community of fishermen as a whole has an incentive to maximise fish stocks in the long term, no individual trawler owner has an incentive to do other than to extract as many fish as possible. If we can imagine an entity that owned the North Sea and that was able to sell fishing rights, then that entity would wish to keep fish stocks high over the long term in order to raise the value of the asset. The owner would have an incentive to sell fishing rights in such a way that conservation was promoted. The owner would also have an incentive to ensure that any entity polluting the sea was prevented from doing so or was required to pay compensation. Private ownership should lead to conservation and a better husbandry of the marine environment.

We can, indeed, envisage private property rights in the sea, just as we have in land – or at least we can envisage mechanisms set up by government, such as are used in Alaska and Iceland, that mimic private ownership in fishing rights (see Gissurarson, 2000 and Morris, 2008). Such systems provide a good example of the application of the concepts of the common good, solidarity and subsidiarity. The common good and the principle of subsidiarity demand that higher communities should *help* lower order communities pursue *the latter's* legitimate ends where they cannot be pursued by individual or voluntary action. The legitimate end of the lower order communities in this case is sustainable fishing. It may not be feasible[15] for individuals to resolve this problem through individual action. So, ultimately, we may

---

[15] Due to transactions costs in the economic jargon.

look to institutions of government to help set up systems whereby fishing rights can be defined and traded. This is quite compatible with the responsibilities laid upon government in Catholic social teaching, as discussed above. Once such a system is set up, individuals and lower order communities themselves decide how to operate and earn their living within the framework set by the higher order community (the government, or supra-national body in the case of the EU) in accordance with the principle of subsidiarity. As Ostrom (2008) has pointed out, those who are intended to benefit from the system, should be allowed to develop and adapt the rules to changing conditions – this again shows subsidiarity in action.

The state or supranational authority should only step in to help when lower order communities are clearly incapable of achieving, for whatever legal, economic or institutional reason, their legitimate ends – sustainable fishing in this example. It is not, if we apply the principle of subsidiarity, for the higher order political community to define the desired ends and neither should the higher-order political community simply step in and regulate to achieve the ends of a particular elite or pressure group. But the government, if no other entity is capable, should ensure that the community can achieve their legitimate aims.

Fishing is, perhaps, an 'intermediate' example of an environmental problem – it is neither local nor global. Problems such as man-made global warming arising from the emission of greenhouse gases are global in nature.[16] Let us assume that greenhouse gas emissions are a problem and that the problem can be ameliorated by policy action. The creation of property rights in the atmosphere is obviously difficult. If we accept the scientific evidence, there are clear effects of $CO_2$ emissions on certain groups of people that arise from the behaviour of other groups of people – and there is no practical way of ensuring that only people who emit $CO_2$ suffer from global warming. In solidarity, people emitting large amounts of greenhouse gases should, in the first place, out of concern for the plight of fellow humans, be prudent in their behaviour and try to limit their impact. Such a voluntary approach, which may well extend beyond individual action to action by intermediate groups within society, may not be sufficient to deal with the problem however.

Thus, also in solidarity, we may, as Christians, propose that action is taken at the political level, perhaps on a supranational basis. This should be a last resort as far as Catholic social teaching is concerned. It should only happen due to sins of omission that undermine the common good – in this case, perhaps, undermine human flourishing by making areas of the earth uninhabitable. Christians can legitimately disagree on whether political action is appropriate – it is a matter for prudential judgement. Political action may make matters worse as a result of the practicalities of political action. Alternatively, action might

---

[16] I shall ignore the scientific and economic debates here. A minority does not accept the science. Others accept the science but do not believe we can reverse the process at a cost that is worth paying.

reduce the chances for human flourishing of vast numbers of people today who rely on electricity produced using carbon-intensive means. No Christian should speak as if government action here (or government inaction, for that matter) is a Christian imperative.

Furthermore, the motivation for the decision to take action at the governmental or inter-governmental level should always be driven by recognition that the lower order communities genuinely wish for some sort of action, for example to stabilise $CO_2$ emissions, but economic and institutional constraints prevent them from taking such action voluntarily. This may seem obvious but it is a thought process that policymakers should go through explicitly. They should not be influenced to too great an extent by campaign groups and those who have a vested interest in political action.

It would also seem appropriate that mechanisms to alleviate the problem are chosen that leave room for the greatest freedom of action at the individual level. Tradable quotas or carbon taxes would seem to be the obvious instruments, but this would lead us into a technical economic area that cannot be explored within the constraints of this chapter. However, the point is that different communities in different situations may wish to achieve a reduction in carbon emissions in different ways. Some may be able to develop and sell alternative methods of producing energy (such as wind or solar power); others may wish to explicitly cut energy consumption. Tradable quota systems and taxes allow individuals, families and other lower-level communities, in accordance with the principle of subsidiarity, to make these decisions in ways that direct regulation of economic activity does not.

## Slogans and muddled thinking

Thus the application of the principles of subsidiarity and solidarity can take us a long way towards understanding how Christians should approach environmental problems and provides us with a framework for considering the issues. Though the approach above is quite compatible with serious works on Catholic social teaching such as the *Compendium, Catechism* (1994) and Charles (1998), it is a long way from the sloganising of many campaign groups. Indeed, it sits uneasily with statements of the local Catholic Bishops' Conference in England and Wales.[17] To take an example of the former, the diocesan newspaper of Arundel and Brighton, in its lead article in February 2008, quoted, uncritically and without qualification, radical campaigner George Monbiot stating that the capitalist system could not protect the environment and 'it had to go'. Such a statement cannot be justified given the evidence, nor can it be justified in terms of Catholic social teaching. Indeed, the appalling environmental performance of communist countries and countries that do not have functioning market economies is now a matter of undisputed record.

---

[17] See the chapter by O'Brien – though it should be recognised that nearly all recent statements by Archbishop Nichols and the Bishops' Conference 2010 pre-election document were well considered and sober. In particular, they tended to stress individual responsibility whilst staying clear of the complex policy issues in which clergy have no specialised knowledge or authority.

Whilst some Christians may feel that a market economy does not provide all the answers to environmental problems, there is no justification for assuming that an economy without a functioning market system will do so. Most indicators of environmental quality have been improving dramatically in the last forty years in those developed countries that have systems of secure property rights and market economies.

It can be perfectly legitimate to examine the facts and theory and, through a process of reason, prudentially come to a view that an interventionist approach to environmental problems is necessary. However, to not go through that careful process can lead to slogans rather than deep analysis being at the heart of policy. All Christian groups have a duty to consider these issues carefully, but they should also understand the consequences of different approaches to policy because it is quite possible to develop policies in this field in such a way that the cure is worse than the disease.

Pope Benedict's World Peace Day message, 2008[7.], is important to bear in mind in this regard: '[it is] important for assessments...to be carried out prudently, in dialogue with experts and people of wisdom, uninhibited by ideological pressure to draw hasty conclusions.'[18] In general, the Christian message should be one of hope. We should avoid the atmosphere of despair that leads us to ignore environmental problems; we should not be facile optimists and idealists; and we should

---

[18] See: http://www.vatican.va/holy_father/benedict_xvi/messages/peace/documents/hf_ben-xvi_mes_20071208_xli-world-day-peace_en.html

not be pessimistic to the extent that we accept aggressive population control as promoted by many environmental groups as a valid mechanism of promoting protection of the environment. God has not only endowed the world with great natural resources but has also endowed human beings with great technical ability.

## Personal and business responsibility for the environment

So far, the discussion has focused entirely on the framework in which we might think about government policy which is the intended focus of the chapter. However, in concluding, it is important to consider the comments that Catholic social teaching has made about the environmental impact of consumers and producers. This is particularly so, as they take us back to our discussion of the proper meaning of solidarity.

We have argued above that environmental problems arise mainly where property rights are poorly defined and price mechanisms do not function properly. Any approach to policy – whether interventionist in nature or based on a comprehensive role for private property rights in protecting the environment – will produce outcomes that are far from perfect. Individuals, businesses and voluntary communities should, in solidarity, go further than their legal obligations in terms of their care for the environment. How far they go is a matter left for prudential, personal judgement. Some people might choose to adopt very simple lifestyles but they should not assume that they should require others to follow them in such a way of living.[19] In a similar way some Christians may wish, out of charity, to give away all the income they do not need for essential goods, but they should not set up political systems which involve taking away income of all other citizens, through punitive taxation, as this completely undermines the nature of the charitable act and the dignity of the person from whom money is taken.

A more difficult problem is that of how businesses should behave in areas of the world where the sorts of structures of law and property rights that we take for granted in the West do not exist and where there are possibilities of environmental destruction resulting from business activity. This takes us into the field of corporate social responsibility which is discussed at length in Booth in Gregg and Harper (eds) (2008). There is much muddled thinking about this subject. I will simply end with a comment that corporations should, in solidarity, not simply assume that, if they behave in accordance with the law in the countries in which they operate, they have discharged their moral responsibilities (whether towards the environment or otherwise) – particularly where property rights are not protected properly by the law. At the same time, it can be counter-productive, to impose upon corporations that

---

[19] Nor, indeed, should they need to accept that such a way of living necessarily benefits the environment: it has its own limits because of the inefficient way such styles of living use all economic resources – including environmental resources.

operate abroad business practices that are normal in the West. The principle of solidarity, properly understood in its non-political context, is highly relevant here. Corporations should have the right attitude towards those who are affected by their actions and owners should do their best, often in very difficult circumstances, to act with well-formed consciences.

## Concluding remarks

The concepts of 'subsidiarity' and 'solidarity' underpin much of Catholic social teaching, but their meaning is often misunderstood. The application of the principle of solidarity requires a change of heart, not a change of government. In all that we do as individuals, families, employers, or as leaders of voluntary organisations, we should show concern for the poor. Government action to help the poor may also be appropriate in some circumstances. However, the principle of subsidiarity, together with other principles that underpin Catholic social teaching, require that government intervention is limited, takes place at the lowest level of government and is designed in such a way that it assists lower order communities rather than displaces their initiative. We can apply these ideas to environmental problems just as we can to other policy areas. The analysis here shows how – as is often the case – an understanding of a free economy is quite compatible with Catholic social teaching.

# References

Bate, R. (2001), *Saving Our Streams: The Role of the Anglers' Conservation Association in Protecting English and Welsh Rivers*, Research Monograph 53, London, UK: Institute of Economic Affairs.

Booth, P. M. (2008), '*Modern business and its Moral and Ethical Dilemmas in a Globalized World*', in S. Gregg and I. Harper (eds), *Christian Theology and Market Economics*, Cheltenham, UK: Edward Elgar.

Boudreaux, K. and P. D. Aligica (2007), *Paths to Property: approaches to institutional change and international development*, Hobart Paper 126, London, UK: Institute of Economic Affairs.

Catechism (1994), *Catechism of the Catholic Church*, London, UK: Geoffrey Chapman.

Charles, R. (1998), *Christian Social Witness and Teaching: the Catholic tradition from Genesis to Centesimus Annus*, Leominster, UK: Gracewing.

Gissurarson, H. H. (2000), *Overfishing: the Icelandic Solution*, Studies on the Environment, No. 17, London, UK: Institute of Economic Affairs.

Hayward, S. F. and A. L. Kaleita (2007), *Index of Leading Environmental Indicators*, Twelfth edition, USA: Pacific Research Institute.

Himes, K. R. (2005), 'Commentary on *Justitia in mundo (Justice in the World)*', in K. R. Himes (ed.), *Modern Catholic Social Teaching: commentaries & interpretations*, Washington DC, USA: Georgetown University Press.

Lamoureux, P. (2005), 'Commentary on *Laborem exercens (On Human Work)*' in K. R. Himes (ed.), *Modern Catholic Social Teaching: commentaries*

& *interpretations*, Washington DC, USA: Georgetown University Press.

Morris, J. (2008), 'When it comes to the sustainability of marine resources, institutions matter', *Journal of Sustainable Development*, Spring 2008, 1,2.

Ostrom, E. (2008), 'Institutions and the environment', *Economic Affairs*, 28(3), 24-31.

Pennington, M. (2002), *Liberating the Land: the case for private land-use planning*, Hobart Paper 162, London, UK: Institute of Economic Affairs.

Pontifical Council for Justice and Peace (2005), *Compendium of the Social Doctrine of the Church*, London, UK: Burns & Oates.

Spencer, N. and J. Chaplin (eds) (2009), *God and Government*, London, UK: SPCK.

Townsend, N. (2009), 'Government and social infrastructure', in N. Spencer and J. Chaplin (eds), *God and Government*, London, UK: SPCK.

Tullock, G., A. Seldon, G. L. Brady (2000), *Government: Whose Obedient Servant? A Primer in Public Choice*, IEA Readings 51, London, UK: Institute of Economic Affairs.

# 11
# CORPORATE SOCIAL RESPONSIBILITY AND THE ROLE OF BUSINESS IN SOCIETY

*Michael Miller*

## Introduction[1]

In the decades since the collapse of communism and rise of the current phase of globalisation, the world has witnessed the development of increasingly commercial societies in Asia, Africa and Latin America, and seen millions of people lift themselves out of poverty. Business and entrepreneurship has played a significant role in this development. Yet the last decade has been marked by volatility, real estate and technology bubbles, ethical failures and massive financial crises that have created scepticism about the role of markets and questioned the contemporary understanding of business. As Pope Benedict XVI wrote:

---

[1] This essay is based on two talks: a paper I gave a conference sponsored by the John Ryan Institute and held at the Pontifical University St. Thomas (Angelicum) in Rome, 2006: The Good Company: Catholic Social Thought and Corporate Social Responsibility; and on a talk given to the Fellowship of Catholic Scholars in 2011. I am thankful for the questions and critiques I received at both of those conferences, as well as from my colleagues S.J. Gregg and C.L. Romens.

Today's international economic scene, marked by grave deviations and failures, requires a profoundly new way of understanding business enterprise. Old models are disappearing, but promising new ones are taking shape on the horizon. Without doubt, one of the greatest risks for businesses is that they are almost exclusively answerable to their investors, thereby limiting their social value. (*Caritas in veritate*, 40)

One of the dominant models of business ethics in the last several decades has been the corporate social responsibility movement (CSR). The CSR movement is rooted in a 'stakeholder' vision of business as opposed to a 'shareholder' view. CSR proponents argue that companies have responsibility beyond mere profit and have constituencies that extend further than the shareholders. The corporate social responsibility movement stresses what is often called the 'triple bottom line' that measures profit, people and the environment. CSR models do not reject the importance of profit but add to the 'bottom line' the impact a corporation has on the environment and a wide range of 'stakeholders' which not only includes shareholders, but also employees, consumers, the local community and anyone on whom the operations of the company has an impact. The CSR model calls on corporations to be attentive to real and potential negative externalities that arise from its business operations, such as environmental pollution, or negative impacts on the community in which it operates, and to take an active role in the community by promoting social welfare and supporting charities and a variety of causes.

The CSR approach draws attention to several important elements. Corporations do have a social responsibility beyond profit and have the responsibility to be attentive to negative externalities caused by their operations and should attempt to prevent or mitigate them and make restitution when necessary. Corporations should pay attention to the unintended consequences of their actions and should see themselves as an integral part of a larger society with ethical and social responsibilities to that society. There is, as Benedict XVI noted in *Caritas in veritate*, 'a growing conviction that business management cannot concern itself only with the interests of the proprietors, but must also assume responsibility for all the other stakeholders who contribute to the life of the business: the workers, the clients, the suppliers of various elements of production' (ibid). In light of the financial crisis that began in 2008, and the ethical failures of corporations in the early 2000s, this conviction has grown stronger, and there is an evident need for a renewed ethical dimension to business. As Pope Benedict noted in Lisbon on May 11, 2010: 'The events of the last two or three years have demonstrated that the ethical dimension must enter into economic activity. Now is the time to see that ethics is not something external, but internal to economic rationality and pragmatism.' While Catholic social teaching had not spoken directly about 'corporate social responsibility' until Benedict XVI used the term in *Caritas in veritate*, there has always been an implicit understanding that businesses have a social responsibility beyond mere profit. We can see this in modern Catholic social teaching from *Rerum novarum* to the present, and in the Church's long tradition of moral and social teaching seen in the ancient Fathers, and specifically in St Thomas Aquinas and throughout the Scholastic period.[2] While the corporate social responsibility movement is only several decades old, the idea of business as a 'community of persons' (*Centesimus annus*, para. 35) that is deeply rooted in society with rights and duties is a part of the Catholic tradition.

The CSR movement highlights important concerns and because of this, there has been some enthusiasm for the CSR movement among some Catholic circles who see it promoting a holistic vision of business that fits in well with Catholic social teaching. At first glance this is understandable, yet a closer look at the current CSR model shows that it has some serious problems that undermine robust business ethics, misunderstand the nature and purpose of business and its role in society, weaken respect for private property and often end up supporting causes that directly support activities that are morally evil. As Benedict XVI wrote:

> Today's international capital market offers great freedom of action. Yet there is also increasing awareness of the need for greater social responsibility on the part of business. Even if the ethical considerations that currently inform debate on the social responsibility of the corporate world are not all acceptable from the perspective of the

---

[2] St Thomas and especially the late Scholastics in Salamanca dealt in a detailed manner with all sorts of ethical questions with business, trade, exchange, price and so on. See, for example, Chaufen (2003), Grabill (2007).

Church's social doctrine... (*Caritas in veritate*, 40)

While the CSR movement does encourage awareness of the social implications of business, I will argue that the current approach is deeply flawed and does more harm than good.

## Critique of CSR

Perhaps the most well know critique of the CSR movement comes from the late Milton Friedman who wrote a scathing critique of CSR in the *New York Times Magazine* in 1970. Friedman's argument was summarised in the title of his essay 'The Social Responsibility of Business is to Increase its Profits'. In this essay and in his book *Capitalism and Freedom*, Friedman argued that in a free society:

> ...there is one and only one social responsibility of business – to use its resources and engage in activities designed to increase its profits so long as it stays within the rules of the game, which is to say, engages in open and free competition without deception or fraud. (Friedman, 'The Social Responsibility of a Business is to Increase its Profits', *New York Times Magazine*, 13 September, 1970)[3]

He argued that the corporation was not the property of the managers, but the property of the shareholders and therefore the managers do not have the right to use other people's property for a purpose other than that for which it was entrusted to them, even it if it is to attain so-called 'social goals'.[4]

---

[3] See also Friedman (1962).

[4] Friedman distinguished between public and private corporations and

Friedman makes some important points, but is incorrect to state that the 'one and only social responsibility' of business is to make a profit. It is clearly *one* of the social responsibilities of corporations: profit is an important indicator of whether the business is serving the needs of others and whether managers are exercising good stewardship over the resources that have been entrusted to them by the owners (shareholders) of the company. This is one of the primary duties and social responsibilities to the shareholders who have entrusted them to be stewards of their capital productively.

However, making a profit is not the *only* social responsibility. Friedman himself maintains that corporations have a responsibility to obey the law, to not defraud, etc. These are not mere instrumental activities that serve profitability. They are clear social and moral responsibilities of the corporation that, if disregarded, have a negative impact on the common good and undermine the moral fabric of a free society. The actions of businessmen and women are moral actions that have repercussion

---

makes an allowance for private companies to do what they wish with the money because it is their property. Friedman writes: 'The situation of the individual proprietor is somewhat different. If he acts to reduce the returns of his enterprise in order to exercise his 'social responsibility,' he is spending his own money, not someone else's. If he wishes to spend his money on such purposes, that is his right, and I cannot see that there is any objection to his doing so. In the process, he, too, may impose costs on employees and customers. However, because he is far less likely than a large corporation or union to have monopolistic power, any such side effects will tend to be minor' (Milton Friedman, 'The Social Responsibility of a Business is to Increase its Profits', *New York Times Magazine*, 13 September 1970). However, it is worth noting that even the owners of a shareholder business may have objectives other than the simple one of profit maximisation – but this should be a matter for owners to determine and not management.

on themselves and on the larger society. Business is not somehow morally different from other types of activities. Following the 'rules of the game' is a social responsibility of business. Secondly, because business operates within society, it has the responsibility to be attentive to any possible negative externalities that may arise – whether it be environmental pollution or something that significantly reduces the quality of life or harms the moral ecology of the area – and business should be ready to remedy the situation and/or make restitution. For example, if a corporation pollutes the local river by its use of pesticides and so directly causes illness, it has the responsibility to make restitution to those individuals or communities that are negatively affected. Indeed, it could be argued that such restitution is merely making up for the business facing what might be described as 'incomplete rules of the game': if the government does not properly protect people's property rights, businesses should not simply ignore those rights. Simply making a profit for shareholders does not fulfill the social responsibility of corporations. It is these types of negative externalities that motivate the CSR model of the 'triple bottom line' even if it has, as I will argue, been deeply compromised.

Further, while profit is important, this idea misses the underlying purpose of a business.[5] Catholic social teaching understands businesses as communities of persons that produce goods and services that meet human needs (i.e. benefit society)

---

[5] I discuss this in more detail in my chapter in Harper and Gregg (eds) (2008).

and meet the needs of the people working in them.
As John Paul II writes (CA35):

> The Church acknowledges the legitimate role of
> profit as an indication that a business is functioning
> well. When a firm makes a profit, this means that
> productive factors have been properly employed
> and corresponding human needs have been duly
> satisfied. But profitability is not the only indicator
> of a firm's condition. It is possible for the financial
> accounts to be in order, and yet for the people
> who make up the firm's most valuable asset to
> be humiliated and their dignity offended. Besides
> being morally inadmissible, this will eventually
> have negative repercussions on the firm's economic
> efficiency. In fact, the purpose of a business firm
> is not simply to make a profit, but is to be found
> in its very existence as a community of persons
> who in various ways are endeavoring to satisfy
> their basic needs, and who form a particular group
> at the service of the whole of society. Profit is a
> regulator of the life of a business, but it is not the
> only one; other human and moral factors must
> also be considered which, in the long term, are at
> least equally important for the life of a business.

## CSR and the problem of private property

While Friedman's understanding of the social
responsibility of corporations has limitations,
he makes the important point that corporate
philanthropy amounts to managers using someone
else's private property to achieve social goals that
are distinct from the ends and purpose of the
business. A public company does not belong to
the managers, but to the shareholders. Friedman

argues that 'a corporate executive is an employee of the owners of the business. He has direct responsibility to his employers...in his capacity as a corporate executive, the manager is the agent of the individuals who own the corporation or establish the eleemosynary institution, and his primary responsibility is to them.'[6]

When a corporate executive uses company funds that belong to shareholders in order to support a particular cause it raises a serious question about the fiduciary responsibility of the managers not just to the shareholders but to other stakeholders. As Friedman notes, when a corporation engages in philanthropy: '...the corporate executive would be spending someone else's money for a general social interest. Insofar as his actions in accord with his "social responsibility" reduce returns to stockholders, he is spending their money. Insofar as his actions raise the price to customers, he is spending the customers' money. Insofar as his actions lower the wages of some employees, he is spending their money' (ibid.).

One of the replies to the objection that CSR is a violation of private property is that shareholders are aware that companies have CSR policies and therefore give implicit approval to corporate philanthropy when they purchase stock. As noted above, shareholders may not simply try to maximise profit, but this observation does not seem to address the problem on a number of levels. Firstly, just because people are aware of something does not make the action morally

---

6 Milton Friedman, 'The Social Responsibility of a Business is to Increase its Profits', *New York Times Magazine*, 13 September 1970.

acceptable. Secondly, CSR has crept in as a social norm over time and many individual shareholders and pension fund holders know very little about it, and some bought stock before it was widely accepted. Further, individuals or even funds of shareholders have very limited means to alter a system dominated by very strong interest groups and activists. I will discuss the interest group problem below. One could argue that the only real form of protest against CSR is through a choice not to buy stock of a certain company, and it is certainly practical for shareholders to exercise that option. A possible alternative solution could be a type of 'opt-out' clause where shareholders could choose to participate or not to participate in corporate philanthropy and the 'losses' or 'expenses' of CSR would fall only on those shareholders who 'opt-in' – yet sorting out the value or losses from CSR would be impossible. This is especially so, as customers might value certain actions taken by the company under the guise of CSR and so those actions may raise sales and profits. In this case, it should be noted, CSR does not achieve anything different from a policy of profit maximisation.

Another problem related to the property rights issue and corporate executives engaging in corporate philanthropy is the problem of subsidiarity. The responsibility of charity lies first with individuals and families, not corporations. It is sub-optimal at best to outsource charity to corporate executives who are neither close to the problem, nor who have any apparent competency for doing charity. When corporations give out philanthropy the effect is that the owners' profit is reduced. This in turn reduces their capacity to engage in charitable work and increases the likelihood that charity will be captured by powerful interest and pressure groups.

The private property argument is one of Friedman's strongest critiques of the CSR model – at least with regard to the corporate philanthropy element – and should be taken seriously by those concerned with business ethics and the social role of business, especially those who work within the traditions of Catholic social doctrine. Modern Catholic social teaching beginning with *Rerum novarum* takes the issue of private property very seriously. Leo XIII gives a long defence of property in *Rerum novarum*[7] that is echoed by other modern popes. Furthermore, private property is presupposed in the Decalogue, clearly understood in the Old and New Testaments, and strongly defended by St Thomas Aquinas.[8] The idea of charity itself presupposes that we are giving something that belongs to us. We cannot be properly 'charitable' with someone else's property.

## Four additional critiques of corporate social responsibility

In addition to the private property critique of CSR I will discuss four other overarching weaknesses of the way CSR is commonly understood and practised.

---

[7]  Leo XIII, *Rerum novarum*, para. 6 et seq.
[8]  St Thomas Aquinas, *Summa Theologica*, Secunda secundae, Article 2.

## Relativism

The first, and fundamental weakness of the current CSR approach, and one that is at the root of most of its other weaknesses is a lack of any coherent ethical vision based on a robust concept of truth and the existence of clear moral absolutes. The problem of relativism is a problem that plagues much of modern ethics and it is no surprise that it finds its way into applied ethics in the field of business. We see the same problems in politics, education, and medical ethics. One of the dominant methods of teaching ethics in business schools is to set before the student a variety of ethical approaches and encourage them to choose one. Ethical relativism is so widely accepted and ostensibly inescapable that the only option is for individuals to choose paths that 'follow their own integrity' or to come to some agreement how corporations should be 'good corporate citizens'. The CSR movement is a product of genuine concern about the role of business in society mixed with relativism that generally avoids controversial issues that deal with moral law. It therefore ends up reducing ethics to whatever is socially or politically fashionable. Since people disagree about morality and a vision of the good life, CSR turns its attention to those things that are currently socially in fashion. Thus we see quite a bit of CSR focused on environmentalism, support for popular charities, and the promotion of diversity. The idea of the 'triple bottom line' has much to commend, but unless it is rooted in a clear ethic of right and wrong and one that accepts the existence of moral absolutes, the 'bottom lines' will be dominated by current fashions and fads rather than by what is actually the right or most prudent course. This is precisely what happens in much of the CSR movement.

This underlying relativism plays out in several ways. Firstly, it is a distraction from serious reflection about ethics. While there are some unique problems that are specific to business ethics, in general most of the issues in business ethics revolve around perennial ethical issues such as lying, stealing, cheating, fraud, greed, avarice, lust for money, sexual misconduct and so on. As John Maxwell's book title aptly states, *There is No Such Thing As "Business" Ethics*. The dominant CSR approaches provide very little in the way of a foundation to address moral issues because there is no coherent vision of truth or the good. Any business ethics worth its salt must engage key moral issues and should provide a template to resolve – or at least engage – them whether it be a religious authority (e.g., this company abides by the moral standards set out in the Bible or the Koran); a natural law approach; or other philosophical alternatives such as the Kantian categorical imperative. The CSR model's underlying relativism provides no means to discuss moral issues beyond fashion, the assertion of emotion or personal predilection.

As noted above, a lack of a coherent and robust understanding of truth often results in CSR models substituting ethics with fashionable social policy. We can see the evidence of this through the types of programmes, charities and movements that receive support from many of the companies that practise CSR. While the impression of CSR is that monies are going to needy organisations or to support clean environments, even a cursory look at corporate philanthropy reveals the tendency for philanthropy to be directed toward those causes which generate the most publicity or that can exert pressure on a corporation.[9] A less insidious explanation may be that the people who fill CSR roles at corporations tend to come from backgrounds and world views that support these policies though this is only speculation.

Attention to the external impact of a corporation is a positive development. Yet even more important for business ethics is attentiveness to the ethical behaviour within the company and the individual and personal moral responsibility of executives and employees. Fashionable social policy is not business ethics. Thus we have seen how CSR regimes often have been ineffective in dealing with ethical problems. Enron is a perfect case in point. The energy company was well known for a very active CSR programme but was unable to deal with a culture of lying, fraud, sexual promiscuity and cheating that brought down the company and financially destroyed thousands of employees and shareholders as well. When ethics is reduced to philanthropy, it creates an easy path to moral breakdown because one can equate morality with charitable giving and supporting the right causes rather than with following ethical norms of right and wrong. Supporting a clean environment is good but it is not a substitute for personal moral responsibility, which requires a commitment to truth and clear standards of right and wrong.

---

[9] See below where I list some of the types of organisations that receive corporate philanthropy.

## Corporate social responsibility misunderstands the social nature of business

The second major flaw of the CSR movement is that it misunderstands the social nature of business and fails to sufficiently appreciate the positive contributions that business makes to the common good.[10] This misunderstanding manifests itself in a number of ways.

One of the common themes around discussions of corporate social responsibility is that of businesses 'giving something back' to the community. As noted earlier, firms do indeed have a social responsibility and duties to the communities in which they operate. However, the idea that firms need to somehow 'give something back' reveals an attitude that presupposes that firms have somehow taken something away from the community in the first place – that their success was somehow built on the backs of the community and that they now 'owe' the community something because they were able to succeed as a business.

While it may be true that a company is able to be successful because it enjoys an attractive business climate, secure property rights, a just and efficient legal system, an educated workforce, etc., the firm fulfills its duty (i.e. gives back to the community) by being a successful company. Indeed, in such an environment a business, in the course of business activity, will be giving something to the community. It tends to be in environments where property rights are poorly protected and legal systems are corrupt that businesses are able to benefit at the

---

[10]  Again, see Harper and Gregg (eds) (2008).

expense of the community. In making profits – which provide incomes for owners – through producing valuable goods and services, the business is doing something for the community by being a business. There are subsidiary benefits too such as the creation of jobs, the payment of just salaries to those bringing up families and the development of roots in a community that allow corporations to contribute to the economic and social well-being of the community in a significant way.[11] The business has already given much to the community by being a business.

It is important to note that, while the contributions of business go beyond mere economic contributions, it is within the economic sphere where businesses have the most competence and a proper role. There are other organisations that contribute to society in other ways, and there is no reason for business to undertake those roles too. Business plays an important, though specific, role in society and its main contribution to society is, and should be, in the economic sphere and this is where the bulk of its social responsibility is found. An analogy to churches may be helpful. While churches do indeed benefit the economy by encouraging ethical behaviour, strong families and responsible individuals, all of which have economic benefit and create a culture of trust and lower transaction costs, this is not the primary role of a church.[12,13] The primary role of a church is

---

[11]  Ibid.

[12]  See Fukuyama (1995).

[13]  Part of the problem may be increasing centralisation that can leave a vacuum in the social area which we may try to fill by having business take

spiritual, not economic. A church need not confer economic benefit on society in order to justify its existence any more than a business need confer spiritual benefit. One of the underlying problems of the CSR movement is the confusion over the different roles and responsibilities that different individuals and organisations have in society. This is often made manifest in the language of business as a family. A business is many things, it does many good things, and it can provide the context for friendship, belonging, and support, but it is not a family. An essential misunderstanding within the CSR approach is that it can tend to see business as having to play a multitude of roles that are outside its competence. Just as in a family the mother, father, children, and grandparents each have different roles it is also the case that business, churches, mutual aid societies, schools, the government, charities and so on have different roles and areas of competence within a society. Generally, this is reflective of a general lack of appreciation for the principle of subsidiarity which would help inform a more organic demarcation of the roles and responsibilities of different groups within society.

The idea of giving back also ignores the many positive externalities that business brings to a local area, building and enriching communities beyond the economic sphere. Most notable is

on more responsibility. This is beyond the scope of this essay but a better approach may be to create public policy that encourages a wide variety of private organisations that handle different problems and issues within the society. Some of this is already happening with the rise of the number of non-profit organisations dedicated to a variety of community activities and causes.

the social cohesion and stability that occurs when employment levels are high and relatively secure. Many cities compete to attract a variety of businesses and industries precisely for these economic and social benefits – to keep employment high, give opportunities for families to stay nearby and not have to move to find work, and to increase tax revenues for public services and cultural development. The importance of business to the community becomes evident when we see the often disastrous impact on communities when businesses relocate. For example, think of formerly thriving manufacturing cities such as Detroit, Michigan, which has seen its population decrease dramatically in the last decades. Using the same 'give back' rubric, one could argue that communities should 'give back' to businesses. Does the community owe more to the business than secure private property rights, good public services, and a fair legal system? Should people in the local community who benefit most from the business decision to operate in their area pay additional fees beyond the market price because they receive additional benefits? This does not even include the charitable and philanthropic work of business owners who often give money and time to charities and cultural endeavours. In the city where I live, for example, there is a world-class ballet company, museums, botanical gardens, music facilities, public and private university facilities, non-profits, and world-class hospital and research facilities. This is not because of government money and it is not primarily because of CSR. Many of these endeavours are supported by private donations from local successful business owners and their families who have a personal commitment to the community and want to make it a better place in which to live. Because I live in a specific town, should I pay more for the goods and services that these companies produce since I reap additional benefit beyond the goods or services themselves? Does a community have the responsibility to 'give back' to the business? Of course the answer is 'no'. But the point is that there is a natural symbiotic relationship that exists between different members and organisations within a community that all benefit one another by operating within their spheres of competence and their proper roles.

Related to this idea of giving back to the community is the idea that a corporation has a debt or somehow 'owes' something to the community because it received a licence or permit to practise business in a particular area. But this confuses a licence or the registration of a business with the *legitimacy* to engage in business. Business may need a licence or permit to operate in a certain area and will most likely need to register the business for tax, legal, or regulation purposes. Though this can be overly burdensome, the ability to register a business is generally positive for economic development.[14] Yet this registration or licence is not the same as legitimacy. The legitimacy to start and operate a business derives from the

---

[14] The ability to register a business is an important facet for development. In many developing economies small business owners find it especially difficult and highly expensive to register a business and therefore are often relegated to the informal sector of the economy. See for example De Soto (2000).

natural right of free association which follows from the social nature of the person. The natural right of free association was developed in *Contra impugnates* where St Thomas Aquinas defended the rights of the mendicant orders to teach and operate universities. Aquinas' argument became one of the foundations for Leo XIII's defence of the right of unions in *Rerum novarum*.[15] Persons have the right to join together to take care of themselves and to engage in something for which they are competent and which benefits the common good. Thus, there is not an absolute right of free association: people do not have the right to form a gang that intends to create mayhem because it destroys the common good. Nor does the right of free association mean that people have the right to join together for the purpose of moral evil. The state may also take certain action to limit freedom of association if the members are working outside their sphere of competence. For example, all members of the public do not have the right to set up a hospital. Whether and how such freedom should be limited is a prudential matter to which Catholic social teaching does not have a definitive answer.

Like trade unions or other voluntary organisations, the legitimacy of a business does not come from the state but from the right of free association. There are countries with a Catholic tradition that have experienced eras where business had to have a licence to operate and such licences were often restricted so that effective statutory monopolies were given. One can understand why

---

[15] Leo XIII, *Rerum novarum* para. 49 et seq. I am thankful to Russell Hittinger for this insight.

the concept of 'giving something back' could arise in such situations. However, such statutory restrictions are not, in themselves, desirable.

There is indeed a duty that comes with this right of free association. Much of this has been mentioned earlier, but business has the duty to obey the moral law, obey the law of the land, treat employees justly, not destroy the environment and produce goods and services for which people are willing to pay. A business does not have the right to exist no matter what. Hence, if no one is willing to pay for the goods or services a company may go out of business. As long as the business fulfills its duties noted above, it retains its legitimacy from the natural right of free association and not from the state or local municipality.

## CSR introduces transaction costs and corrupts the moral ecology of business

The third major problem with the current CSR model is that its focus on charity and 'giving back' can end up becoming a transaction cost and, in its worst case, a type of legal protection racket where companies give out charitable donations (i.e. pay-offs) to various types of interest groups in exchange for positive public relations and/or not being bothered at shareholder meetings.[16]

There is an understandable public relations dimension to certain donations that support local charities or public sporting events. This can demonstrate a firm's commitment to the

---

[16] Theodore Malloch discusses this in his book Spiritual Enterprise, *Doing Virtuous Business*, (Malloch, 2008). Elaine Sternberg also discusses the idea of the protection racket in Sternberg (2009).

community in which it operates and can have a net positive effect on profitability. However, we should label these activities 'public relations' rather than 'social responsibility'. In addition to these types of company donations, there are often much more insidious types of donations – both from a general viewpoint and especially from the viewpoint of Catholic moral and social teaching.

Some of the fruits of the CSR movement have already been mentioned. An examination of corporate philanthropy reveals that many of the recipients are politically correct causes or powerful interest groups such as Greenpeace, the Sierra Club, UNICEF, and a number of gay and lesbian organisations. From a Catholic moral and natural law perspective, much worse than the political correctness is that some of the recipients actually fund and promote intrinsic moral evils. Planned Parenthood, for example, has received corporate donations from a number of large, well-known corporations. Additionally, while some of the organisations who receive corporate philanthropy are needy schools or charities, this is not always the case. One could reasonably doubt the level of need of organisations such as the National Wildlife Turkey Foundation and the New York City Gay Men's Hockey League, both of which were reported to have received corporate donations from Tyco and Time Warner respectively. The fruits of CSR giving in practice are less than promising.

In addition to the morally problematic issues addressed above, we also can see 'charitable' donations going to a host of different types of

354

interest groups. CSR donations can become a type of 'protection racket' whereby corporations feel that they need to give 'donations' to a wide variety of interest groups to avoid public relations attacks or shareholder activism. Thus, we see corporations paying off all sorts of interest groups – often those that are socially fashionable or adopting and promoting their programmes. Support for CSR causes can become a cost of doing business in developed economies much like a bribe to a local government official is a 'normal' cost of business in much of the developing world. Certain elements of the CSR movement end up being a highly sophisticated and institutionalised type of 'protection racket' to pay off interest groups to leave them alone. These types of payments undermine the moral foundations of a free economy and do not promote a socially responsible way of doing business or using company profits. Such activities often tend to reward the very people who fail to recognise the positive contributions of business to the common good and incentivise the type of shareholder activism that is used as a type of thuggery to intimidate corporations. It should be noted that any group has the right to campaign about issues that concern them. Similarly, companies have the right to use funds to support such groups, as long as management is transparent in accounting to shareholders. However, we should not pretend that such support is exercising a form of 'social responsibility'. Once again, such support is a sophisticated form of public relations – though often focused on rather narrow interest groups.

### A new model of corporate social responsibility

The final flaw or weakness of the current CSR movement relates to how the current model of CSR detracts from the actual social responsibilities of business to contribute to and help sustain a free economy and a virtuous citizenry. Some critics of CSR have tended to 'throw the baby out with the bathwater' and reject CSR in general. But, as we have discussed, there are clear social responsibilities of businesses; the problem is they are rarely if ever discussed within the current CSR framework. I can only give a sketch of these in this chapter. Some of the key social responsibilities of business are discussed below.

Businesses should help to maintain a free, competitive, and just market economy that enables innovation and allows new entrepreneurs to compete fairly. Big businesses must resist the temptation to look to governments for protection or try to influence regulation in their favour through lobbying. A great deal of the financial crisis of 2008, as well as the anger that it generated, was the result of crony and managerial capitalism where big businesses and government colluded often at the expense of others. One of the social responsibilities of business is to resist the temptation to 'partner' with governments. This may mean short term losses – and even being overtaken by competitors – but it has widespread and long-term benefits for consumers and society. Businesses clearly have the capacity and competency to do this, and this type of action falls more precisely within their role as a business than trying to support social causes.

Businesses should promote a healthy moral

ecology by eschewing crass, vulgar, or sexually objectifying advertising. The type of free enterprise system that John Paul II speaks about in *Centesimus annus*[17] requires a moral culture to support it. As noted above, families, churches, and schools have a primary role in creating the moral culture but business has a role to play as well. This is especially strong in the area of advertising. Business should avoid advertising strategies that undermine parental authority, objectify women, or appeal to base desires merely to sell a product. While the motto 'sex sells' may be true, it also weakens the moral foundations of a society, encourages promiscuity, and can break down marriages – all of which have serious social, moral, and economic costs. Companies would do much more for society and for children by monitoring their advertising than by giving money to schools. Omni Hotels is an example of this proper type of social responsibility. Omni made the decision to not offer pornography in their hotels because of the negative effects it has on women, men, marriage and children.[18] They did this realising that they would lose money but thought the social benefits would far outweigh the loss. This is an example of real social responsibility, a private business, in an area where it has competence and influence, making a decision to choose a moral good over profit. This can be contrasted with other hotel companies that

---

[17]  See *Centesimus annus*, para. 42.
[18]  See Robert P. George's excellent essay on the negative impact of pornography (George, 2002). For the story of Omni Hotels see: http://www.zondervan.com/Cultures/en-US/Product/ProductDetail.htm?ProdID=com.zondervan.9780310894872&QueryStringSite=Zondervan

sell pornography but fulfil their CSR by supporting fashionable causes. In the end, as it happens, Omni did not lose money as a result of their decision. It is important to notice that their decision to avoid pornography was rooted in a non-relativist ethics that sees pornography as something that is morally disordered, not merely something that is a choice. There are many other examples of where corporations can promote the common good in a way that fits within their business strategy, remains within their competence and respects the moral law.

## Conclusions

In a global economy, business will continue to play an important role in society and, as Pope Benedict XVI notes, we need to rethink the ethical understanding and place of business within society. The CSR model in its current relativist form does not achieve this end and it distracts from serious discussions about business ethics. While recognising the importance of profit, the tradition of Catholic social teaching is quite clear that businesses do indeed have a social responsibility beyond profit. The current model of CSR has raised awareness and encouraged serious reflection about the social responsibilities of business. Nevertheless, as it is understood and practised by many, the CSR model fails to understand the nature of business and society. It misses the actual and potential contributions of business to the common good. At best, it becomes a distraction for serious reflection on ethics in business. Even worse, CSR actually undermines true business ethics; is largely ineffective; substitutes fashionable social policy for real ethical reflection; creates a 'protection racket' culture; increases transaction costs; breaks down a healthy and moral business culture; and funds morally evil social causes that do real harm to all aspects of society. Furthermore, and quite ironically, because CSR is captured by current social fads that tend to be suspicious of business and markets, businesses are distracted from the real possibility to assume their authentic social responsibilities and contribute to the common good where they are most competent. Any serious discussion of corporate social responsibility must begin with the existence of definite truth and recognition of the existence of moral good and evil.

## References

Chaufen, A. (2003), *Faith and Liberty: The Economic Thought of the Late Scholastics*, Lanham, MD: Lexington.

Grabill, S. (ed.) (2007), *Sourcebook in Late-Scholastic Monetary Theory*, Landham, MD: Lexington.

Friedman, M. (1962), *Capitalism and Freedom*, Chicago: University of Chicago Press.

Harper, I. R. and S. Gregg (eds) (2008), *Christian Theology and Market Economics*, Cheltenham: Edward Elgar Publishing.

Fukuyama, F. (1995), *Trust*, New York: Free Press.

De Soto, H. (2000), *The Mystery of Capital: Why capitalism triumphs in the West and fails everywhere else*, London: Black Swan.

George, R. P. (2002), *The Clash of Orthodoxies:*

*Law, Religions, and Morality in Crisis,* Delaware:Intercollegiate Studies Institute.

Malloch, T. (2008), *Spiritual Enterprise, Doing Virtuous Business,* Tennessee:Encounter Books.

Sternberg, E. (2009), 'Corporate social responsibility and corporate governance', *Economic Affairs,* 29(4), 5–10.

# 12
# EDUCATION AND THE CATHOLIC CHURCH IN ENGLAND AND WALES

*Dennis O'Keeffe*

## Introduction

The Catholic Church's great intellectual gift to mankind has been the individualism implicit in the doctrine of the unique, immortal soul of each person.

Of all history's institutions the Catholic Church embodies the greatest intellectual and cultural achievement. The Church has been itself a vastly accomplished teaching agency, as befits a body in receipt of Christ's instruction that Catholics should teach all nations. One essential strand in this pedagogic success has been the Catholic tradition of the individual soul. Xavier Martin has argued that traditional Catholic approaches to education are far more individualist than the philosophy of the French Enlightenment, which in the main espoused a view of man as manipulable.[1] He quotes Jacques Maritain on the Thomist

---

[1] Martin surveys all the main voices of the French Enlightenment and finds in them an anthropology according to which the human animal needs direction by experts, employing a programme external to the person being taught. See Martin (2001).

educational doctrine that 'in any discipline and in any form of teaching the master merely offers external assistance to the principle of immanent activity which is present in the pupil' (quoted in ibid.: 78). Such 'external assistance' will include a knowledge of subject matter and of the rules and conventions of scholarship superior to those possessed by the pupil. It is this knowledge which creates the teacher's authority. The pupil is the active focus, however, in whom crucial powers of learning and human creativity are located.

Even sceptics have often agreed subsequently that the unique individualism of the West, without which the Renaissance, the Enlightenment and the extraordinary economic development of recent centuries would all have been impossible, is a bequest to the world of the Christian doctrine of the individual human soul (Minogue, 2003).

Presenting Catholic influence on civilisation in this way is in marked contrast to the better-known modern tendency to dichotomise Catholic experience, between pre-Vatican II and post-Vatican II notions. The traditionalists claim that modern Catholic education is an empty set, leaving the Catholic population disastrously ignorant of their religion. The modernists claim that traditional Catholic schooling involved little more than unenlightened rote learning and stifling bigotry. The traditional versus modernist claims are well presented in Gerald Grace's book on modern Catholic education (Grace, 2005: chs 2, 3). Professor Grace does not, however, deal with the incomparably more important question of the role of Catholicism in the protection of civilisation.

This chapter examines the most crucial features of present Catholic teaching on education alongside the practice of teaching in Catholic schools. How well do Catholic educational attitudes and practice secure our vital civilisation and heritage?

We cannot pursue at length the question of how far there is a global Catholic view of education or how far Catholic educational practice differs between countries. There is no comprehensively binding educational consensus among Catholics in individual countries, let alone worldwide agreement. The only manageable focus of this essay is Catholic education in its British context, though it must necessarily pay some attention to opinions from Rome and elsewhere. It seems entirely proper to look at the variations in British Catholic opinion on education. We need also to examine how well our Catholic schools in general seem to transmit the Catholic faith. In practice, education in England and Wales must serve as an approximate guide for a general British account. As we shall see, England and Wales have learned useful lessons from Scottish experience. While the ideal would be to examine Catholic education at all levels, I will speak mostly about the bedrock primary and secondary levels. The Catholic Church in this country does not have a very large presence at the tertiary level.

The practical situation in England and Wales appears generally a good one. There is now a very strong and successful Catholic middle class in this country. Many well-known figures are Catholics, and the ancient prejudices seem mostly buried. Catholic schools have enjoyed a large growth in numbers (Burn, 2001: 37). Moreover, from north of the border we have the admirable example set by the late Cardinal Winning, ensuring that the shortcomings of Catholic teaching in Scotland were brought to public attention, and reform set in motion for his Glasgow diocese.

Winning spoke of 'post-conciliar confusion' and pointed to the virtual collapse of doctrinal transmission in the schools in the 1970s – 'a catechetical desert' in the Cardinal's words – making it impossible for many parents to participate subsequently in the Catholic education of their children.[2] This observation – of unplanned incompetence – should be flanked by another one, made to me in May 2006 by the headmaster of a Catholic independent school in southern England, to the effect that many parents, including nominally Catholic ones, are interested only in the secular education Catholic schools provide. There have long been non-Catholic pupils at Catholic schools, including maintained ones. It was also clear in the past that many nominally Catholic children did not go to church, yet clearly their parents wanted them at a Catholic school. Today, however, the numbers of non-Catholics and even non-Christians at Catholic schools are higher than ever. As to tokenism by Catholics, how could we ever really know its magnitude? In any event, it seems that it is often the trace elements of Catholic education, the famous discipline, intellectual rigour and community ethos, which appeal to Catholic and non-Catholic parents alike. How far the system

---

[2]  Eric Hester, 'Religious education in crisis', *Catholic Times*, October 2004.

and its attraction to parents is driven by Catholic spirituality is debatable.

## Our depleted spiritual resources

Gerald Grace believes that the spiritual resources of the Catholic Church in this country have been greatly depleted.[3] I would agree with his analysis. The implication would seem to be that the spirituality of our Catholic schools has at the very least been attenuated. Grace has very usefully assembled much invaluable factual and analytical material on modern British Catholic education. What he calls depletion I would call 'decline'. There are still, nevertheless, powerful reserves available. The printed and intellectual materials we need for successful Catholic aspirations are not lacking. Unfortunately, we have often used inadequate material, such as *Weaving the Web*.[4] Nor does the primary text *Here I Am* inspire much enthusiasm. Few traditional Catholics speak highly of that other Catholic text, *Icons*, whose use spans primary and secondary schools. Book 1 defines twelve Hindu terms for the edification of young children. Book 3, which is the approved text for pupils aged eleven to fourteen, gives a careful explanation of the five pillars of Islam. It is hard to see much justification for this in basic Catholic texts, given the obvious time constraints and ongoing anxiety about how

---

[3] Grace (2005). Professor Grace's concerns are articulated through the notion of 'spiritual capital', a borrowing from the 'cultural capital' of Pierre Bourdieu, of which more later.

[4] Ibid. One Catholic head I spoke to, however, claimed that *Weaving the Web*, while a limited resource, is satisfactory if it is backed up by more profound and central notions.

much our children know of their own faith. Such excursions may be well intended, but seem likely to cause further depletion.

Yet in secular terms praise of the Catholic schools is still due. Research findings supplied by official reporting reinforce the popular view. Catholic schools, like other Voluntary Aided Schools, are superior in academic terms to the non-denominational Maintained Schools on the secular front; Catholic schools maintain a varying but distinct margin of advantage. Morris puts it thus: 'The superiority of Catholic schools, in respect of measures adopted by OFSTED [Office for Standards in Education] is very noticeable.'[5]

In the popular view this connects with the stronger moral ethos in the voluntary aided sector. This perception has served to increase the popularity of Catholic schools and to swell the numbers of non-Catholics who attend them. The Holy See has, moreover, long looked with favour on applications of the voluntary principle. The non-private Catholic schools are clear exemplars of mutual compromise and understanding between the Roman Church and the British state.

Their secular superiority does not, however, make Catholic schools effective in religious education. Mr Ken Connelly, formerly Head of English at St Benedict's, Ealing, later Deputy Head at the Oratory School and subsequently employed as a civil servant specialising in the drafting of

---

[5]  A. B. Morris, 'Catholic and other secondary schools: an analysis of OFSTED inspection reports, 1993–1995', *Educational Research*, 40(2): 181–90; quoted in Grace (2005: 106).

government bills,[6] has been active on the Education Committee of the Catholic Union. He has a distinctly low opinion both of the general secular legislative apparatus that affects *all* schools and of the religious teachings in the ascendant in Catholic ones. He thinks most educational legislation is at best useless and at worst highly destructive.[7] Given the officially available evidence on the millions who have emerged both illiterate and innumerate from the system (Bartholomew, 2004), we are surely entitled to wonder just how all this legislation can be represented as aiding the learning activities of our schools.

It is the weakness and distortion of *Catholic* teaching which most worry Connelly, however. This is seen, for example, in many of the English and Welsh Bishops' public statements, which seem to interpret the promotion of the 'common good' in socialist terms, despite papal teaching that emphasises the importance of achieving the common good through institutions such as the market economy, voluntary exchange and the family. Despite more emphasis in recent years on the importance of charity, community and the 'Big Society' in promoting the common good, the general view of the Catholic Bishops of England and Wales with regard to education remains that the prime movers should be the Bishops' Conference bureaucracy in partnership with the state – this was very clear in the national pastoral letter on education issued in 2007.

More correctly, the emphasis on the family

---

[6]   For the Department of the Environment.
[7]   In a private interview with the author, 14 May 2006.

is supremely important. It is the family, not the state, which the Church sees as the prime agency for promoting basic morality. In his attempt over many years of retirement to promote a traditional teaching of Catholic morality and values, in particular with regard to the role of the sacraments and grace, Connelly's criticisms of current teaching and its emphasis on secular themes were generally met with great hostility. It is ironic and regrettable that those who are often described by their opponents as 'liberals' seem to be most defensive and dogmatic in maintaining the status quo that has now been established if it comes under attack. The first Catholic priority is the redemption of the individual soul. Each individual salvation is unique. It is the facilitation of individual salvation *collectively* which constitutes the common good. It is this perspective which must underlie the Catholic view of curriculum and pedagogy. It is far from clear that all or even most Catholic school practice reflects these perspectives. Hence the anxiety felt by Professor Grace and Mr Connelly.

## The *Compendium of the Catechism of the Catholic Church* published by the Catholic Truth Society

It has been precisely deficiencies and strange priorities reflecting an overemphasis on secular themes which alarm some Catholics. Despite these shortcomings, good Catholic teaching material has recently become available. On the question of good texts for teaching, things are distinctly looking up. We now have at our disposal *The*

*Compendium of the Catechism of the Catholic Church*
(Catholic Truth Society, 2006). Eric Hester, a very
experienced former headmaster of Catholic high
schools, has described the reissue of this book as
'a gift from God, a treasure, a precious jewel'.[8]
Like the familiar catechism of generations ago, the
*Compendium* is a model of clarity and simplicity,
set out in straightforward question-and-answer
form. The book contains the profession of faith,
with all the main prayers, the celebration of the
sacraments, life in Christ, with the elucidation of
the Ten Commandments, and Christian prayer.
The main prayers are in English and Latin. Then
there are the Formulas of Catholic doctrine: the
Eight Beatitudes; the Gifts of the Holy Spirit; the
Fruits of the Holy Spirit; The Four Last Things;
The Corporal and Spiritual Works of Mercy.

Hester insists that the *Compendium* should be
used in *all primary and secondary classes* (my italics)
in our Catholic schools. This would much relieve
those of us who worry about the teaching of the
faith. After all, there could scarcely be a clearer
exposition of the Church's teaching. We need
more traditional Catholic teaching on faith and
morals and less by way of self-indulgent posturing.
It is perfectly proper for children to understand the
evils of prejudice between races and sexes. It is also
imperative, however, that pupils should learn that
opposition to such evils is fundamentally subsumed
in the Ten Commandments. Does racism need
any further indictment than that implied by all
humanity being made in God's image? Should not

---

[8]   Eric Hester, 'Compendium of the Catechism of the Catholic Church',
*Catholic Times*, 23 April 2006.

sexual prejudice fall at the first Christian fence too? We also need some hard-headed thinking on the political economy of education, a point to be driven home later.

## Difficulties: Catholic, educational, sociological and economic

The central need is a resumption of catechesis. The *Compendium* is available and the spiritual resources are depleted. These opposite facts are our initial markers. How well do our primary and secondary schools explain, justify and propagate the Catholic religion? I note with regret that I have not come across any specifically Catholic modern teachings such as might, if they were followed, play some part in attending to the notorious deficits in modern educational practices, those affecting all the advanced Western societies, these having long had predominantly market economies, combined oddly and *discontinuously* with mainly state-financed school systems. The level of illiteracy and innumeracy in the British case as elsewhere is of alarming proportions. Conservative scholars have long complained about this. These days it is the everyday stuff of official pronouncements. Two-thirds of the children taking public examinations in England and Wales in the General Certificate of Secondary Education (GCSE) do not pass in English or mathematics.[9]

Other deficits include lack of historical knowledge and widespread moral and intellectual relativism.

---

[9] 'GCSE tables expose the truth about maths and English', *Daily Telegraph*, 11 January 2007, p. 1. Most of the candidates are sixteen years old.

These also connect with the bad behaviour now so widespread. Moreover, there is a neglected economic aspect to the problem. These deficits are indices of economic inefficiency. They suggest that resources involved in educational and intellectual transmission are seriously misused (O'Keeffe, 1999). Indeed almost no one would presume to argue that school standards have risen over the last half-century. The one undenied truth is the vast increase in resource input. The implication is a drastically falling trend in productivity (see O'Keeffe and Marsland, 2003: 1–28; O'Keeffe, 1999). The question is not whether but why these things are so. I have located no Catholic opinion on this vital issue.

Activists in Catholic education tend to fall into the same division between conservative and socialist which occurs in other fields of concern. The reflex conservatism I remember from childhood reflected the Church's very active, indeed *unbending*, hostility to Marxism and communism, a hostility long since abandoned by many Catholics. Thus the error obtains of treating the Marxist challenge as possessing intellectual authority. Indubitably learned writings make references to Marx (Harvey et al., 2005: 28) and Hobsbawm (ibid.: 47). The Catholic writings on education I have been reading mostly fall in with the correct general Western academic convention that Nazism and fascism are beyond the intellectual pale, such that pronouncements by their ideologues are simply absent from discourse, though James Hanvey's fine book does mention Martin Heidegger (ibid.: 88). There is *perhaps* a case for allowing any Catholic writer to refer to *any scholar of any persuasion*, provided the intention is to strengthen the Catholic viewpoint.

If we conclude, however, that the anathema on writers of Nazi persuasion is too strong to overturn, then at least we could extend the same treatment to Marxism and communism. In terms of the almost countless millions slaughtered by communism and its rabid hostility to our Christian faith, the argument here seems unanswerable. My case would be helped along if one could find among Catholic radicals any recognition of the common anti-totalitarian view that Nazism and its half-brother fascism are fundamentally *Marxist heresies* (Pipes, 1994: ch. 5). Pipes is not a Catholic, though he is Polish by birth. In Catholic Poland the identification to which he inclines is widely made. If we were intellectually consistent we would maintain a general rule that no writer having totalitarian persuasions should feature in the literature of Catholicism, except by way of hostile analysis. In fact, however, much of the non-totalitarian radicalism one encounters in that literature is deeply suspect too.

The rejection of Marxism should follow from the empirical facts of communist experience, but even more crucially from the ferocious intolerance of the theory itself (see Kolakowski, 1988). This stance is precisely what many Catholic activists have *not* adopted. Since the 1960s such activists have not been outright communists: anti-anti-communist would be a better label. Indeed, the overall Catholic voice on politics is not even socialist in any society-wide sense. What many Catholic intellectuals want is a *socialist education system*. They want public finance and egalitarian ideology, the socialisation of mind as a surrogate for socialised property. This is not Marxist politics any more; rather it is a residual version, what the French call *Marxisant* politics.

The atmosphere of discussion in most Catholic educational circles is immediately recognisable to me, however, no matter how we label the ideology. There is much talk of 'gender'. Whatever arguments were employed when this term was plucked from its grammatical context, it is now merely an unjustified replacement for 'sex'. Grace does not use it extensively in his much-regarded text, though it appears in a subhead as an unproblematic category in bold type, Gender, Leadership and Catholicism (Grace, 2005: 229). Of the extensive use of the term in radical Marxist feminism as far back as the 1970s, and its hold today on virtually all feminist literature, however, there is no doubt. The modern use of the term perhaps comes from the seminal essay by Gayle Ruben, 'The traffic in women: notes on the political economy of sex', in which she coins the phrase 'sex/gender system' (Ruben, 1975). The use of the word 'gender' rather than 'sex' was strongly criticised by Cardinal Ratzinger in his booklet, because it attempted to diminish the importance of the created differences between the sexes (see Ratzinger, 2004).

The penetration of Church thinking on education by secular themes of a soft radical kind now reaches back nearly half a century. Thus the Declaration on Christian Education (*Gravissimum educationis*) proclaimed by Pope Paul VI on 28 October 1965 bears witness to the influence of secular speculation on human rights, a speculation since grown to gigantic proportions, harking back to the adoption by the General Assembly of the United Nations, on 10 December 1948, of the Declaration of the Rights of Man. Pope Paul VI noted in *Gravissimum educationis* that the rights of men to an education, particularly the primary rights of children and parents, are being proclaimed and recognised in public documents. On page two we learn that 'men of every race, condition and age ... have an inalienable right to an education'.

This proposition is grossly false. Perhaps MacIntyre's view that 'rights' are one with unicorns and fairies is too severe (MacIntyre, 1999). Perhaps our being human does entail limited rights. More important are the *duties* laid upon us by the Catholic faith as commands, vis-à-vis our treatment of others. We have inalienable duties as to other people. Inalienable rights are merely the shadows of these. So-called rights to education are non-existent. They presuppose individuals whose duties include the requirement that they educate others. This can be true only of parents. It cannot be true for others except by way of contract. So-called rights are mostly contractual and conventional, not inalienable.

*Gravissimum educationis* compounds this problem by saying that Catholics have an inalienable right to a Catholic education. Again this is only true in the sense that Catholic parents have a duty to educate their children in the Catholic faith where they can. Where parents are unable to educate their own children, it is difficult to see upon whom such a duty can fall. Certainly it is not clear that it should fall on the taxpayer. The truth is that people have a duty to permit religious freedoms to others, save where these others restrict the freedoms of other persons to perform their duties. We can pursue the goal of Catholic education for our children only because of our mutual reciprocal duties with regard to people of other persuasions. Thus parents do have a right to be allowed to educate their children in the faith. This is different from a right of children to a Catholic education. More generally, these aspects of the Vatican II Decree on Education are not very tightly argued, betraying a capitulation to lay fancies.[10]

## What the Church does not talk about: Catholicism and tough social science

If Rome has positions on compulsory attendance, standards, private or state finance, vouchers, intellectual competition between students and between institutions, none seems to be on the agenda here at diocesan level. We know that Vatican statements on education have specifically stated that parents who use private education should get the same support from the state as those parents who use state schools – indeed, this is stated in the recent *Compendium on the Social Doctrine of the Church* (see also Chapter 6). This might, for example, imply a voucher system of support for education but it does not seem to

---

[10]   The development of teaching on rights was most explicitly articulated in *Pacem in terris* (John Paul XXIII, 1963). There is room for debate about the merit of specific rights articulated in that document but, whilst it is clear that Catholic parents have a duty to provide Catholic education for their children, how can children have a right to a Catholic education financed and provided by the generality of the population that is not Catholic?

figure in our diocesan debates. Indeed, there is in Catholic quarters a general failure to address crucial questions of economic and intellectual efficiency.

It is also the case, however, that Catholic writings on education do not seem to put any emphasis on a clear-sighted *economic* analysis of education more generally. The central structure of Grace's book is borne by his interviews with 60 teachers across three English archdioceses. On Grace's own admission, most of the heads of schools interrogated about the importance or otherwise to them of market-style competition denied any trust in such competition, though one bold spirit went so far as to say that the hierarchy was hypocritical in its opposition to severe competition and attempts to maintain superiority by certain schools by way of competitive ethos. He also said outright that it is the children who benefit most from competition and that schools 'do not look after each other', that is do not maintain mutual solidarity, proclamations to the contrary constituting a sham (Grace, 2005: 191).

If education is often malfunctional – doing proper things inadequately – or even dysfunctional – doing improper things – the economic context is important. Failure to teach reading exemplifies the malfunctional, while worrying children about what race or which sex they belong to exemplifies dysfunctionality. We have been trying to manage education without property rights. In the absence of mechanisms of complaint, exit and correction, these faults are precisely the outcomes we encounter, often for decades on end, once the elite abandon competition. Education systems manifestly function less efficiently than they would if property rights did indeed obtain in schools and colleges and if competition existed within the system (O'Keeffe, 2003). Some Catholics, however, seem to have the problem precisely the wrong way round.

## Markets versus centralised state control of resources

Where education is involved, some Catholic authors say there is a tension between the efficient operations facilitated in theory by market transactions – and most economists worldwide would now say in reality – and the 'common good'. This latter concept is much in favour with the Catholic Bishops' Conference of England and Wales. Indeed, they have produced a critique of 'market education' called *The Common Good in Education* (Catholic Education Service, 1997). There is nothing amiss with a belief in and promotion of the concept of the common good, of course. What is wrong, however, is to deny that the common good can be achieved through the mechanisms and institutions of competition and the marketplace – in education as elsewhere. The common good and family autonomy, leading to choice in education, should be in harmony, not in conflict. Grace too speaks of an 'attempted colonisation' of education by market ideologies in the 1980s and 1990s (Grace, 2005: 180). Those many writers hostile to market forces in education are, however, vulnerable on many counts. We now know beyond doubt that central power is a wholly inefficient means of organising scarce resources, above all because there is no way of knowing what the public wants. As Hayek has shown, no one knows, nor could know, this information (Hayek, 1948). Discussion of this problem is simply missing in this Catholic literature.

Why, we may ask, should education be held to escape the proven results, some might call them 'iron laws', of socialism? Private enterprise works far better than the socialist planning of communism. Why should not free enterprise work better in education for the same reason than do our socialist arrangements? The centralisation of power, the abolition of markets, the absence of property rights, the reduction of money exchanges and varying degrees of suppression of the division of labour did not lead to human emancipation but to murder and wickedness and vast waste. If these are the results of society-wide socialism, on what grounds is socialism to be applauded and furthered in relation to the transmission of knowledge and culture in free societies? If socialism must be pursued in education, why not also in the wider society? If not in the wider society, why should it be pursued in education? There is no question as far as the empirical evidence is concerned – parental autonomy (choice of school) in education improves standards. It particularly improves standards for the poor and those with disabilities and so on. The reason for this is clear. When there is an educational monopoly based on catchment areas, it is only by moving house or articulating one's needs to the headteacher that improvement can come. Give the poor the right of exit and the results are clear.

The mantra runs that something about education necessitates public finance. But what? It cannot be the necessity of education, since economic science knows no distinction between necessary and luxury goods. Anything said about education as a special case can equally be said about food or holidays. Some argue that education is a public good, and therefore subject to externalities that require public finance. I cannot retain for myself all the benefits of being educated, therefore the state must pay some contribution to the cost of my children's education.

In fact education is a thoroughly private good. It is not even certain that the overall outcomes of mass-financed education are not dysfunctional. Such eminent scholars as Milton Friedman and E. G. West thought so and provided a substantial body of historical evidence and economic analysis to back up their case. It may be the case that zero action by the state, with neither public funding for education nor compulsory attendance for children, would secure better outcomes.[11]

There is another, in some ways even more important, mistake made by progressive educationists. They seem to assume that socialised education must be hostile to competition. This is not so. Indeed, the key difference between free enterprise and socialism is that the former is always competitive, while the latter is so only under special circumstances.

There was little talk of markets in the 1940s and 1950s when I received respectively my elementary and secondary-school education. In my elementary

---

[11]  Much of this can be found at the website of the E. G. West centre: www. ncl.ac.uk/egwest/

school, by the age of eleven every child could read. That is rather rare in primary schools today in my very extensive experience.[12] The fierce and non-stop competition, backed up by ferocious discipline on the part of the nuns who dominated the school, forced standards upwards. At my private Catholic secondary school, competition was equally fierce, though the discipline was much milder. Perhaps there are comprehensives today which match its standards, but these are few and far between, and rare in London.[13]

It is also a commonplace that competition in education was far fiercer under the communist regimes than it is in the education systems of most market economies. The reasons need not concern us. While it is hard to imagine any kind of private production which is not competitive, in the case of publicly financed education the intentions of the elite are all-important. Competition, often savage competition, is not inconsistent with socialised schooling, whether we mean by this publicly funded compulsory education in predominantly market economies, or straightforwardly socialist education as in generally socialist societies. The elites decide. It is not that communist education systems were not corrupt. But the freewheeling pseudo-bourgeoisie of state schooling in the free societies, who experiment using *other people's money* and are never or rarely held to account for their offences (O'Keeffe, 1990), were absent

---

[12] See the evidence of children unable to pass the basic English examination for sixteen-year-olds, above. This presupposes low English standards in primary schools.

[13] I had 27 years' experience as a teacher of education in London.

in communist societies proper. The communist elite simply forbade such freewheeling. Under the *patina* of Marxism on the communist curriculum there was an old-fashioned set of European ideas. Add this reality to a continued reliance on didactic teaching and the secret of communist education stands revealed. It is not that communist education systems were good overall. But for a complex set of reasons they functioned better than our kind of socialist educational arrangements do.

Gerald Grace believes that the spiritual resources of the Catholic Church in this country have been greatly depleted. I have agreed completely. Grace speaks of a declining 'spiritual capital' on the lines of Bourdieu's famous 'cultural capital' (Grace, 2005: 65). Here we part company somewhat theoretically. The original explicit suggestion from Bourdieu was that the 'cultural capital' of those who possess it works alongside 'economic capital', in the differential social positioning of the population. I object not to the proposition that culture or spirituality can be capitalised, but to the category error in Bourdieu's contrast.

## Category errors, wrong theorising and the loss of the sacramental

The trope itself in cultural or spiritual 'capital' is in error. All capital is economic by definition, in the sense of deliberated and costly decisions having been made in pursuit of economic advantage. Bourdieu and Grace may be referring to uncalculated stocks, formed spontaneously in the ordinary lives of children in educated families, conferring undoubted economic advantage, but involving no capital calculus. Alternatively, they may be referring to pondered capital formations, with regard to education. The very use of the word 'capital' presupposes this latter case. Thus 'cultural' and 'spiritual' capital are *sub-categories* of the general category 'capital'. In the functional (*sic*) sense this matters not a jot, of course, and Grace is quite correct that the Church has run down its intellectual and spiritual reserves. Nevertheless, it is worth pointing out the mistaken terms in which some functionally correct arguments are sometimes put.

Such category errors seem trivial when we compare them with the dysfunctional fare of contemporary sociology, and even this latter fault fades into insignificance alongside my central anxiety, namely that Catholic education has today lost most of its sacramental character and that those who should support its reassertion prefer a soft radical alternative secular agenda. In my view, these disasters cannot be corrected within the present structure. Let us conclude with a brief examination of why this is so.

## The socio-economy of public finance

Since the time of Schumpeter few economists have dabbled much in the borderlands of economics and sociology. This absence has largely vitiated the contemporary sociology of knowledge, especially the Marxian version till recently so common in the study of education (O'Keeffe, 1999; O'Keeffe and Marsland, 2003). The key variable requiring investigation is public finance. In a free society the public finance of the transmission of knowledge and culture has a number of most undesirable results once public and elite opinion become separated, as in this country happened in the 1960s.

First, public finance affects educational decision-making. It hugely enhances the power of the educational elite, especially in a free society with a tradition of reverence for experts. Using resources that are not its own, this elite becomes a kind of irresponsible pseudo-bourgeoisie, which privatises education decisions according to its own priorities and predilections, socialising the costs when policies fail. The rise of soft social science at all educational levels is a function of the activities of this elite, as is the disastrous 'progressive' education and a teaching of mathematics as woeful as the way we have been teaching reading.

On the crucial demand side consumption motives are magnified at the expense of investment. This is exemplified in the choice of soft rather than hard subject matter, with students choosing sociology rather than physics or modern languages. From the supply side inferior teaching and curriculum cause waste, often by under-equipping the children or by baffling parents and children alike, by rendering the activities of the classroom opaque to non-initiates of the progressive scene, a point Bernstein noticed 30 years ago, though he did not object to the mystification (Bernstein, 1975). It is hard to see how the system can be rectified without an infusion of property rights, unless the elite are converted wholesale.

In all these cases the absence of property rights and of the institution of bankruptcy effectively prevent exit. These defects are, like the other shortcomings of our educational arrangements, largely a result of the operations of public finance. No policy that does not include a very substantial element of privatisation has any hope at all of improving things. Markets can breed improprieties. These are dwarfed by those of socialism. Nor should we forget that an aim of many forms of socialism has been the eradication of all kinds of religion, perhaps especially in the case of the Church of Rome. This is becoming increasingly clear as the political and educational establishments become more radically secular in the UK.

There is an attenuation of Catholic tradition in Catholic schools, illustrated at its most frightening by the absurd claim that Catholic schools are themselves somehow the new Church (quoted in Grace, 2005). This contention is utterly heretical. The schools are the instrument of the Church. Not least an issue is that people are forced to go to schools but they are not forced to go to church. Having an institution that people are forced to attend as the main focus for worship and witness is completely contrary to free will.

## Markets, Catholicism and mercy

Most important of all though is the perverse misunderstanding of markets on the part of Catholics and in particular their failure to grasp that economic efficiency is imperative to those who view the predicament of their fellow human beings in a spirit of mercy. There is above all a grave loss of spontaneity in socialised education. As Bastiat puts it: 'Let men work, trade, learn, form partnerships, act and react upon one another, since according to the decrees of Providence, naught save order, harmony, and progress can spring from their intelligent spontaneity.'[14]

It is very clear that Catholic teaching demands parental autonomy in the field of education and that requires a 'free economy' in education, even if not a 'market economy'. Canon Law says: 'Catholic parents have also the duty and the right to choose those means and institutes which, in their local circumstances, can best promote the Catholic education of their children ... Parents must have a real freedom in their choice of schools'. Bishops, as has been pointed out by the Catholic Education Service in the current debate in the UK over 'free schools', can choose whether to give a school the title 'Catholic'. But the spirit of subsidiarity is not just applied in the political domain. There is no reason why dioceses should be the sole or even main provider of education that is designated Catholic. Canon Law also says: 'If there are no schools in which an education is provided that is imbued with a Christian spirit, the diocesan bishop has the responsibility of ensuring that such schools are established'. In other words, bishops may establish schools if necessary, but this responsibility is not a reason for putting impediments in the way of parents, lay movements and other groups who

---

[14]   Frédéric Bastiat, *Harmonies*, trans. W. Hayden Boyers, ed. George B. du Huszar, Princeton, NJ, 1964, p. 12.

wish to develop a school with a distinctly Catholic character. Indeed, in the spirit of Vatican II bishops should encourage the laity to be active in education. While the bishops have every right to be cautious in allowing new schools to be formally described as 'Catholic' they should not be deliberately obstructive.

As we have noted, Catholic social teaching in the matter of school financing is also interesting. The *Compendium* argues that it is an injustice for the state not to support attendance at non-state schools, that a state monopoly of education offends justice and that the state cannot merely tolerate private schools. The right to economic initiative in education is just as clear as in other areas of life. Local bishops should not obstruct that.

Indeed, what Christian charity is there in rejecting so notable a gift of Divine Providence as the spontaneously operating free economy, the only system known to history which can replace poor societies with rich ones?

## References

Bartholomew, J. (2004), *Getting out of the Welfare State We're In*, London: Politico's.

Bernstein, B. (1975), 'Class and pedagogies: visible and invisible', *Class, Codes and Control*, vol. 3, part II, ch. 6, Routledge & Kegan Paul, pp. 116–56.

Burn, J. (2001), 'Church schools: a critique of much current practice', in J. Burn, J. Marks, P. Pilkington and P. Thompson, *Faith in Education*,

Civitas, p. 37.

Catholic Bishops' Conference of England and Wales (1997), *Catholic Schools and Other Faiths*.

Catholic Education Service (1997), *The Common Good in Education*.

Catholic Truth Society (2006), *The Compendium of the Catechism of the Catholic Church*.

Grace, G. (2005), *Catholic Schools: Mission, Markets and Morality*, London: Routledge and Falmer.

Harvey, J. et al. (2005), *On the Way to Life: Promoting and Supporting Catholic Education in England and Wales*, Catholic Education Service.

Hayek, F. A. (1948), 'Economics and knowledge', in *Individualism and Economic Order*, London: Routledge.

Kolakowski, L. (1988), *Main Currents of Marxism*, Oxford: Clarendon.

MacIntyre, A. (1999), *After Virtue*, Chicago, IL: Open Court Press.

Martin, X. (2001), *Human Nature and the French Revolution*, trans. P. Corcoran, London: Bergbahn Press.

Minogue, K. (2003), 'Christophobia in the West', *New Criterion*, 21(10).

O'Keeffe, D. (1990), *The Wayward Elite*, Adam Smith Institute.

O'Keeffe, D. (1999), *Political Correctness and Public Finance*, Studies in Education no. 9, London: Institute of Economic Affairs.

O'Keeffe, D. (2003), 'Education and modernity', *Economic Affairs*, 23(2), June 2003, pp. 34–9.

O'Keeffe, D. and D. Marsland (2003), *Independence or Stagnation: The Imperatives of University*

*Reform in the United Kingdom*, London: Civitas.

Pipes, R. (1994), *Russia under the Bolshevik Regime*: 1919–1924, London: Harvill.

Ratzinger, J. (2004), *On the Collaboration of Men and Women in the Church and in the World*, Congregation for the Doctrine of the Faith, London: Catholic Truth Society.

Ruben, G. (1975), 'Notes on the political economy of sex', in R. Reiter (ed.), *Towards an Anthropology of Women*, New York: Monthly Review Press.

## 13

# CATHOLIC SOCIAL TEACHING AND THE FINANCIAL CRASH[1]

*Philip Booth*

## Prudence – the importance of not saying too much

Christian leaders responded to the financial crash in various ways. Some notable figures made wholesale denouncements of greed; others called for more regulation or for completely new financial structures. Some commentary emphasised the moral issues – a line that can best be summarised by the phrase 'a good world needs good people'. An early comment by Pope Benedict XVI, which others have echoed, suggested that the crash was a good time to reflect on the relative unimportance of material possessions.

The role of the Christian commentator can be difficult when discussing these issues. Sometimes great discernment is required when coming to a judgement on technical economic points – indeed a definitive judgement on a particular issue is often not possible. This leads to a legitimate question of what, if anything, Christians can bring to the

---

[1]   An earlier version of this chapter appeared in Booth (ed.) (2010).

discussion of the problems in financial markets that manifested themselves in recent years. This general question has been dealt with in papal encyclicals and other documents. For example, John Paul II in *Centesimus annus* (43) wrote:

> The Church has no models to present; models that are real and truly effective can only arise within the framework of different historical situations, through the efforts of all those who responsibly confront concrete problems in all their social, economic, political and cultural aspects, as these interact with one another. For such a task the Church offers her social teaching as an indispensable and ideal orientation, a teaching which, as already mentioned, recognizes the positive value of the market and of enterprise, but which at the same time points out that these need to be oriented towards the common good.

Thus there is a tradition in Catholic social teaching of identifying problems which might merit action and then leaving it to those knowledgeable in the field to debate, prudentially, what the best course of action would be. In other words: 'Of itself it does not belong to the Church, insofar as she is a religious and hierarchical community, to offer concrete solutions in the social, economic and political spheres for justice in the world. Her mission involves defending and promoting the dignity and fundamental rights of the human person.'[2] Though there are groups of Christians that look for a specifically 'Christian third way', this is not the general disposition of the Catholic Church.

---

2   *Justitia in mundo*, World Synod of Bishops, 1971, 37.

As such, Cardinal Pell of Sydney spoke wisely in the wake of the financial crash when he said: 'The only thing we can say is to repeat the central teachings of Christ. When men and women over-reach themselves...trouble often follows... The financial crisis is enormously complicated, and I would hope that we don't attempt to say too much.'

There are important Christian perspectives on the financial crisis and the application of these perspectives can, no doubt, lead to better public policy for promoting the common good. However, we should proceed with humility and prudence. In the remainder of this chapter we examine these issues. To a greater extent than elsewhere in this book, we draw on comments that have been made by non-Catholic Christians to illustrate certain points.

## The 'common good'

The financial system, it is often pointed out, should promote the 'common good'. Promoting the common good is not about making society more equal, nor even about making everybody better off in material terms. The common good has been defined in Catholic social teaching as 'The sum total of social conditions which allow people, either as groups or individuals, to reach their fulfilment more fully and more easily' (Pontifical Council for Justice and Peace, 2005, 164).

We must resist the temptation to assume that we can control and design political and economic systems in order to achieve the common good. We must also guard against assuming that the common good is something that can be measured: it is not possible in some utilitarian way to weigh up the increase or decrease in the common good that arises from changing this or that financial regulation, for example. Different people will have different goals and callings and thus the phrase 'allow people to reach their fulfilment more fully and more easily' is important. Promoting the common good is not necessarily about governments taking positive action as much as governments allowing the conditions to exist in which people can thrive and reach fulfilment.

The financial system is part of a free economy that can help people live a flourishing life – not just in material terms. The sheer inconvenience and drudgery of life where financial systems do not facilitate payments and long-term saving or ensure that people can borrow money to start a new business are unbearable. On the other hand, if the financial system has developed so that it allows some to profit *at the expense of* others or so that it excludes most people from its benefits then the common good might not be fulfilled also.

## The regulation of the financial system

Christian leaders have been at the forefront of calls for more financial regulation in the wake of the crash of 2008. The Archbishop of Canterbury, for example, suggested in March 2009 in an article in the *Guardian*:

> [G]overnments committed to deregulation and to the encouragement of speculation and high personal borrowing were elected repeatedly in

Britain and the United States for a crucial couple of decades. Add to that the fact of warnings of some of the risks of poor (or no) regulation, and we are left with the question of what it was that skewed the judgment of a whole society as well as of financial professionals.[3]

Furthermore, several of the Archbishop of York's comments implied that participants in financial markets should be kept on a tighter rein. For example, he said: 'To a bystander like me, those who made £190 million deliberately underselling the shares of HBOS, in spite of its very strong capital base, and drove it into the bosom of Lloyds TSB Bank, are clearly bank robbers and asset strippers.'

In March 2009, leaders of the major non-conformist churches called for increased regulation of financial markets, tax havens and more regulation surrounding accounting and reporting standards.[4]

We should be careful, as Christians, not simply to echo the cacophony of secular reactions to events. Just because the financial system has gone through a number of problems, it does not follow that regulating it more will facilitate the common good

---

[3] http://www.archbishopofcanterbury.org/2324# (accessed 9 October, 2009). This is one of several unfortunate interventions in this debate by the Archbishop of Canterbury. He stated, for example, that Pope Benedict supported a transactions tax. This intervention was very significant but completely inaccurate. The Wikipedia page (now corrected) came to state that the Pope was in favour of the tax and there are 333,000 responses to the google search 'robin hood tax pope'. The BBC has also claimed that the Pope was in favour of the tax. The facts are rather different. The Justice and Peace Commission published a document (which the Pope might never have read before publication) in which it suggested that we may wish to reflect on the idea. It is very difficult to understand how the Archbishop could get such an elementary matter wrong.

[4] http://www.standrewsurcsheffield.org.uk/node/329

more effectively: this is especially so, of course, if many of the problems resulted from regulation in the first place. Certainly, Catholic social teaching alone cannot lead one to that conclusion.

If we are to think about where the government might intervene to a greater degree, one starting point is to ask ourselves a series of questions that might establish a prima facie case that a particular matter is worthy of serious reflection and possible policy action by government. The chapter by Townsend in Spencer and Chaplin (eds) (2009) discusses the sorts of criteria that Christians might use to make such a judgment. The authors start with the proposition that the *raison d'être* of government action is the promotion of the common good. However, that does not mean that any government action we feel will make a society a better place is justified. Even changes to regulation that, on the basis of rational calculation, might appear to increase human welfare, might be seen as circumscribing the freedom of some and preventing them from promoting the common good. Furthermore, as Townsend points out, the Christian polity – and not government – is the primary mode by which God wishes to bring about the kingdom here on earth.

Nevertheless, in creating the conditions for the common good, government does need to act in certain ways, argues Townsend. He reiterates the traditional Christian principles for legal action: governments should act to ensure that nobody is forced to do what is wrong or is prevented from participating in the promotion of the common good. This would imply, for example, that families' property must be protected from expropriation and contracts must be enforced. As a parallel, Townsend also suggests that governments should respond to some sins of omission. This would normally include ensuring that all had the basic necessities for dignified living, where the charity of fellow human beings omitted to provide for this. However, this might also include, to take the case cited by the Archbishop of York, government action to prevent people from rigging financial markets. Thus the Archbishop of York's argument *may* be justified on this ground, though it should be noted that rigging financial markets is already illegal and the short selling that the Archbishop criticised cannot be said to have fallen into the category of rigging the market (see the chapter by Copeland in Booth (ed.) 2009).

Applying these theological constructs, Townsend himself suggests that the financial crisis mainly suggested that action at the moral rather than at the governmental level was necessary, though he does make some policy suggestions.

If we are to propose more regulation of the financial system based on the principle of promoting the common good then we need to assess the practical and prudential realities. For example, relating to financial regulation, we should ask whether problems in the financial sector arose as a result of a lack of regulation or, perhaps, too much regulation of the wrong type. Does the problem have an upstream cause (such as mismanaged monetary policy – see chapter 2 by Booth in Booth (ed.) 2010) which should be fixed first? Do the problems arise from a legal system which prevents those working in the industry from being made financially accountable for their decisions? Again, if this is so, the correct response might be to fix this problem, rather than to regulate the banking system to a greater degree. Finally, we can ask whether greater regulation will actually lead to more harm than good, knowing the imperfections that also pervade regulatory agencies.

These questions are essentially empirical economics questions about which theologians do not have any particular value to add in their role as theologians. The matters are also highly subjective. Different people will interpret the facts differently and come to different conclusions about how to act.

On balance, it is difficult to make a *prima facie* case from Catholic social teaching that there *must* be a regulatory response to the crash, except in one or two senses that will be discussed below. At the same time, a Christian cannot come to the view that increased regulation should definitely be ruled out. There are areas where a regulatory response *might* be justified but whether to go forward and regulate in these areas is essentially a prudential judgement on which Catholic social teaching would give limited guidance. In other words, there is a relatively wide field on which Christians of goodwill can conduct debates about these issues. This may seem like a long chain of reasoning to get to an inconsequential conclusion. However, it is an important conclusion. When ministers of religion, priests, and so on, use their authority to propose policy action in particular fields in which they lack the specialist knowledge to come to a wise prudential judgment, they are in danger of undermining their authority in those areas where their voices should have special resonance.

In the remainder of this chapter, we will discuss in less abstract terms how we might respond to the financial crash in a way that is consistent with Catholic social teaching.

## Should banks be bailed out?

Christians will be instinctively concerned by the government bail-out of banks that took place around 2008. In an emergency situation, the bail-outs could be justified as being compatible with the common good. But, once that emergency is over, most Christians would want the government to take action to prevent such a situation arising again.

Arguably, there is a potential (or actual) injustice in a situation where the managers, owners and creditors of banks can obtain the benefits of success in good times but have their failures underwritten by taxpayers. Taxpayers then put their property at risk if the bank fails. Taking the income of future taxpayers in order to bail out banks is depriving the former of their property and may prevent them participating fully in the common good – especially if higher taxes lead to higher unemployment: the case of Ireland in the aftermath of the crash is an obvious example of such a problem.

It is, of course, possible for a Christian economist to conclude, prudentially, that nothing can be done to improve on the current situation where banks are implicitly or explicitly underwritten by the state without damaging the common good.

They might argue that deposit insurance, a central bank providing lender of last resort facilities, and government support for banks whose failure could bring the banking system down are a price we have to pay for a modern financial system from which everybody benefits. Other Christian economists might conclude that regulation is the solution to the problem in order to restrict the activities of banks.

However, there is, I believe, a strong *a priori* case that there should be effective legal mechanisms to make banks financially accountable for their mistakes so that bail-outs would no longer take place. It can be argued that justice demands that those who make mistakes and who provide finance to banks should bear the cost of those mistakes. It is also the case that, if they do bear the cost of those mistakes, the self interest of the participants within financial markets will run with the grain of the interests of society as a whole. This is because the incentives will exist for providers of capital to banks to be prudent and make decisions that add value for both consumers and financial institutions. Indeed, a precondition for a reasonably efficient economy is that participants in markets bear the costs of the decisions that they take. In the particular case of the banking industry, the implicit guarantee that the government provides to financial institutions is likely to lead them to indulge in more risky behaviour and lead financial institutions to grow larger and less personal – especially if larger institutions are more likely to be bailed out.

Thus, whilst Catholic social teaching does not lead unequivocally to this conclusion, I believe that there is a strong *prima facie* case for giving serious consideration to mechanisms that ensure the orderly winding up of financial institutions that are facing insolvency.[5] It is therefore perhaps surprising that Pontifical Council for Justice and Peace (2011) proposed a worldwide bail-out fund for large financial institutions that failed. Surely, both justice and good economics demand that we find safe ways to wind up banks that have failed. It is partly the continual bailing out of financial institutions – especially in the US – that leads to reckless and imprudent behaviour and the growth of ever-larger financial institutions. Do we want a world bailout fund that would enable JP Morgan and Goldman Sachs to compete unfairly with the smaller players?

Indeed, this observation provides a potential application of one of the proposals in the Justice and Peace Commission's document that was instantly dismissed by many commentators. The document called for an international financial regulatory authority, but the details were not at all clear. There are, of course, many international regulatory authorities in the field of finance and banking and it is a moot point whether they contributed to the crash. There could, however, be a role for such an international authority in *co-ordinating legal systems* to ensure that banks operating on a transnational basis could be wound up when they get into trouble. This might have helped deal, for example, with the Icelandic banking crisis. This

---

[5] See the chapter by Lilico in Booth (ed.) (2010) on the Christian aspects of this issue and an excellent paper by Lilico (2011) on the economics of this subject.

would seem to be completely compatible with long-enunciated principles of Catholic social teaching as it would both assist in providing the necessary legal framework within which the financial system operated whilst not directly regulating the sector – something that Catholic social teaching argues is not primarily the responsibility of the state, still less global bodies.

## The provision of credit – is credit a Christian issue?

There has been widespread concern that the availability of credit was one of the causes of the financial crash. The Archbishop of Canterbury also took up this theme in the *Guardian* article referred to above, saying: 'A badly or inadequately regulated market is one in which no one is properly monitoring the scarcity of credit. And this absence of monitoring is especially attractive when governments depend for their electability on a steady expansion of spending power for their citizens.'

It is certainly legitimate for Christians to raise the problem of credit as a potential public policy issue. Though it is not just a public policy issue – it is a moral issue too. Indeed, it is extraordinary how rarely the moral aspect of the subject is mentioned by clergy when giving pastoral advice to their flock.[6] The over-extension of credit may happen, of course, as a result of somebody finding themselves in very difficult circumstances through no fault of their own. But, notwithstanding this, indebtedness

---

[6]   US churches and some of the evangelical churches in the UK are exceptions.

creates a potential situation of dependence on others and, in many cases, will imply an attachment to material goods. Prudent behaviour, not becoming attached to material goods to such an extent that huge debts are incurred, and so on, are virtues that should be cultivated at all times. Furthermore, good pastoral advice might also encourage saving – though not simply for the sake of accumulation. Saving reduces our reliance on others in old age, in the event of unemployment, etc. Saving is also a discipline which, by its nature, requires us to *wait* for material goods. It also provides capital that enables an economy to thrive.

Nevertheless, what might Christians contribute to the public policy debate on the market economy? The Archbishop of Canterbury blamed the problems of credit expansion on a badly or inadequately regulated market and on governments wishing to expand the spending power of their citizens in order to be re-elected. He seemed to be implying that it is possible for some kind of omniscient being to decide how much credit should be granted. However, one of the main factors in the expansion of credit was the way in which monetary policy was conducted by the US Federal Reserve Bank and, to a more limited extent, by the Bank of England in the UK. It is difficult to argue that this was pursued – certainly in the UK – to make economic conditions more favourable to the re-election of governments. Indeed, arrangements making the Bank of England independent in 1997 were designed largely to prevent government using monetary policy to create a credit boom for political ends. More pertinently, though, many actions were taken by the US government to facilitate the extension of credit to the poor and to underwrite mortgage lending in the US. Arguably, this was also a significant cause of the crash of 2008. This was done largely to try to improve housing conditions for the poor without using taxation directly. It was certainly a mistaken policy but it is notable that those who are calling for more regulation of markets today did not speak against the guarantee of housing finance for the poor in the run up to the crash. There is, nevertheless, no view on these matters that can be uniquely claimed as legitimate Catholic social teaching.[7]

Related to consumer credit, of course, is the question of usury which has concerned the Church throughout the ages. Catholic Church teaching on usury is formally documented and therefore changes in the doctrine – or, strictly speaking, changes in the application of the doctrine – are relatively easy to follow (see Charles, 1998, Woods, 2005 and Gregg, 2007 for discussions of Catholic interpretations of usury, interest, credit and money). Various interpretations of the concept of usury have applied at different times. These have included the charging of interest in any circumstances; the charging of interest when there is no sharing of risk by the lender; the charging of excessive interest to those who are vulnerable; and the charging of interest on the lending of money for which the lender has no use and which is

---

[7] Some Austrian-school economists would claim that fractional reserve banking is incompatible with good ethics and back up that view using the theories of early Catholic writers including the late scholastics (see De Soto, 2011).

not put to productive use by the borrower. The modern view on usury generally holds that that the charging of interest is not wrong in principle, especially where capital is put to productive use by the borrower. However, Christians may feel that loans that involve exploitation of somebody who is indebted or consumer credit transactions which do not involve lending being put to productive use are potential areas that may merit either voluntary restraint or legislative restrictions.

Of course, it does not follow that, simply because Christians regard a particular form of behaviour to be wrong, there should necessarily be legislative prohibitions on that behaviour. Indeed, Catholics involved in public life should understand the unintended consequences of legislation in any field. Legislators are not omniscient angels who can foresee all the implications of their actions. Furthermore, regulatory bureaus can become vested interests that work for their own benefit rather than for the common good or they can become captured by the firms they are supposed to regulate. Legislative caps on interest rates, for example, encourage black markets and the brutal enforcement of illegal contracts: indeed, prohibitions in many areas have led to dreadful unforeseen consequences. Proposals that have been made in the UK to limit mortgage lending as a proportion of income may well further encourage lying and dishonesty on mortgage proposal forms and this, in turn, will increase risks to lenders and increase interest rates for borrowers. Thus, once again, there is no unique position with regard to the government's role in regulation that is consistent with Catholic social teaching, even if we see behaviour of which we do not approve.

Views should, however, coalesce more on the moral aspects of certain forms of consumer credit. Both the morality of consumers over-extending credit and the morality of sales people deliberately tempting individuals with offers of credit knowing that the potential debtor is already over-extended are matters on which clear moral guidance can be given.

## Debt and equity finance

Interestingly, the Archbishop of Canterbury, in his *Guardian* article also called for a 'return to the primitive capitalist idea' of risk-sharing. Others have also pointed out that our monetary and credit systems confuse savings with money and discourage people from taking risks with their savings.[8] This, in turn, means that debt finance tends to be more easily available to entrepreneurs than equity finance. If debt finance is more easily available than equity finance it raises the probability that a business will go bankrupt. If this happens in the case of banks and related financial companies, there can be serious systemic effects.

The problems of debt finance are a key concern within the usury debate and equity finance is exempt from the prohibition on interest even within Islamic financial systems. As ever, these are matters for prudential judgement, about

---

[8]  Again, this is the basic position of the Austrian school of economics.

which different Christians could disagree. It is, though, worth mentioning that the taxation system in nearly all developed countries strongly discourages equity finance and encourages debt finance. Perhaps this is something which, if it once served the common good (a doubtful proposition itself), no longer does so and should be the focus of policy action. One of the obstacles to dealing with this problem, however, is that there tends to be intellectual hostility on the left to the idea of making profits – as such, governments find profits easier to tax than interest, something which may cause great damage.

## Government borrowing

It is interesting that Christian commentators seem to be much more sanguine about the problem of government borrowing than they are about private borrowing. Private borrowing is generally undertaken to allow people to spread their consumption over their lifetime – thus many of us borrow to buy a house, for example. The effects of private borrowing are generally beneficial and benign though, of course, there are exceptions. Government borrowing, on the other hand, normally involves one generation outspending its income and imposing the burden on a future generation, without that future generation having any say in the matter. At times – for example, Japan in the current era and South American governments in earlier decades – such government borrowing imposes a burden on future generations that is potentially crippling. It is legitimate to ask whether many EU governments and the US are going down that path today.

Most would agree that there are some reasons for government borrowing that do not raise public policy issues of a particularly Christian nature. For example, the government may wish to borrow during a period of temporary economic downturn or in emergencies such as wartime. However, the structural budget deficits of the UK, the rest of the EU, Japan and the US do not fall into those categories.

The problem of government borrowing certainly passes at least one of Townsend's tests of whether a subject might be a legitimate area for public policy intervention: future generations may be prevented from participating in the common good because of the burdens placed upon them by the current generation. Whilst this issue is not sufficiently clear cut to suggest that there is an *a priori* case in Catholic social teaching for, for example, constitutional rules to prevent government borrowing, we should certainly consider this possibility. One of the weaknesses of a democracy is that it allows current generations to impose financial obligations on future generations (who cannot vote) and some constraint on such decisions would be justifiable. It is surprising, though, that there has been so little comment about the problem of structural budget deficits amongst all the concern expressed about private borrowing by Christians.[9]

---

[9] Interestingly, Archbishop Rowan Williams did criticise increases in borrowing caused by the recession but not the structural deficit, but he is one of the few people to have mentioned the issue at all. Interestingly, also, there is much Christian comment and comment in Catholic social teaching about

## 'New' financial institutions and Christian social movements

Catholic social action is not primarily about changing public policy. There is a long history in the Catholic Church[10] of social movements in the fields of health, education and also in financial and insurance services. These social movements do not only serve Christians and they may or may not be based around profit-making institutions. Such movements were discussed in Pope Benedict's encyclical *Caritas in veritate.*[11] Credit unions are perhaps the best-known current example of financial institutions with a Christian foundation that lie outside the mainstream proprietary sector in the UK.

Professor Stefano Zamagni[12] has summarised very effectively how these institutions of civil society promote well-being – not just material well-being – but are also not profit-maximising proprietary firms. Profit maximising institutions in the market economy have contractual obligations and agreements as their *modus operandi*. Charitable organisations have love at their heart: we do charitable acts expecting nothing in return. Governmental action has coercion at its heart: if I do not pay my taxes I go to prison. On the other hand, the institutions of civil society have reciprocity at their heart: individuals and communities perform acts for each other without contractual obligations,

the inter-generational effects of environmental problems.
[10]   As in other Christian denominations.
[11]   Especially in section 3.
[12]   Zamagni advised the Pope during the writing of *Caritas in veritate* and probably particularly influenced section 3.

altruism or coercion defining all aspects of those actions. This is the basis of friendly societies, mutual building societies and credit unions many of which have been important in UK financial markets at different times.

In the financial sector, the economic issues surrounding such institutions can be complex. Sometimes there will be an aspect of charity involved in their management: people give their time to the management of credit unions freely, for example. Sometimes, the institution will make some profits and its employees will be paid but it will have a particular ethos, such as wishing to remain small and rooted in the community.

Because trust is so important in ensuring that the financial system functions properly, there will often be significant economic benefits from institutions where supporters and members have a common bond and a sense of trust between them, though this can limit their size. Institutions built on reciprocity might be expected to thrive in this context. It can be difficult to distinguish between the exercise of Christian fraternity, charity and self interest in such organisations. However, it is not necessary to make such distinctions as these financial institutions arise to meet human need – whether they are primarily motivated by charity, fraternity or self interest, or some combination, is beside the point.

There is general agreement about the importance of these forms of institution. Many Christian socialists favour them; as has been noted, these institutions were explicitly mentioned in *Caritas in veritate*; they find favour with supporters of a free economy; and they find favour with the Catholic distributist movement.[13]

Interestingly, distributists argue that market economies lead inexorably to large uncompetitive firms crowding out social movements and institutions of civil society that can provide financial and other services. There is, however, little empirical evidence in support of this position. Proponents of a free economy recognise that a free economy does not just involve profit-maximising business corporations acting within markets. In our free economic and social lives, we can interact with a huge range of institutions with a wide range of different objectives and motivations. Whilst there are technical reasons why financial institutions have grown bigger and have thus have been more likely to use the proprietary form of organisation, some of the institutions of civil society (particularly in the insurance field) have disappeared simply because the government has taken over their function. Friendly societies, for example, arose because they were effective at monitoring and helping claimants in the mass provision of health, unemployment and disability insurance: these functions have been taken over by the state.

In addition, serious research suggests that the hugely increased level of financial regulation in recent decades also played a major part in making our financial scene look more uniform. In the days before regulation and government guarantees for financial institutions, such institutions had to demonstrate to those using them that they

---

[13]   Perhaps best represented by Phillip Blond at the current time in the UK.

were 'sound'. They no longer have to do so – the regulator has taken over that function. Before the days of extensive financial regulation, many financial institutions remained relatively small, rooted in the community and owned by their member-customers. Life insurance companies were often owned by their policyholders, as some still are, as a way to avoid conflicts of interest between owners and policyholders: these conflicts are now managed by statutory regulation. Thus, the institutions of civil society often performed the function of signalling trust and reliability and this function has been taken over by regulation. In addition, the increased volume of regulation also makes it more difficult for new entrants to come into the market and compete with the existing giants – there are huge economies of scale in the costs of complying with the thousands of pages of statutory financial regulation. Large institutions have also been given additional implicit guarantees by the state that smaller institutions do not get as we have discussed above.

Therefore, although there is widespread agreement about the need for financial institutions with a different ethos, different corporate forms and objectives, we do have to consider the political, legal and regulatory framework that will allow such organisations to thrive. Christian economists' perspectives can complement philosophical and anthropological observations about the importance of the institutions of a civil society and might help us understand how they can once again be nurtured.

## Conclusion

In two of his first three encyclicals, Pope Benedict XVI stressed the necessity for all social action to have the correct moral orientation. These ethical issues are of crucial importance in our response to the crash as Christians.

Arguably, ethical failings were not the main cause of the crash – though they may have contributed. It is also likely that ethical compasses were severely distorted by the perception of government bailouts and certain aspects of regulation.[14] But, there is a sense in which none of this matters. Ethical behaviour should not just be reserved for occasions when we think it will have a profound impact on the success of the financial system. Every 'liar loan', every transaction undertaken by a trader in his own interest rather than in his company's interest, every loan that is 'oversold' to a consumer who cannot afford to repay it, and so on has its effects on others. Furthermore, a breakdown in trust amongst those working within the financial system seriously degrades its operations.

In general, however, if the goal is a higher standard of ethical behaviour, government regulation is the wrong instrument. Immorality requires a change of heart not a change in the law. If immorality and unethical behaviour abounds, one cannot assume it will not pervade regulatory bureaus. It is certainly a mistake to have, as a default position, the view that more regulation is the answer to problems

---

[14]   See 'Ethics alone will not prevent financial crises', Philip Booth, *Financial Times*, 12 November 2009: http://www.ft.com/cms/s/0/49310344-cfb6-11de-a36d-00144feabdc0.html

in financial markets – human institutions cannot be perfected by giving power to other human institutions.

Christians generally will argue that the particular policy responses to the crash are matters reserved for prudential judgement: two Christians of goodwill could legitimately disagree about the appropriate action to be taken. However, it is important that we have a public policy framework that works with the grain of human nature so that, when making ethical judgements, we are not pushing water uphill. The policy framework must, of course, promote the common good – that is, as far as it can, allow human flourishing. It is also important that we recognise the limitations of public policy in terms of its ability to perfect the world. Nevertheless we should be questioning a policy framework that affords special privileges to providers of capital to large financial institutions, that penalises the provision of equity versus debt capital and that makes it difficult for alternative financial institutions to establish themselves. One of the dilemmas, of course, is that this alternative framework, though it will give rise to a marketplace that is richer in many dimensions, may give rise to more failures of financial institutions, even if such failures have fewer systemic effects. However, Christians would be ill advised to follow the modern trend of trying to eliminate risks and failure – the pursuit of perfection in this respect may well be the enemy of the good: perhaps, indeed, the enemy of the common good.

## References

Booth, P. M. (ed.) (2009), *Verdict on the Crash: causes and policy implications*, Hobart Paperback 37, London, UK: Institute of Economic Affairs.

Booth, P. M. (ed.) (2010), *Christian Perspectives on the Financial Crash*, London, UK: St Pauls.

Charles, R. (1998), *Christian Social Witness and Teaching: The Catholic Tradition from Genesis to Centesimus Annus*, Leominster: Gracewing.

De Soto, J. (2011), 'Economic recessions, banking reform and the future of capitalism', *Economic Affairs*, 31.2.

Gregg, S. (2009), *The Commercial Society: foundations and challenges in a global age*, Maryland, USA: Lexington.

Lilico, A. (2011), *Bank Creditors, Moral Hazard and Systemic Risk Regulation*, London, UK: Policy Exchange.

Pontifical Council for Justice and Peace (2005), *Compendium of the Social Doctrine of the Church*, London: Burns & Oates.

Pontifical Council for Justice and Peace (2011), *Towards reforming the international financial and monetary systems in the context of global public authority*, Rome: Pontifical Council for Justice and Peace.

Spencer N. and J. Chaplin (2009), *God and Government*, London, UK: SPCK.

Woods, T. E., Jr (2005), *The Church and the Market: A Catholic Defense of the Free Economy*, Lanham, MD: Lexington.

Part Three

# SUBSIDIARITY AND SOLIDARITY –
# THE ROLE OF THE INDIVIDUAL, THE
# COMMUNITY AND THE STATE

# 14

# THE SOCIAL TEACHING OF BENEDICT XVI

*Samuel Gregg*

## Introduction

Most pontificates, however short or long, tend to be dominated by particular themes that shape much of its teaching. The magisterium of Paul VI, for example, was dominated by the motif of a Catholic dialogue with modernity. Likewise John Paul II's long reign consistently underscored the idea of the importance of authentic Christian anthropology and its application to a range of contemporary political, social, cultural and economic problems. In each case, these reflected long-standing concerns of both men which they brought to the office of the successor of Peter.

In the case of Benedict XVI's pontificate, the dominant themes were clear from its very beginning. As a young theologian, Joseph Ratzinger was interested in the idea of renewing the Catholic Church through returning to the original sources of Christian inspiration, most notably Sacred Scripture, Tradition and the Church Fathers. Associated with this endeavour were a number of influential twentieth-century Catholic theologians including Henri de Lubac SJ, Hans Urs von Balthasar, Jean Danielou SJ, and Jorge Medina Estévez. This movement of 'return' to the sources – commonly referred to by the French term *ressourcement* – was considered essential by Ratzinger if the 'updating' of Church practices (sometimes described as *aggiornamento*) was to be consistent with Catholic faith. Ratzinger and his colleagues were not interested in constructing a Catholic ghetto or somehow returning to the Middle Ages. Nor were they dismissive of the insights offered, for example, by modern sciences such as physics or economics. They were, however, convinced that unless the Catholic Church spoke *in distinctly Christian terms*, the uniqueness of Christ's message was bound to be lost.

Another cluster of theologians, however, had a different starting point. They argued that Church renewal meant looking to the modern world for guidance. It included figures such as Edward Schillebeeckx OP, and Hans Küng. On one level, they were concerned with making the Christian message comprehensible to self-consciously 'modern' people. But most eventually went further and argued that the modern world itself contained the hermeneutic for how Christians should engage the earthly city and even defined what it meant to be Christian.

The problem with this approach is that it quickly degenerates into a set of circular propositions such as the following: the modern world (as defined by, for example, Hans Küng) says that equality à la John Rawls or Karl Marx is the content of justice; the modern world defines Christian self-understanding; therefore the Christian concern for justice should be Rawlsian or Marxist in nature. In this schema of reasoning, there is no obvious way of testing whether a particular modern proposition accords with Divine Revelation because the modern world itself is regarded as somehow summarising the content of Revelation. In effect, whatever is considered to be modern – and, more disturbingly, whoever sets himself up as defining the content of modernity – becomes the arbiter of what is and is not Christian.

A deep awareness of these problems was central to Joseph Ratzinger's long and ultimately successful struggle against Marxist versions of the now largely-defunct liberation theology. When we look, for example, at the documents on liberation theology produced by the Congregation for the Doctrine of the Faith in the 1980s (as well as independent articles authored by Ratzinger on the subject), we soon discover that neither these magisterial texts nor Ratzinger had much to say about the precise policy implications of liberation theology (which were in any case rather vague). Instead they concentrated on the ways in which liberation theologians departed from, and often directly contradicted, orthodox Christian belief about subjects such as the person of Jesus Christ, the nature and purpose of the Church, the origin and character of sin, the interpretation of Scripture, and the understanding of the place of the poor in Christian theology and practice.

Upon becoming Pope, Benedict XVI's *ressourcement* approach was quickly brought to bear upon almost every question that he believed the Magisterium needed to address. Whether the subject was the ends and character of liturgy or the origins and nature of international law, Pope Benedict's method was primarily one of asking what insights into a given question arose from the sources of Christian Revelation. A significant effect of this method when it came to social and political issues was to allow Benedict's social teaching to offer perspectives on a range of thematic and policy issues that do not fit easily into contemporary secular category oppositions of left versus right, progressive versus conservative, or liberty versus equality. This is especially apparent in Benedict's treatment of a key issue around which Catholic social teaching has revolved: the nature of justice and its implications for human relationships, especially in the economy.

## Justice, truth and love: a 'trinity of principles'

The question of justice has been a perennial concern of Catholic social ethics, both before and after Leo XIII's *Rerum novarum* (1891). In part, this reflects elaboration upon the commandment to love thy neighbour as well as a number of principles found in Sacred Scripture such as the prohibition against theft. By the Middle Ages, Catholic theologians had identified three categories of justice: legal justice (what the citizen owes in fairness to the community); distributive justice (the manner according to which goods and services are distributed to individuals and groups on the basis of criteria such as need, merit, function, desert, etc.); and commutative justice (what primarily concerns strict observance of promises and contracts into which people have freely and reasonably entered). The term 'social justice' entered into usage within Catholic social ethics in the nineteenth century. The content of social justice, however, is very similar to that which the Catholic Church has traditionally associated with the common good insofar as social justice is concerned with providing 'the conditions that allow associations or individuals to obtain what is their due, according to their nature and their vocation' (CCC, 1928).

The precise relationship between these different modes of justice has received considerable attention from Catholic thinkers over the centuries. If anything, this attention to justice intensified in the twentieth century. This partly reflected perceived injustices in the distribution of wealth within nations and between the developed and developing worlds. After the Second Vatican Council, Catholic involvement in movements for justice arguably intensified. Entire religious orders, for example, made the pursuit of social justice (often vaguely or incorrectly defined) their primary concern, even regarding it as taking priority over evangelisation. By the 1980s and 1990s, it is arguable that the concern for justice constituted the very essence of the Catholic faith for a good number of Catholic social justice activists, with core Catholic dogmas and doctrine being simultaneously 'relativised' or ignored altogether. In many instances, the situation was exacerbated by the fact that the understanding of justice prevailing among the same Catholics had more in common with that of the left-liberal philosopher John Rawls or the decidedly materialist understanding of justice found in Karl Marx's thought than with the visions of St Augustine and St Thomas Aquinas.

There is no question that Benedict XVI believed that justice in all its forms – legal, distributive, commutative, and social – must be a central concern for any serious Christian. Indifference to genuine injustices is simply not an option. Yet Pope Benedict is acutely aware that not every understanding of justice is compatible with the Catholic faith. Nor does the identification of an injustice, be it relational or systematic in nature, automatically suggest how it is best addressed.

Rather, however, than enter into the details of these matters – many of which fall very much into the realm of prudential judgment – Benedict's social teaching primarily dwelt on how specifically Christian insights should shape the Catholic concern for justice. As noted in Chapter 16, Benedict's first encyclical *Deus caritas est* (2005) underscored the limits of the state's efficacy in dealing with problems of injustice. In part, this reflected Benedict's Augustinian appreciation of the fact that the state, like everything else, bears the mark of sin. Nonetheless, Benedict was also determined to remind Christians that the virtue of love – which is ultimately a theological virtue – must inform, and in many ways take precedence over, the pursuit of justice. Love of neighbour, Benedict insists, propels us beyond the limits of what is strictly owed to others. Moreover, love reminds us that all humans have needs that cannot be met by the strict fulfilment of justice. Many human needs only find an answer in 'loving personal concern'.

*Caritas in veritate* (2009) takes this theme further, but invests it with even more theological significance. At the very beginning of the encyclical, Benedict observes that Sacred Scripture, Tradition, and the Church Fathers tell us that Jesus Christ reveals himself simultaneously as *Agápe* and *Lógos* (CV 3). 'Love – *caritas* – is an extraordinary force which leads people to opt for courageous and generous engagement in the field of justice and peace. It is a force that has its origin in God, Eternal Love and Absolute Truth' (CV 1). As if to ensure that his readers do not miss the importance of this point, the Pope adds:

> Charity is at the heart of the Church's social doctrine. Every responsibility and every commitment spelt out by that doctrine is derived from charity which, according to the teaching of Jesus, is the synthesis of the entire Law (cf. Mt 22:36–40). It gives real substance to the personal relationship with God and with neighbour; it is the principle not only of micro-relationships (with friends, with family members or within small groups) but also of macro-relationships (social, economic and political ones). For the Church, instructed by the Gospel, charity is everything because, as Saint John teaches (cf. 1 Jn 4:8, 16) and as I recalled in my first Encyclical Letter, 'God is love' (Deus caritas est): everything has its origin in God's love, everything is shaped by it, everything is directed towards it. Love is God's greatest gift to humanity, it is his promise and our hope. (CV 2)

A number of consequences flow from this. The first is the need to be aware that the Christian concern for justice arises from very different sources than the understandings of justice found in the works of, for example, John Locke, Thomas Hobbes, Thomas Jefferson or John Rawls. The centrality of love to the Christian Gospel makes the Christian understanding of justice different from that of virtually every other religion or philosophical system. The second implication is that Christian love is not to be confused with sentimentalism or emotionalism. This is revealed by that other aspect of Christ as Absolute Truth and Divine Reason. Truth is central to the Christian vision of justice, and truth for the Christian is not determined by feelings or majority consensus. Truth – including moral truth – is regarded as knowable to the human mind through natural reason and, in all its fullness, the Divine Revelation of Jesus Christ.[1]

By drawing upon these ancient and eternally relevant conceptions of *who* Christ is, Benedict creates a powerful framework through which Christians can reflect upon justice. This reflective lens may be summarised in the following way. Justice that is not grounded upon truth inevitably becomes arbitrary, relativistic and thus an exercise in injustice. Justice delinked from truth becomes subject to the whim of the fashionable and the tyranny of the strong. Likewise, justice that closes itself to the ultimate horizons revealed by divine love can easily degenerate into a harsh formality that is deeply depersonalised and which denies the possibility of forgiveness and redemption. Justice

---

[1] This was the key message of Pope Benedict's speech to leaders of civil society at Westminster Hall in 2010: http://www.vatican.va/holy_ father/benedict_xvi/speeches/2010/september/documents/hf_ben-xvi_ spe_20100917_societa-civile_en.html

delinked from love also darkens our ability to see the one whom we help as truly our flesh-and-blood neighbour, weak and fallible like myself. While justice is 'an integral part of the love "in deed and in truth"' (CV 6), Christian love demands that we go beyond the demands of strict justice. Though, as Benedict writes, 'charity demands justice', it also 'transcends justice and completes it in the logic of giving and forgiving' (CV 6).

Of course, the Christian God *is* a God of Justice. Christ Himself assures us that there *will* be a final reckoning and that all of us will be judged. Not everyone will enter heaven (Mt 25: 31–46). But even more than justice, the Christian God is also the God of Mercy. Christ Himself reconciled justice and mercy by dying on the Cross. While his execution represented a just atonement for the sins of man, it was also an exercise in divine mercy because Christ took man's place on the Cross.

The positing of Christ as the ultimate dispenser of the justice that will truly settle all accounts also allows Benedict to incorporate a penetrating critique of utopian aspirations, from whatever source they come. This is central to Benedict's second encyclical *Spe salvi* (2007). As a Christian, Benedict understands that fallen humanity cannot realise perfect justice in this world: 'We can try to limit suffering, to fight against it', Benedict writes, 'but we cannot eliminate it' (SS 37). This Christian truth helps us to realise, like St Augustine, that what fallen humanity can achieve 'is always less than we might wish' (CV 78). But the same truth reminds us that, Benedict argues: 'The *earthly city* is promoted not merely by relationships of rights and duties, but to an even greater and more fundamental extent by relationships of gratuitousness, mercy and communion. Charity always manifests God's love in human relationships as well, it gives theological and salvific value to all commitment for justice in the world' (CV 6).

In a certain sense, these are not new Christian insights. The theological virtues of faith, hope and love have always been understood as giving new depth, meaning and teleological purpose to the classical virtues of prudence, justice, temperance and fortitude identified by the thinkers of antiquity as central to the good life. But Benedict's way of making this point is a classic example of the *ressourcement* method. Having reminded us of the unique significance of Christianity's stress upon love, he then uses this idea to show us how the good life and the good society is about far more than protecting rights (a concern that dominates contemporary secular public discourse) and fulfilling duties (about which rather less is said today, perhaps because many of us have been all too content to delegate our responsibilities to and for others to the state). Rights and duties are crucially important if a society is to merit the description of being a just community. Yet they are not enough for what Benedict XVI, echoing the language of Paul VI, calls 'integral human development'. This is nothing more and nothing less than the all-around flourishing of each and every person that is the summit of human freedom which is ultimately realised in the kingdom of heaven.

## Justice, truth and charity in the marketplace

Initially it might seem that Benedict's analysis of the relationship between justice, truth and love is primarily helpful for exploring some of the major philosophical debates that have occupied human minds since the beginning of human civilisation. But does it have implications for more mundane, but nevertheless important, matters such as the question of how to live the good life in the conditions of a market economy?

Perhaps one of the most important points missed by virtually all commentaries concerning the nature of *Caritas in veritate*'s treatment of the market economy is that Benedict appears to assume that markets are simply a given feature of the economic landscape in which, for the foreseeable future, most people will live. There is no suggestion that alternative economic systems, such as socialism or corporatism, ought to be contemplated. Even when Benedict discusses forms of business that differ in their approach to profit-orientated associations, he does not suggest that these should supplant the more traditional business model, let alone argue that the power of the state should be employed to realise such an end. Indeed a whole variety of business models is compatible with a free economy. It is the relationship between the state and human action in the economic sphere that determines whether an economy is free, not the particular business models that evolve. The Pope is helping his audience think about how economic life might further conform to the principles of truth, justice and love.

When it comes to the demands of truth, Benedict

is uncompromising: the market economy *cannot* be based on just any value-system: 'The economic sphere', the Pope reminds us, 'is neither ethically neutral, nor inherently inhuman and opposed to society. It is part and parcel of human activity and precisely because it is human, it must be structured and governed in an ethical manner' (CV 36). Against all relativists, of whatever political predisposition, Benedict maintains that market economies *must* be underpinned by commitments to particular basic moral goods and a certain vision of the human person if it is to serve rather than undermine humanity's common good: '*The economy needs ethics in order to function correctly* – not any ethics whatsoever, but an ethics which is people-centred' (CV 45).

From this standpoint, we see that Benedict does not regard the market or market exchanges as morally problematic in themselves. Indeed the Pope actually dismisses a number of common myths about domestic and global free markets. He describes, for example, as 'erroneous' the notion that the wealth of developed countries is predicated on the poverty of poor nations (CV 35). *Caritas in veritate* also decries how foreign aid can produce situations of dependency (CV 58) and notes the damage generated by protectionism (CV 42). 'In and of itself'. the Pope states, 'the market is not... the place where the strong subdue the weak. Society does not have to protect itself from the market, as if the development of the latter were *ipso facto* to entail the death of authentically human relations' (CV 36). What matters, Benedict claims, is the *moral culture* in which markets exists. At the heart of the economy are human persons. People whose minds are dominated by crassly hedonistic cultures will make crassly hedonistic economic choices. 'Therefore', Benedict comments, 'it is not the instrument that must be called to account, but individuals' (CV 36).

The consequences of a serious appreciation for truth for the moral culture within which modern market economies operate do not, however, stop here. For Benedict, it is a lens through which to assess ideas such as 'business ethics', 'ethical investing' and 'corporate social responsibility'. The notion that investment and business choices have a moral dimension is hardly new. Benedict does nevertheless stress that careful attention ought to be given to the precise understanding of morality underlying these schemes. He is very clear that an assessment should be made as to whether a given scheme's conception of morality is grounded in a confidence that truth – and not merely of the scientific variety – is knowable through reason (and, for the believer, faith). Merely labelling an investment scheme as 'ethical', Benedict notes, hardly tells us whether it is moral (CV 45).

Seriousness about truth, then, has serious importance for the choices made by producers, consumers and entrepreneurs in a market economy. At the same time, it is also clear that Benedict believes that any society that commits itself to integral human development ought to allow market-orientated relationships of exchange to be supplemented and undergirded (rather than replaced) by relationships based on charity and justice. Though commutative justice is central to assessing the justice of a given exchange (CV 35), Benedict affirms that this is compatible with an attention to the demands of love. For Benedict, love and justice are both ultimately derived from the same source – Jesus Christ. Nevertheless they are also shaped by somewhat different – without being contradictory – logics. Justice, the entire Catholic tradition maintains, is primarily about rendering to others what they are due, regardless of whether the mode is distributive, commutative, legal or social. The internal logic of love, however, is one of gift. As Benedict states, '*Charity goes beyond justice*, because to love is to give, to offer what is "mine" to the other' (CV 6). Put another way, the demands of commutative justice (or even the demands of distributive justice that can be realised not only through the state but also through associations of civil society) do not exhaust the content of our relationships with others that we encounter in the marketplace. Ultimately, 'if it is to be authentically human', Benedict writes 'economic, social and political development...needs to make room for the *principle of gratuitousness* as an expression of fraternity' (CV 34).

What might this mean in practice? To give an example, let us consider the workings of contract. The demands of commutative justice require me to fulfil all the implied, formal and reasonable promises that I freely make when I enter into a contract with others. Fulfilling the demands of commutative justice is essential if contracts are to perform their crucial coordinating and regulatory function in a market economy. But there is also a sense in which I can fulfil the demands of a contract in a legalistic manner whereby I do the bare minimum that is required. If, however, I strive to fulfil the commandment to love my neighbour, then in many instances, I will realise that I have the opportunity to go beyond these minimal requirements and give to the persons with whom I am contracting something that is in fact 'mine' to offer them, sometimes at no extra cost, and sometimes by voluntarily assuming an extra cost. It is even arguable that this occurs on a regular basis in many if not most contractual arrangements insofar as even the most tightly written contract presumes that the contracting parties are willing to extend each other a trust that no amount of expectation of commutative justice can generate on its own. As the Pope himself observes, '*Without internal forms of solidarity and mutual trust, the market cannot completely fulfill its proper economic function*' (CV 35).

For Benedict, it is not a question of somehow attempting to legislate the logic of gift into economic transactions. By definition, such policies would destroy the very nature of the gift since no gift can be compelled. Though Benedict does call for economic space for business enterprises that consciously seek to embody the logic of the gift (CV 46), such as non-profit enterprises associated with the economy of communion, his prime interest is in helping to make the realm of the economy an arena in which the virtue and habits of love of neighbour can be exercised alongside the demands of justice. Benedict, it seems, sees a strong link between all forms of justice – including commutative justice and love. He insists, for example, that 'I cannot "give" what is mine to the other, without first giving him what pertains to him in justice. If we love others with charity, then first of all we are just towards them' (CV 6). From this perspective, we may say that no amount of generosity can substitute for basic violations of commutative justice, such as failing to perform agreed-upon promises without reasonable cause.

## Hope, utopia, and eschatology

Though *Caritas in veritate* contains examples of the application of distinctly Christian ideas and emphases to a number of concrete situations, it would be a mistake to see this approach as typical of Benedict's social teaching. Benedict does make a number of prudential judgments about social and economic questions to which, like all prudential judgments offered by the Magisterium on any number of prudential policy questions, Catholics are not bound in conscience to adhere. But the emphasis of Benedict's social teaching does not lie upon making such suggestions. When it comes to social ethics, Benedict XVI is primarily concerned with helping Christians to rediscover the social implications of the ultimate horizon of Christian faith. This was central to his earlier disputes with the liberation theologians. Ratzinger took issue with the liberationists' understanding of eschatology and their tendency to reduce the kingdom of heaven to very earthly-focused utopian programmes. Much of the liberationist heresy, to Ratzinger's mind, lay partly in the liberation theologians' adoption of an understanding of hope that contradicted the classical Christian understanding of this theological virtue. The relevance of this point, however, is not confined to arguments about these largely defunct theologies. It has direct implications for justice in this world.

In *Spe salvi*, Benedict XVI argued that Christianity's insistence upon the hope and possibility of eternal life fundamentally re-orientated human history by saving pagan Europe from an understanding of life as essentially purposeless. Christianity encouraged people to view the world as one in which things made sense (SS 2). The same God who gave man hope of eternal life was understood to be a thoroughly rational deity – the *Lógos* – rather than a willful, capricious divinity. Thus astrology began giving way to astronomy, as humans accelerated their quest for truth, confident that humanity's existence was not the work of mere chance or a master clock-maker, but rather came from a God who was simultaneously Caritas and Veritas.

But Benedict then poses the question of what happens when Christian hope begins to fade from a society's cultural horizon. This, he suggests in *Spe salvi*, is what occurred when some Enlightenment thinkers, exemplified by the scientist-philosopher Francis Bacon, began to believe that human reason could eventually solve all of humanity's problems (SS 16–17). This ideology of progress, Benedict suggests, resulted in people imagining that ultimate justice – the Kingdom of God – could be realised on earth. Unfortunately, Benedict cautions, 'Anyone who promises the better world that is guaranteed to last for ever is making a false promise' (SS 24).

The French Revolution, Benedict holds, was the first political attempt to implement this ideology and it ended in bloodshed (SS 19). The same logic, he argues, was central to the Marxist project. In Benedict's view, Marxism could not help but leave behind 'a trail of appalling destruction' (SS 21). Marx, Benedict says, was virtually silent about the end-state of his promised heaven-on-earth because he 'forgot man and he forgot man's freedom' (SS 21). In other words, once we accept the reality of human liberty, we know that society can never be static, never perfect, and never completely just. There is no human-engineered 'end of history'. Ironically, Benedict states, Marxism's denial of liberty meant that its politics could never get beyond the 'dictatorship of the proletariat' phase. Thus, Benedict observes, 'having accomplished the revolution, Lenin must have realised that the writings of the master gave no indication as to how to proceed' (SS 21).

This linkage between eschatological hope, human justice, and human liberty has, from Benedict's standpoint, both 'positive' and 'negative' aspects. The 'negative' effect is to induce a sober Augustinian realism into how we think about justice in the temporal order. Though the Christian's hope in salvation through Christ's death and resurrection provides us with a sense of the eternal happiness of heaven that God offers us, Benedict draws upon St Augustine to point out 'we do not know the thing [eternal life] towards which we feel driven. We cannot stop reaching out for it, and yet we know that all we can experience or accomplish is not what we yearn for' (SS 12).

This means that while we ought to strive to make life more just, we should also be very wary of any impulse within ourselves or others that would lead us in the direction of attempting to realise the fullness of justice in the here-and-now. Utopia, as St Thomas More well knew when he gave his famous book its title, means 'no-place'. And that is where justice disassociated from an authentically Christian understanding of hope leads us: the no-place of relativism, despair, and tyranny.

This tension between what is possible for human beings, their desire for eternal happiness, and their inability to imagine eternal life in all its fullness is not the most satisfying of situations for humans to find themselves in. It is, however, part of the condition of living in a human world that, being human, can only prefigure the kingdom of heaven. Yet there is also a positive dimension to this conception of the relationship between the heavenly and temporal orders. This concerns human freedom. The anti-earthly utopian dimension of Benedict's thought also translates into a powerful concern for preserving and promoting human liberty that any aspiration for justice must take into account. Humans need space to make free choices. 'These decisions', the Pope insists, 'can never simply be made for us in advance by others – if that were the case, we would no longer be free' (SS 24). Obviously the Pope's understanding of liberty is not one of free will detached from natural reason and truth (i.e. the conception of freedom that prevails in most secular thought and among many self-identified 'liberal Christians'). His point, however, is to note that while the structures of justice are important and necessary, 'they cannot and must not marginalise human freedom' (SS 24). Any structure that 'could irrevocably guarantee a determined – good – state of the world' would mean denying 'man's freedom'. Hence, Benedict concludes, 'they would not be good structures at all' (SS 24).

Paradoxically enough, the same circumstances also create situations that actually allow space for a flourishing of the spiritual, moral and material goods that can be attained through human freedom. It permits, for example, 'every generation' to 'make its own contribution to establishing convincing structures of freedom and of good, which can help the following generation as a guideline for the proper use of human freedom' (SS 25). It also leaves us free to enter into relationships of love – including our relationship with the loving God – that, by definition, transcend and complete relationships of justice. Lastly, structures that respect rather than repress human freedom open up the path for authentic human flourishing to which all are called, but which each person must decide for themselves whether or not to choose. '*Integral human development*', Benedict reminds us, '*presupposes the responsible freedom* of the individual and of peoples: no structure can guarantee this development over and above human responsibility' (CV 17). No amount of structural change in the name of justice can possibly compensate for people freely choosing the good. This is especially the case if, as the Second Vatican Council teaches, our liberty should be the occasion for the spreading 'on earth [of] the fruits of our nature and our enterprise – human dignity, brotherly communion, and freedom' that contain intimations of the kingdom of Heaven and which will be taken up 'but freed of stain, burnished and transfigured, when Christ hands over to the Father: a kingdom eternal and universal, a kingdom of truth and life, of holiness and grace, of justice, love and peace' (GS 39).

The economist John Maynard Keynes is famous for many things, including the saying that 'in the long run, we are all dead'. The horizon of Benedict XVI's sense of the long-term is rather different. When it comes to social questions, Pope Benedict asks people to live their political and economic lives in the short, medium, and long-term as if living in the truth is *eternally* important, as if relative justice can be realised in this world, and to take seriously the commandment of love by seeing it as something that completes what justice alone cannot. A more radical message is different to imagine. It is, however, integral to the Christian Gospel.

## 15

# SUBSIDIARITY AND SOLIDARITY

*Denis O'Brien*

## Introduction

The concepts of subsidiarity and solidarity arose in the context of concern about the distributive implications, and the working conditions, in nineteenth-century economies, especially in northern Europe. While the full implications will be clear only from a detailed discussion, it will perhaps be helpful to indicate briefly what these terms mean.

By *subsidiarity* is meant the principle that responsibilities should be devolved to the lowest viable level – the individual if possible. This stems directly from the Christian concept that the individual is of overriding importance because the individual is unique, born with free will, and is of infinite value to God. The principle of subsidiarity is therefore rooted in a Christian understanding of the nature of the human person made in the image of God. By *solidarity* is meant the idea that no man is an island, and that mankind has the need and duty to bind together in common action to achieve aims that cannot be achieved by single individuals. Subsidiarity then requires that the smallest possible level of communality necessary to achieve a particular end should be employed. Action at state level is essentially a last resort. This is essentially because the Church has always favoured voluntary association, springing from individual decisions to act in conjunction with others. Action by the state carries with it a number of dangers, notably that the inescapably coercive character necessarily overrides individual decision-taking – and thus individual moral autonomy.

## Leo XIII and Pius XI

Leo XIII was alarmed by nineteenth-century economic developments, with the appearance of a huge urban proletariat, and a small wealthy class (*Rerum novarum*, 2). Unconsciously echoing J. S. Mill, he stressed that it was the poor that needed protection in the dangerous situation which had come about (RN 32). The rich were well able to protect themselves. He sought to work out remedies for these developments, in the context of Catholic teaching, in his great encyclical *Rerum novarum* of 1891; and he was followed 40 years later by Pius XI, who in his *Quadragesimo anno* of 1931 also sought remedies for the inequality he observed in industrial society (QA 25, 63).

Both popes were not merely clear but strongly emphatic that socialism provided no answer to the problems that had emerged. It was truly dangerous and based upon false premises (RN 3–12, 15). Socialism involved 'a remedy far worse than the evil itself, [which] would have plunged human society into great dangers' (QA 10). Capital and labour worked together and labour had no right to be the sole claimant on income (QA 53). Class conflict should be avoided, not fostered; at the same time, employees should be treated as equals by those who hired them (RN 16). Indeed, though a competitive labour market was legitimate, it was desirable to work towards a system of profit sharing and partnership (QA 64–5) (another unconscious echo of J. S. Mill – Mill, 1923 [1848]: 764–94).

Socialism was even worse than the evil that it purported to remedy; and at a time when members of the influential British left, notably George Bernard Shaw, were in denial over this, Pius XI referred trenchantly to the horrors of communist regimes. Where socialism had led to communism, the results had been terrible:

> Communism teaches and seeks two objectives: Unrelenting class warfare and absolute extermination of private ownership. Not secretly or by hidden means does it do this, but publicly, openly, and by employing every and all means, even the most violent. To achieve these objectives there is nothing which it does not dare, nothing for which it has respect or reverence; and when it has come to power, it is incredible and portentlike in its cruelty and inhumanity. The horrible slaughter and destruction through which it has laid waste vast regions of eastern Europe and Asia are the evidence; how much an enemy and how openly hostile to Holy Church and to God Himself is, alas, too well proved by facts and fully known to all. (QA 112)

Pius insisted that fundamentally socialism, even in its toned-down form, was irreconcilable with the teachings of the Catholic Church. 'Whether considered as a doctrine, or an historical fact, or a movement, Socialism, if it remains truly Socialism … cannot be reconciled with the teachings of the Catholic Church because its concept of society itself is utterly foreign to Christian truth' (QA 117).

The fundamental reason for this, which is indeed the key to the whole intellectual apparatus constructed by the popes, is that it is the individual who should be at the centre of consideration, and whose salvation provided the ultimate moral standard. The ultimate aim was the salvation of individual souls: 'Socialism, on the other hand, wholly ignoring and indifferent to this sublime end of both man and society, affirms that human association has been instituted for the sake of material advantage alone' (QA 118). The individual must never be regarded as a cog in a machine, with the guiding standard being instead some kind of measure of state achievement.

Leo began his encyclical with a forceful defence of private property as of central importance to the family, the family being the context of the individual (RN 5–7, 9–10, 35). In turn this was echoed by Pius XI (QA 44–5, 49). Recognition of the importance of private property in Catholic teaching goes back as far as Aquinas (RN 19), but it assumes much greater prominence in the two encyclicals. At the same time, possession of property, it was emphasised, was not an absolute right; its possession implied social obligations. But this did not justify collectivisation. The property right was fundamental (QA 46–7).

The state did have a role in providing good

government based upon moderate taxes and protecting the stable ordering of economic life (RN 26–35). But it should not interfere with families, except to alleviate distress (RN 11). This was stressed very strongly by Leo. Subsidiarity – the primacy of the individual – must be overriding. It was entirely wrong to interfere with it. But the same principle applied at every level of organisation from the individual upwards. 'Just as it is gravely wrong to take from individuals what they can accomplish by their own initiative and industry and give it to the community, so also is it an injustice and at the same time a grave evil and disturbance of right order to assign to a greater and higher association what lesser and subordinate organisations can do' (QA 79).

Precisely because the state was incapable of regulating itself, it must be hesitant about interfering (QA 88). Moreover, it was not the only source of material welfare when assistance was required; the Church had an important role as well (RN 24). Leo stressed that state intervention should go no further than was required to equilibrate a disequilibrium situation. Private interests were paramount. In particular, the state had no authority to swallow up either the individual or the family (RN 28–9). It could certainly help them in a crisis; but there was also an important role for charity in addition to the state (QA 137).

Both encyclicals, however, encouraged not only the establishment of trade unions – an exercise in worker solidarity – but also the development of labour laws. Leo's encyclical undoubtedly led to the development of these, and this was approved in turn by Pius XI (RN 34; QA 28). There was a natural right of association with which the state should not interfere (RN 37). At the same time many trade unions were socialist in orientation, with an emphasis on class conflict; and the popes looked to the development (which did follow) of Catholic trade unions (RN 38–44; QA 36).

Such an exercise in solidarity would in turn help to provide a level of wages which not only supported the family but (and this is of great importance in Leo's encyclical) provide also a sufficient margin for saving, leading to the accumulation of property by the wage earner (RN 35). Thus a more equal distribution of income would lead to a more equal distribution of property, something which both popes considered to be vital (QA 61–3, 74). In addition, and both popes stressed this as well, taxation should be at moderate levels in order to leave scope for saving and the acquisition of property (RN 35). This was designed to raise the welfare of the lower-income groups. According to Pius XI, 'it is grossly unjust for a State to exhaust private wealth through the weight of imposts and taxes' (QA 49).

The wage level had not only to be sufficient to leave a margin for thrift: it had also to be at a level to provide both for the employee *and his family*. (This comes out much more clearly in the encyclical by Pius XI; QA 71.) Women should not be forced to undertake paid work when they would prefer to nurture the all-important family.

The popes thus looked to reform rather than to an overturning of property rights. There is a root-and-branch condemnation of socialism; but acceptance of the operation of a market economy is qualified.

It was an absolutely fundamental requirement that the market should operate within a framework like that envisaged by the English classical economists, one of law, religion and custom, which limited the pursuit of self-interest through competition, in order to protect social interest (RN 26; QA 49, 88). Without this restraint, free competition was not acceptable. The market system was 'not of its own nature vicious'. But it was so if the owners of capital hired labour 'scorning the human dignity of the workers, the social character of economic activity and social justice itself, and the common good' (QA 101).

Nonetheless, *given* such a framework, there was no objection to increasing wealth in a just and lawful manner through the operation of the market system (QA 136).

## John XXIII and John Paul II

The themes in the encyclicals of Leo XIII and Pius XI were further developed in four major encyclicals in the second half of the twentieth century: *Mater et magistra* (1961) from John XXIII, and *Laborem exercens* (1981), *Sollicitudo rei socialis* (1987) and *Centesimus annus* (1991) from John Paul II. Socialism was again explicitly rejected; it was the individual who was of prime concern, the focus of attention and not a mere cog in a machine (CA 13). The class struggle was contrasted with the achievement of genuine social justice, which must be the aim (CA 14).

Social justice involved recognition of human rights to take private initiative, to property and to freedom in economic life (MM 109; LE 52; SRS 86; CA 24, 30, 31, 43). It was again argued that workers should be given scope to save in order to become property owners, and indeed the state should encourage widespread property ownership (MM 109, 115). As in the earlier encyclicals, ownership of property is qualified by the social obligations that it imposes (MM 119–20; CA 6, 30); but the right to own property is an important part of the consolidation of the power and initiative of the individual vis-à-vis the state (MM 105–9).

Nonetheless, and despite the fact that inequality should be reduced as prosperity increased (MM 73), there was a continuing need for solidarity, and individuals should recognise the need to commit themselves to social as well as individual aims. Solidarity was based upon the need to recognise a common humanity. In particular, the poor needed protection, and solidarity should help to provide this (SRS 38–40, 74–80; CA 10). Catholic trade unions should deploy countervailing power in this cause, rather than seeking to pursue a class struggle (MM 100–101; LE 26–7; CA 7, 15, 24, 34).

But solidarity extended beyond trade union activity to social reforms. Such reforms were achieved through employing the agency of the state (MM 60–61; CA 16); but John Paul II, like Leo XIII and Pius XI, stressed the priority of the individual, of the family and of society over the state (CA 11). The state should provide a framework, including labour laws; and it should provide things like unemployment relief (MM 52, 54; CA 15). But it should not seek to control individuals. The family, as the nurturer of individuals, and as the primary level of solidarity, had a key role (CA 39). Like earlier popes, John Paul II stressed that women should not be forced to enter the labour market and forsake their role as the centre of the family (SRS 69; CA 8, 34, 43).

All this, then, involves a forceful restatement of the principle of subsidiarity. This principle is contrasted with its diametrical opposite, totalitarianism, of which John Paul had first-hand experience, first as a subject of the Nazis, and then of the communists. Totalitarianism was identified as the antithesis of subsidiarity (CA 44–5).

John Paul went well beyond his predecessors in asserting the efficiency of the *free market*. Although 'there are many human needs which find no place in the market', nonetheless, 'It would appear that, on the level of individual nations and of international relations, the *free market* is the most efficient instrument for utilizing resources and effectively responding to needs' (CA 34; emphasis in original).

Indeed, he pointed to the damage done by the suppression of the pursuit of self-interest. 'In fact, where self-interest is violently suppressed, it is replaced by a burdensome system of bureaucratic control which dries up the wellsprings of initiative and creativity' (CA 25).

Moreover, he stressed the importance of entrepreneurial ability. '[T]he role of disciplined and creative *human work* and, as an essential part of that work, *initiative and entrepreneurial ability* becomes increasingly evident and decisive' (CA 32; emphasis in original).

He recognised a legitimate role for profit. 'When a firm makes a profit, this means that productive factors have been properly employed and corresponding human needs have been duly satisfied' (CA 35).[1]

If individual economic initiative were suppressed, this harmed the common good. The damage occurred through a process of 'levelling down', and through dependency creation (MM 55–7; CA 13).

> In the place of creative initiative there appears passivity, dependence and submission to the bureaucratic apparatus which, as the only 'ordering' and 'decision-making' body – if not also the 'owner' – of the entire totality of goods and the means of production, puts everyone in a position of almost absolute dependence, which is similar to the traditional dependence of the worker-proletarian in capitalism. This provokes a sense of frustration or desperation and predisposes people to opt out of national life. (SRS 24)

Of course, it was necessary that the free market should operate within a framework of law, religion and custom, to distinguish it from raw capitalism. 'Economic activity, especially the activity of a market economy, cannot be conducted in an institutional, juridical or political vacuum' (CA 35, 48).

In the choice of an appropriate economic system, the presence or otherwise of such a framework was decisive. In considering whether 'capitalism' should be the way forward, this was the key issue:

> If by 'capitalism' is meant an economic system which recognises the fundamental and positive role of business, the market, private property and the resulting responsibility for the means of

---

[1] The role of profit as a resource allocation signal seems to be recognised here.

production, as well as free human creativity in the economic sector, then the answer is certainly in the affirmative, even though it would perhaps be more appropriate to speak of a 'business economy', 'market economy' or simply 'free economy'. But if by 'capitalism' is meant a system in which freedom in the economic sector is not circumscribed within a strong juridical framework which places it at the service of human freedom in its totality, and which sees it as a particular aspect of that freedom, the core of which is ethical and religious, then the reply is certainly negative. (CA 42)

John Paul stressed that such limits could be at the level of subsidiarity through the exercise of consumer choice (CA 36). He explicitly mentioned drugs and pornography as things through which consumers, by not choosing them, could help to limit the operation of the market for the better. A sense of solidarity could also temper the profit motive (SRS 38). Insofar as the framework of economic activity involved legislation, it must involve sovereign law, which could not be subverted by the arbitrary will of individuals (CA 44). In this he was unconsciously echoing Adam Smith (1979 [1776]: 825–6); but the lessons, no doubt learned in communist Poland, are of far wider application in an era when tax authorities seek to make retrospective changes to tax regimes.

The role of the state is thus carefully circumscribed. In particular both John XXIII and John Paul II warned against the excessive development of the welfare state. Such development offends against the principle of subsidiarity. Indeed, according to John Paul it posed the danger of the 'social assistance state'.

> In recent years the range of such [state] intervention has vastly expanded, to the point of creating a new type of State, the so-called 'Welfare State' ... However excesses and abuses, especially in recent years, have provoked very harsh criticisms of the Welfare State, dubbed the 'Social Assistance State'. This development is the result of an inadequate understanding of the tasks proper to the State. Here again the *principle of subsidiarity* must be respected: a community of higher order should not interfere in the internal life of a community of a lower order, depriving the latter of its functions. (CA 48; emphasis in original)

John XXIII warned too of the danger of creating dependency (MM 63–5). This was unacceptable, because it made the individual permanently subservient to the state and its decisions.

Thus we return to the idea that the state can assist, but must not take over, people's lives. It can support and coordinate, but it must not directly interfere (CA 48, 49).

It can legitimately provide public goods (CA 40). These include justice, and sound money, both of which are mentioned by several popes. But the scope for public goods may be rather constrained by the discovery that the category itself is far more limited than had previously been thought – in particular there is the famous case of lighthouses, endlessly invoked by economists as a classic case of a public good that turns out to have been initially provided largely by private enterprise (Coase, 1974).

## The economic model

The basic model which emerges from all this is remarkably similar in a number of aspects to that found in the writings of the British classical economists. This is a parallel which the popes would not have recognised; it is evident that they believed northern Europe to be in the grip of an extreme form of laissez-faire. German economists, as devotees of what they regarded as a morally superior *Sozialpolitik*, caricatured English classical economics as advocating an extreme form of unregulated competition which they called 'Manchesterism' (Schumpeter, 1954: 765, 888); and this caricature seems to have been taken at face value south of the Alps.

Yet the basic model which emerges from the papal documents shares with the classical economists an emphasis upon security of property and decentralised decision-taking. In both cases the importance of individual initiative is stressed. The state should remedy defects in the competitive system as they emerge, but should not seek to take over the system. The labour market should respond to the preferences of individuals, not only in the provision of acceptable working conditions – stressed from Leo onwards – but also, and even more fundamentally, in not forcing women out of the home and into the labour market. Taxes should be at a moderate level (see also Chapter 6); this is consistent not only with the idea of encouraging individual initiative, but also reflects the concern to allow a margin for capital accumulation. The diffusion of property, which is a major concern of the encyclicals, is also one which accords with the outlook of the classical economists, who certainly did not see capital accumulation as the preserve of just a few individuals in society, and who witnessed the rise of many individuals from humble origins to commercial success.

At the same time, while stressing the importance of legal and other frameworks for economic activity, the papal encyclicals are strong in their objections to state encroachment on individual activity, and emphasise that state assistance should be temporary and not become a permanent feature of economic activity. This has a parallel in the agonising of the classical economists over the Poor Law in England and Wales.

Again, while the classical economists fully recognised the need for a legislative framework for economic activity, they were very wary of direct state involvement outside limited areas, such as the provision of the currency. This accords with the outlook of the encyclicals. Indeed, Pius XI emphasised in 1931, decades before neoclassical economists had got away from the idea of the benevolent, omniscient state, that the state has one fundamental weakness above all in the economic sphere – it is incapable of regulating itself.

The emphasis by John Paul II on the supremacy of the rule of law, with its implication that economic activity must take place within a framework that is certain and not arbitrary (something which has come under threat in Britain in the last few years with the emergence of retrospective tax changes), is entirely in accord with Smith's view in the

*Wealth of Nations*, one which was accepted by his successors. It is a corollary of the idea that security of property is vital, this in turn springing from the concept of the central role of the individual.

There are other aspects of the encyclicals which sit less easily with the liberal model. For instance, the social obligations of property ownership are mentioned from 1891 onwards, yet remain undefined and vague. The idea does, however, seem to reflect an aversion to the concept of the grim-faced entrepreneur, and a desire not only for harmonious relations in the workplace but also for profit-sharing and for cooperative enterprise. While this would have reflected the preferences of J. S. Mill, it cannot be said that Mill's views have enjoyed widespread support among economists or that cooperative enterprise has a particularly glorious history – or indeed that it necessarily provides better conditions for employees. Moreover, the emphasis on the encouragement of trade unions, entirely understandable as it was in 1891, and indeed in 1931, may seem a little strange to those who lived through the 1970s, particularly in Britain. But this may be something which can be interpreted in terms of the distinction in the encyclicals of Leo XIII and Pius XI between the activities of Catholic trade unions and those of socialist ones.

In addition, the British trade unions had remarkable legal privileges, and enjoyed, by virtue of these, powers of compulsion which effectively altered their character from that of voluntary associations to ones enjoying state sponsorship.

## Lessons not learned – *Gaudium et spes*

Despite these problems, however, it is clear that the body of ideas worked out over a century provides an excellent guide to Catholic teaching on economic activity. It is then unfortunate that much of what was painstakingly built up seems to have dropped out of sight.

The starting point for this process would seem to be the document *Gaudium et spes* (1965), which was the product of the Second Vatican Council, and promulgated as *The Pastoral Constitution on the Church in the World of Today*. This document bears all the hallmarks of a committee document, and reflects very little of the carefully worked-out teaching previously discussed in this chapter. In particular it is imbued with 1960s corporatism, with an emphasis on state coordination, and with little emphasis indeed on the central concept of subsidiarity. It is clear that, where definitive statements are made on subjects such as economics and other social sciences, those making the statements have often gone outside their field of expertise and competence.

Though it defines the common good as individual fulfilment (GS 26), it does not relate this to concerns about the individual of the kind which informed the encyclicals of 1891 and 1931, and which were to be revived in the encyclicals of John Paul II. Sometimes the argument verges on the comic. At one point the reader is solemnly informed that 'Meanwhile every man goes on, obscurely recognising himself as an unanswered question' (GS 21).[2]

The document contains standard 1960s clichés about foreign aid (see also Chapter 4) and the arms race (GS 85–6). In connection with the former it becomes apparent that there is serious ambiguity concerning the concept of solidarity, one which also surfaces at some points in the encyclicals of John XXIII and of John Paul II (MM 157; CA 22, 28, 51).[3] For both they and the authors of *Gaudium et spes* interpret solidarity as the protection of poor countries by richer countries (GS 87–8). Solidarity then becomes a top-down, government-driven, political exercise, a view which is consistent with the general 1960s corporatist outlook of the document (GS 65).[4] In the encyclicals of Leo XIII and Pius XI, however, and elsewhere in the encyclicals of John XXIII and John Paul II, solidarity is a bottom-up concept, originating in voluntary action, not state intervention. It is rooted in recognition of a common humanity, not in the political equivalent of *noblesse oblige*. The initial expression of solidarity is the family. Next there

---

[2] This is not written with regard to economic or social teaching but in the context of the difficulties that may face man in his life on earth. But it is an example of the kind of language in this document which is unintelligible and not typical of papal documents.

[3] See also Paul VI, *Populorum progressio*, 43, 62–4.

[4] This not unnaturally attracted some astringent criticism, notably from Peter Bauer (Charles, 1998, vol. 2: 455). Bauer concentrates his fire on Paul VI's *Populorum progressio* (1976) and on the Pontifical Letter *Octogesima adveniens* (1971). He notes in particular the reliance on 'top down solidarity', grounded in the naive belief (once held by economists) that governments always work for the best, the 1960s conventionalism resulting in recommendations that were neither distinctively Christian nor distinctively Catholic, and observes witheringly that 'Envy is traditionally one of the seven deadly sins. Vocal modern clerical opinion endows it with moral legitimacy and intellectual respectability' (Bauer, 1984: 73, 76, 78, 87).

are associations for the promotion of particular objectives, and then the trade unions. Moreover, it is stated quite clearly that subsidiarity requires that, wherever possible, functions should be left with such low-level expressions of solidarity, and that the state should involve itself only where it is quite clear that these lower-level associations are not achieving desired aims.

In addition, *The Pastoral Constitution* appears willing to depart from papal teaching in the direction of what its authors believed to be new developments in social sciences. Thus the reader is assured that 'recent psychological studies explain human activity more deeply' (GS 54) and sociology is also recommended. Indeed, in view of what has recently been revealed about the role of psychology in bringing about the scandals that have afflicted the Church in the USA (Rose, 2002: 9, 31–40, 129–44), it is deeply disturbing to find that the authors of The *Pastoral Constitution* suggested that those teaching theology in seminaries should 'cooperate intellectually and practically with experts' in psychology and related subjects (GS 62). At the very least, it is now clear that the naivety exhibited by those involved in drafting *The Pastoral Constitution* should be rapidly discarded and, just as Pope John Paul II looked again at the economic theory underlying pronouncements in *Gaudium et spes* in his encyclical *Centesimus annus*, the time has come to look critically at its pronouncement on other aspects of social sciences.

## The Hierarchy of England and Wales

Local Bishops' Conferences produce statements from time to time on matters that are related to economics and politics. These statements are intended to guide the lay faithful and politicians in their thinking by setting out the view of the hierarchy on particular matters. In this section some statements made by the England and Wales Conference are examined, and it is saddening to discover that an outlook of the kind to be found in *Gaudium et spes* seems to have exercised a greater influence on the local hierarchy than the papal encyclicals that both preceded it and followed it. For various pronouncements of the England and Wales hierarchy on the one hand pay no more than lip-service to the concept of subsidiarity while, on the other, endorsing a wide range of contemporary clichés.

This is all the more surprising because the 1994 *Catechism of the Catholic Church* followed correctly the lines of the encyclicals.[5] The *Catechism* rejects socialism, as did the encyclicals (para. 2425), emphasises subsidiarity (paras 1883–5, 2209, 2424, 2431), the family (paras 2209, 2434), the framework of market activity (paras 2425, 2431), and the legitimacy of a profit reward (para. 2432). In particular, it emphasises the importance of the individual, and the danger of excessive intervention

---

[5] It is, however, rather interesting that neither *Rerum novarum* nor *Quadragesimo anno* is cited in the *Catechism*. This omission has only now been remedied with the publication by the Pontifical Council for Justice and Peace of the *Compendium of the Social Doctrine of the Church*. But full details of these and other encyclicals were available to the bishops in the magnificent study by Rodger Charles (Charles, 1998).

by the state, and explains that the principle of subsidiarity is opposed to all forms of collectivism and sets limits to state intervention (paras 1883–5).

Yet, in the pronouncements of the bishops of England and Wales, there is a generalised distrust of the market economy and little scepticism about the level of taxation which, as a proportion of national income, is five times the level in the UK in 1891, when Pope Leo warned against excessive taxation sapping enterprise. This approach may well reflect, in part, pressure from the Catholic left in Britain,[6] which has been very prominent in British public and Catholic intellectual life. In the contributions to the debate in the 1990s and early twenty-first century, subsidiarity is hardly mentioned. In this, the England and Wales hierarchy is faithfully reflecting the tone of *Gaudium et spes* (GS 75).

Indeed, the hierarchy, in contrast to mainstream Catholic teaching, seems to turn instinctively to paths involving taxation and the consequently inescapable state coercion. Documents produced by the hierarchy have disregarded voluntary association, despite the wealth of evidence concerning the good that this has done, especially

---

[6]  Thus, in response to the publication by the bishops of *Taxation for the Common Good*, a writer in the *Tablet* (as reported by the Catholic Communications Service, which, oddly, gives no precise source) claimed that 'Taxes pay for almost every amenity that makes life bearable in modern Britain', and concluded with a swipe at Mrs Thatcher. We should perhaps note, however, the irony of a body – the Church – supported by charitable donations, and thus exempt from tax on its income, being enthusiastic about tax. (It is interesting that the record of responses provided by the Catholic Communications Service included only favourable responses to the bishops' document.) Again, in *Vote for the Common Good* (Bishops' Conference, 2001: 5), we find the old canard about Britain having the highest prison population per head of population in Europe, whereas the relevant denominators are per criminal conviction or per crime.

in fields such as health and education. This is particularly marked in *Taxation for the Common Good*, which accepted without question the huge range of goods and services financed by taxation in the UK.

The bishops have also provided a ringing endorsement of EU enlargement in a document that is, more generally, highly supportive of the EU as an institution (Bishops' Conference, 2004: para. 1), apparently unaware that both the Rome (Article 3) and Amsterdam (Protocol 7) treaties explicitly endorse subsidiarity but that in practice this is conspicuous by its absence from the operations of the EU.

The Bishops' Conference document *The European Common Good* (ibid.) mentions more than once the opportunity that enlargement will give rich nations to transfer resources to poorer nations. In doing so it cites the apparent success of this strategy in assisting the development of Ireland. Yet the main spur to the development of Ireland was significant reductions in tax rates: the rapid rate of growth began about 25 years after Ireland entered the EU. Regional policy of the sort recommended by the document has simply not succeeded. More crucially, nowhere in Church teaching is the application of the principle of 'solidarity' intended to imply that rich nations should assist slightly less rich nations through the transfer of money taken from families through taxation. Assisting the very poorest countries to develop is a continual theme of papal teaching, but such countries are not members of the EU. The bishops are so concerned with 'global poverty and deprivation' that they have offered the view that considerations of this kind could affect whether a Catholic would vote for a pro-abortion candidate (Bishops' Conference, 2001: 3) – yet they fail to notice that the EU, through its trade restrictions and discrimination, is a major contributor to global poverty and deprivation (Bishops' Conference, 2003: para. 5), though there is a minor reference to the need for 'fairer trading conditions' in *The European Common Good*.

Not only is the EU credited with being a source of peace and prosperity (ibid.: para. 2) and EU travel held to have 'helped the UK immeasurably' (ibid.: para. 10) (hardly incontestable claims, and ones on which the bishops have no particular expertise), but in the debate surrounding the EU constitution, the hierarchy went as far as to hope that the proposed EU constitution would promote democracy (ibid.: para. 12). This aspiration is clearly at odds with the contents of the then-proposed constitution.

A possible, though contestable, case can be made that, for many countries in Europe, the EU and other European institutions have helped to preserve peace, democracy and justice. This, together with the importance of Europe's cultural and Christian heritage, has been a theme of both Pope Benedict and Pope John Paul II (see, for example, *Ecclesia in Europa*, 2003). The England and Wales Bishops' Conference statements may possibly be seen in that context. But there surely should be recognition that the political structures and economic policies of the EU are simply not conducive to implementing Catholic teaching on subsidiarity and solidarity.

Furthermore, the England and Wales Bishops' Conference documents go much farther in praising the economic agenda of the EU than the related papal documents.

The bishops appear untroubled by the profoundly secularist agenda of the EU, culminating not only in the refusal to acknowledge Europe's Christian heritage in the constitution, but in the refusal to confirm a European Commissioner in office simply because he was a Catholic who had *private* beliefs that the EU establishment regarded as unacceptable. Such an action, taken on the basis of the private religious beliefs of an individual, would be serious enough; but, in addition, and in contravention of the principle of subsidiarity, the political structure of the EU enables its officials to impose this secularist agenda on citizens of member nations through regulation.

But the absence of any discernible influence of the encyclicals on the England and Wales hierarchy's pronouncements up until recently was nowhere more apparent than in its treatment of the family. The importance of the family is a major theme in encyclicals and in the developed position of the Catholic Church on social and economic issues. It is also an urgent policy issue in the UK. Yet the England and Wales hierarchy has shown a solicitude for single mothers (Bishops' Conference, 2001: 3), and apparently sees no conflict between this solicitude and the need to strengthen family life.[7]

---

[7] Such solicitude is all the more surprising in the present context, given the well-documented bias of the tax and benefit system against marriage. In fairness it should be added that in a later election document (Bishops'

Again, there is little evidence in public statements that what many regard as the nationalisation of childhood taking place in Britain, a most flagrant violation of subsidiarity, concerns the hierarchy. Yet there is ever-more detailed state control, in accordance with the criteria of the left-liberal agenda, of the upbringing of children in Britain. This is coupled with the relentless pressure on women coming both from regulation and from the tax and benefits system to hand over the care of their children to nurseries (themselves the subject of considerable state control, including Ofsted inspections, even when privately owned). Nor is there any apparent concern that the complex tax and benefits system created in recent years has produced the kind of welfare dependency against which both John XXIII and John Paul II emphatically warned.

A further document that shows vividly how the England and Wales hierarchy have trodden in areas where they have no special expertise, have not properly applied the concept of subsidiarity and have not taken on board developments in economics that are compatible with subsidiarity is the bishops' document on the environment (Bishops' Conference, 2002). We are told (Section II) that the environment is breaking down, cities are afflicted by smog, and so on. The section continues to deplore the apparent scarcity of

<hr />

Conference, 2005) both the concern for single mothers and the possibility of voting, with implied episcopal approval, for a pro-abortion candidate do not appear. There is, however, little that is explicitly Catholic about the document and, in particular, the support for marriage and the family is justified not on grounds relating to Catholic teaching but by sociological criteria.

natural resources that is 'threatening international stability' and expresses concerns about global warming threatening the planet. All the policy proposals in the document relate to government and international action through regulation. Kyoto is particularly recommended (Section V).

Pronouncements on this subject are justified by an appeal to solidarity; but a consideration of subsidiarity might have alerted the bishops to the potential loss of national income, were countries honestly to implement the Kyoto agreement, which is hardly a trivial consideration when balancing the costs and benefits of different courses of action, particularly for the 27 per cent of the world's population who do not have access to electricity. For such people the absence of energy supplies rather than global warming is the most urgent problem. Furthermore, most indicators of environmental quality have been improving dramatically in the last 40 years in developed countries that have systems of secure property rights and market economies. Market economies use resources more efficiently, including environmental resources. They are able to access cleaner technologies that can deal with environmental problems as they arise. The price mechanism promotes conservation and the development of alternatives to finite resources in the face of scarcity. Perhaps most importantly, environmental exploitation is generally a symptom of property rights not being properly defined or enforced – rainforests being an outstanding example of this. A true appeal to subsidiarity would have identified this problem.

Instead, there is a single statement on property rights suggesting that *strict limits should be put upon private ownership*. Private ownership is vital for the safeguarding of the long-term sustainability of environmental resources. This can be seen from comparing the ability of privately owned land to produce crops year after year with the perilous state of fishing grounds, access to which is generally government controlled. The way in which the *absence* of property rights in many jurisdictions and over many environmental resources is leading to environmental degradation is not even considered in the document.

There is an urgent need for the England and Wales Bishops' Conference to think more carefully about these issues, taking on board both the principle of subsidiarity and an improved understanding of economics. If the 2010 pre-election document of the bishops can be taken as representative of recent developments in thinking, there is evidence of progress. This document stressed how a good society needed people to behave virtuously in economic life; it commented on the inadequacies of regulation as a substitute for virtue; and it criticised state interference in family life. In most economic areas – education perhaps being the one area where the document deviated from the tradition of Catholic social teaching – the document indicated the dilemmas and stressed where Catholics should give careful thought in making prudential judgements in policy issues. This is a welcome departure from earlier documents issued in recent decades.

## Conclusion

The concepts of su.bsidiarity and solidarity are absolutely central to Catholic social (and indeed economic) teaching. They provide powerful tools in dealing with a wide range of questions, and form the twin foundations of an impressive intellectual structure developed over a century in major encyclicals. It is abundantly clear that awareness of this structure, which is ably summarised in the *Catechism of the Catholic Church*, would be of considerable benefit to the hierarchy of England and Wales bishops, not only in dealing with social and economic questions, but indeed in indicating which areas fell within its competence. From such a start, other considerations might follow.

For example, the hierarchy might consider, when dealing with taxation, that the replacement of estate duty by legacy duty might well increase the dispersion of property ownership, as urged in the encyclicals. Again, the need for a certain and not arbitrary legal framework would not only call into question retrospective changes in tax regimes, but the whole operation of the secret family courts in which children can be removed from their families and put up for adoption. The general level of taxation, about which the hierarchy appears remarkably sanguine, and the provision of private (as distinct from public) goods by the state, notably in the fields of education and health, are areas where current policy would appear to conflict with the tenor of the encyclicals. Perhaps a start might be made by returning to the whole concept of subsidiarity. This should be embedded in the thinking behind all the hierarchy's documents and combined with an attempt to understand the compatibility of subsidiarity with different economic and political structures. From Catholic teaching it is also clear that subsidiarity should be balanced by solidarity but that solidarity progresses from the individual to the family through voluntary organisations. Only in the last resort should it be necessary to use the coercive forces of government to promote the common good. Furthermore higher levels of government should not act in areas that can be left to lower levels. There is evidence – in between the publication of the first and second editions of this book – that this more rigorous way of thinking is now infiltrating the England and Wales Bishops' Conference. This is welcome as it is this approach that is compatible with the pursuit of the common good and with the Christian understanding of the human person who is, at once, unique and autonomous but also interdependent and part of a wider community.

## References

Bauer, P. (1984), *Reality and Rhetoric: Studies in the Economics of Development*, London: Weidenfeld and Nicolson.

Bishops' Conference (2001), *Vote for the Common Good*, London: Catholic Bishops of England and Wales.

Bishops' Conference (2002), *The Call of Creation: God's Invitation and The Human Response. The Natural Environment and Catholic Social Teaching*, London: Catholic Bishops of England and Wales.

Bishops' Conference (2003), *Trade and Solidarity*, London: Catholic Bishops of England and Wales.

Bishops' Conference (2004a), *Responses to Taxation for the Common Good*, London: Catholic Bishops of England and Wales.

Bishops' Conference (2004b), *The European Common Good*, London: Catholic Bishops of England and Wales.

Bishops' Conference (2005), *The General Election. A Letter from the Bishops' Conference of England and Wales*, London: Catholic Bishops of England and Wales.

Catholic Church (1994), *Catechism of the Catholic Church*, London: Geoffrey Chapman.

Charles, R. (1998), *Christian Social Witness and Teaching: The Catholic Tradition from Genesis to Centesimus Annus*, Leominster: Gracewing.

Coase, R. H. (1974), 'The lighthouse in economics', *Journal of Law and Economics*, 17(2): 357–76.

Mill, J. S. (1923 [1848]), *Principles of Political Economy*, (ed.) W. J. Ashley, London: Longman.

Rose, Michael S. (2002), *Goodbye, Good Men: How Liberals Brought Corruption into the Catholic Church*, Washington, DC: Regnery.

Schumpeter, J. A. (1954), *History of Economic Analysis*, London: Allen and Unwin.

Smith, A. (1979 [1776]), *An Inquiry into the Nature and Causes of the Wealth of Nations*, (ed.) R. H. Campbell, A. S. Skinner and W. B. Todd, Oxford: Oxford University Press, 1979, reprinted Indianapolis, IN: Liberty Press, 1981.

# 16
# CATHOLICISM AND THE CASE FOR LIMITED GOVERNMENT

*Samuel Gregg*

## Introduction

Jesus Christ's famous words recorded in Luke's Gospel, 'render to Caesar what belongs to Caesar – and to God what belongs to God' (Luke 20:25), were literally revolutionary in their implications for how we understand the state. With good reason, Luke's Gospel records that Christ's 'answer took [his questioners] by surprise' (Luke 20:26). For, as observed by the nineteenth-century English Catholic historian Lord Acton, 'in religion, morality, and politics, there was only one legislator and one authority' in the pre-Christian ancient world: the polis and later the Roman state (Acton, 1948: 45). Separation of the temporal and spiritual was incomprehensible to pagan minds because categories such as 'temporal' and 'spiritual' did not exist in the pre-Christian world. As the twentieth century's leading historian of Catholic social teaching, Rodger Charles SJ, notes:

> ... in saying that God had to be given his due as well as Caesar, [Christ] asserted the independence

of the spiritual authority from the political in all matters of the spirit, of faith, worship and morals. This was a new departure in the world's experience of religion. In the pagan world, the State had controlled religion in all its aspects. The kingdom of God that Christ had announced was spiritual, but it was to have independence as a social organization so that the things of God could be given at least equal seriousness to those of Caesar. … When events led to conflict with the State on this issue, and the Christians faced martyrdom, the political effects in theory and in practice did much to determine the shape of European political culture and through it that of the modern world. (Charles, 1998: 36)

Throughout the Graeco-Romano world, the widespread ascription of divine characteristics to the polis or the Roman state was often paid lip-service. The Roman authorities, recognising the strength of Jewish resentment concerning the token emperor-worship required of all the empire's subjects, exempted Jews from such acts. Yet there were times when the pagan synthesis of religion and state caused immense difficulty for people in the ancient world. People were not, for instance, able to appeal to a divine law that transcended the polis or the state.

By universalising the Jewish belief that those exercising legal authority were as subject to Yahweh's law as everyone else, Christianity achieved the hitherto unthinkable: the de-sacralisation of the polis and the Roman state. From Scripture, we know that early Christianity was respectful of the Roman state's authority. Both St Paul and

St Peter underlined the divine origin of the state's legal authority (Romans 13:1–6; 1 Peter 2:13–17). Nevertheless, Christianity also quietly insisted that Caesar was not a god and might not behave as if he was God. Though Christians would pray for earthly rulers, it was anathema for Christians to pray to such rulers. While Christians regarded the state as the custodian of social order, they did not consider the state itself to be the source of truth and law (Ratzinger, 2006: 59). Thus, as the then Cardinal Joseph Ratzinger once observed, Jews and Christians viewed the state as an order that found its limits in a faith that worshipped, not the state, but a God who stood over the state and judged it (ibid.: 240). When Constantine gave religious liberty to the Church in his Edict of Milan (AD 313), he did not subject Christianity to himself. Instead Constantine effectively declared that Caesar was no longer God.

Throughout the centuries, there were instances when the Catholic Church associated itself with the exercise of temporal power to varying degrees. Charles notes that both the post-Constantinian Roman state and its successors used the Church's organisation and personnel to address many social and economic problems. Church courts, for example, were notoriously more efficient than the empire's civil courts, and noted for giving fairer judgments (Charles, 1998: 63). In the wake of the breakdown of political order after the Western Roman Empire's gradual disintegration following the waves of barbarian infiltrations and invasions that began in the late fourth century AD, the Church was perhaps the only institution capable of wielding significant moral and legal authority throughout much of western Europe during this period. Hence, it was not surprising that Catholic clergy such as St Ambrose of Milan and St Augustine of Hippo found themselves assuming social and political roles once reserved to Roman officials.

And yet despite this association the vital distinction between the claims of God and Caesar, with its implicit limiting of state power, has persisted in Catholic belief and action in ways that are less obvious in some other Christian communities' teaching and practice. The links between a number of the Eastern Orthodox churches and the rulers of the nations in which they dwelled remained exceptionally strong until the twentieth century – so much so that *caesaropapism* became a tendency deeply ingrained in the consciousness of some Orthodox believers. In the West, the doctrine of the Divine Right of Kings enjoyed considerable favour in Anglican communities and some Lutheran confessions, and even received some support from a number of absolutist Catholic monarchs. This doctrine, however, found very few supporters among Catholic clergy and bishops precisely because of the manner in which it diminished the Church's autonomy from the state and blurred the spiritual–temporal distinction. The sixteenth-century scholastic theologian Francisco Suárez SJ, wrote powerfully and strongly against the idea (Suárez, 1944). Another sixteenth-century theologian, St Robert Bellarmine, later proclaimed a Doctor of the Church, specifically refuted the divine right arguments articulated by one of the theory's most famous proponents, James I of

England, and also penned the famous *Tractatus de potestate Summi Pontificis in rebus temporalibus adversus Gulielmum Barclaeum* (1610) in opposition to Galician tendencies (which involved, among other things, the extension of the French state's powers over ecclesiastical affairs) in the Catholic Church in France (Brodrick, 1950: 224). Nor were divine right theories ever accepted by the popes, primarily because of the manner in which they blurred the spiritual and temporal realms.

A great English saint, Sir Thomas More, understood this point very well. His careful but unambiguous opposition to King Henry VIII and Thomas Cromwell as they drove the Church in England into schism was motivated by several factors (Gregg, 2007). But one element was More's conviction that the Catholic Church's authority in religious matters such as the indissolubility of marriage and the Pope's dispensing power was greater than the demands of the state's laws. 'The custom of the Christian people', More wrote, 'in matters of the sacraments and of faith has the force of a more powerful law than has any custom of any people whatsoever in civil matters, since the latter relies only on human agreement, [while] the former is procured and prospers by divine intervention' (More, 1969: 415). More considered patently absurd the claim advanced by the distinguished legal scholar Christopher St Germain that Scripture and conscience should be subject to the demands of English common law as determined by the king-in-parliament. He also recognised that these and other assertions made to legitimise the Henrican legal revolution of the 1530s would expand the state's power beyond fundamental limits long established in the Catholic Church's authoritative sources of knowledge: Scripture, tradition, magisterial teaching and the natural law.

The very nature of the Catholic Church's own self-understanding therefore means that it cannot accept a state that purports to have no theoretical or practical limits, regardless of whether the absolutist claims are made by an eighteenth-century monarch, a nineteenth-century Jacobin, a twentieth-century Bolshevik or a 21st-century radical secularist. This was dramatically underlined by Pius XI in his encyclical *Mit Brennender Sorge* (1937) protesting about the Nazi regime's treatment of the Catholic Church in Germany:

> Whoever exalts race, or the people, or the State, or a particular form of State, or the depositories of power, or any other fundamental value of the human community – however necessary and honourable be their function in worldly things – whoever raises these notions above their standard value and divinizes them to an idolatrous level, distorts and perverts an order of the world planned and created by God; he is far from the true faith in God and from the concept of life which that faith upholds. (MBS 8)

The roots of a Catholic vision of limited state power, however, go beyond the desire to maintain the Church's own rightful autonomy and its understanding of the correct relationship between the spiritual and temporal realms. It also owes much to (a) the Catholic understanding of the human person as a free, social, sinful and responsible creature, called to choose moral greatness but capable of profound degeneracy; and (b) the Church's stress on the importance of each person pursuing human flourishing by choosing to live in the Truth definitively revealed by Christ to His Church and rejecting the path of evil.

## Freedom and the call to perfection

Each human person, it appears, is designed by nature to want to be free. But what, we should ask, is so special about human freedom? Why is it *worth* being free? Responding to such questions, the Catholic Church maintains that human freedom is important because, as the Second Vatican Council taught in its Declaration on Religious Freedom, *Dignitatis humanae* (1965), 'man's response to God in faith must be free … The act of faith is of its very nature a free act. Man, redeemed by Christ the Saviour and through Christ Jesus called to be God's adopted son, cannot give his adherence to God revealing Himself unless, under the drawing of the Father, he offers to God the reasonable and free submission of faith' (DH 10).

Freedom is not only important because it allows people to respond to God's grace. Catholicism underlines human liberty as an essential pre-requisite for people freely choosing and acting as they ought to act. In his encyclical on the Church's moral teaching, *Veritatis splendor* (1993), John Paul II stressed that God made man free not only so that each person can find God, but so that we might 'freely attain perfection'. The Pope immediately added, 'Attaining such perfection means *personally building up that perfection in himself*. Indeed, just as man in exercising his dominion over the world shapes it in accordance with his own intelligence and will, so too in performing morally good acts, man strengthens, develops and consolidates within himself his likeness to God' (VS 39). The perfection to which John Paul II – consistent with the entire Catholic tradition – states all people are called is one which the Swiss theologian Servais Pinckaers OP, describes as 'freedom for excellence' (Pinckaers, 1993: 354–78). This is the 'self-command' that comes when a person, having discerned the moral goods knowable through reason and the Catholic faith, directs his will to these goods and acts freely and consistently to realise them in his life, aided by God's grace. It amounts to a freedom that Christ's call to each person to live the life of the Beatitudes is both possible and enriching, and a foretaste of the beatific vision that is God.

Liberty, then, in the sense of liberty from unreasonable coercion, is – from the Catholic standpoint – not an end in itself. It is a means for attaining the higher freedom that is called self-mastery: that is, when we discern through faith and reason what is and is not compatible with Christ's call to perfection, and then, through exercising our rational free will, we choose morally good acts and assimilate the truth about the good into our very being.

While Catholicism holds that humans need to be free to choose the higher freedom to which Christ calls everyone, it also teaches that we are social creatures who need other people and who have real concrete responsibilities to others. This much is evident from our everyday experience. From the moment of our conception, we depend upon our mother for sustenance. As babies we are helpless, utterly dependent upon others' goodwill, especially that of our families. As we grow, our associations become less exclusively familial. They increasingly become the outcome of human reason and choice. This reflects our condition as a social being whose capacity for self-reliance is limited. St Thomas Aquinas highlighted this truth when he wrote:

> It is not possible for one man to arrive at knowledge of all these things by his own individual reason. It is therefore necessary for man to live in a multitude so that each one may assist his fellows, and different men may be occupied in seeking, by their reason, to make different discoveries – one, for example, in medicine, one in this, another in that. (Aquinas, 1948: I, 6)

Nor did Aquinas imagine that our dependence upon associational life is confined to our immediate circumstances. When we engage in shaping material, be it physical or intellectual in nature, we almost always draw upon a common stock of human knowledge. This can range from something as fundamental as language to a specific technique developed over time by particular professions.

At the same time, the Church teaches that these same free and associational human beings sometimes make sinful choices that damage themselves and others around them. As Thomas More wrote, we all possess the capacity to abuse our liberty and concoct many 'worldly fantasies' of our own making (More, 1976: 226). While Catholicism does not teach that we are somehow 'free from' the demands of truth, it acknowledges that, as creatures marked by sin, we have the capacity to rebel against the truth revealed by faith and reason. Such rebellion, however, only leads us to neglect what is reasonable and true – and therefore reality – and enter into the prison of untruth and escapism. In More's words, 'Is it not a beastly thing to see a man that has reason so rule himself that his feet may not bear him, but ... rolls and reels until he falls into the gutter?' (More, 1931: 495).

The situation is further complicated by the fact that in any given society of persons, the range of different, sometimes incompatible, possibilities for reasonable choice by individuals and associations continues to expand. It therefore becomes increasingly difficult to reconcile all choices with each other. Decisions thus need to be made concerning the rules and policies that reconcile different reasonable choices and address problems arising from unreasonable choices.

In certain areas, various procedures emerge to resolve particular problems. Though no serious Catholic would sacralise the market economy, John Paul II noted that the market economy has thus far proved to be the most efficient human means for meeting the basic material needs of entire societies (*Centesimus annus*, 32, 34). Likewise, the price mechanism's ability to reflect the supply-and-demand status of goods and services provides people with some of the information they need in order to choose what to purchase. But even here, judgements need to be made concerning what to do when, for example, a person reneges on their promise to pay the agreed-upon price.

The legal philosopher John Finnis observes that

there are only two ways to resolve such conflicts: unanimity or authority (Finnis, 1980: 231–3). The voluntary undertakings agreed upon in a contract, for example, are grounded upon unanimity inasmuch as the contracting individuals adhere to the original agreement. When there is a breakdown of unanimity, the parties to the contract must either decide to dissolve the contract (unanimity), or admit to the authority of a law demanding completion of agreed undertakings, or be held to their undertakings by some organisation wielding a recognised authority (ibid.: 232).

The ongoing increase of possible reasonable and unreasonable choices in most societies decreases the possibility of achieving unanimity on a range of questions. While this may mirror increasing dissension about the proper ends of people, it also reflects an increase in the incompatible but nonetheless reasonable ways of pursuing incompatible but reasonable ends. It is true that traditions, customs and other non-governmental mechanisms often assume a role in providing resolutions to some of these issues. In other cases, however, there may be need for recourse to an authority that can bind people with the force of law – something which markets cannot do. This especially concerns deterring and prohibiting, for instance, criminal behaviour, and more particularly the administration of justice. The very nature of legal justice is such that it involves investing a particular community (the state) with authority, giving particular institutions of that community the responsibility of exercising that authority (legislatures, executives and judiciary), and defining and delimiting the powers of these institutions (constitutions, statute law and common law).

The preceding analysis makes it clear that, from a Catholic and natural law perspective, the legitimacy of the state and political life as a whole is rooted in two elements. The first is each person's natural call – whether they realise it or not – to freely pursue human flourishing and the subsequent need to resolve what might be called 'coordination problems'. The second is the administration of justice, most particularly legal justice (right relations between the individual and the community) and commutative justice (voluntary relations between individuals, especially as mediated through the form of contract). As Benedict XVI reminded his readers in his encyclical *Deus caritas est*, 'The just ordering of society and the State is a central responsibility of politics. As Augustine once said, a State which is not governed according to justice would be just a bunch of thieves: "*Remota itaque iustitia quid sunt regna nisi magna latrocinia?*"' (DCE 28).

In both theory and practice, however, the two often overlap. This becomes clear when we think of instances of legal coercion that may be legitimately exercised by state authorities. On one level, the use of state coercion against, for instance, thieves and murderers is rooted in society's need for an institution to be charged with realising restorative and retributive justice. But the deterrent effect of these powers is such that they help people to understand the moral evil involved in such acts and discourage them from choosing these actions. To this extent, the state's coercive powers help people to choose good rather than evil acts. In other words,

Catholic teaching holds that even the coercive powers associated with the state are grounded in the state's responsibility to assist people to pursue perfection. Nevertheless, the Church recognises that these considerations need to be balanced against the fact that people can assimilate the good only if they can freely choose the good for themselves.

We see, then, that Christ's call to all people to choose freely the higher freedom of human perfection is central to understanding how the Catholic Church understands the state's role as well as its limitations. This becomes clearer when we reflect upon Catholic teaching about what is described in Church teaching as the 'common good' of a political community (i.e. a sovereign nation).

## The state and the common good

The phrase 'the common good' is regularly referenced by popes, bishops and theologians when discussing the nature of the state and the purposes of politics. The expression is not, however, a paraphrase for collectivism or socialism. It does not equate with the tenets of any particular ideology, precisely because the Catholic Church grounds the political community's common good in Christ's call to all to pursue human perfection.

In its *Pastoral Constitution on the Church in the Modern World, Gaudium et spes* (1965), the Second Vatican Council defines the political community's common good as embracing the 'sum of those conditions of the social life whereby men, families and associations more adequately and readily may attain their own perfection' (GS 74). As a form of human association, the political community may thus be understood as existing to assist all its members to realise human perfection. Its ways of doing so might include interacting with other political communities, protecting its members from hostile outsiders, vindicating justice by punishing wrongdoers, and defining the responsibilities associated with particular relationships, such as contractual duties. What these activities have in common is that they are all conditions that *assist*, as distinct from directly cause, people to achieve self-mastery. It is harder, for example, to choose to pursue the good of knowledge in a situation of civil disorder. Likewise, we know that the incentives for us to work are radically diminished if there is no guarantee that our earnings will not be arbitrarily confiscated through taxation or otherwise.

These conditions thus constitute a political community's common good. A particular characteristic of this common good is that it is not the all-inclusive end of its members. Rather it is instrumental as it is directed to assisting the flourishing of persons (Aquinas, 1997: III, ch. 80 nn. 14, 15). The political community's common good thus helps both to define its legitimate authority and to limit it. For the political community's authority does not derive its power from itself. It always proceeds from the responsibility of state institutions to serve a political community's common good, which is in turn directed to a higher end – assisting rather than supplanting people as they pursue human flourishing and disdain evil.

Given the state's responsibility for the political common good, it would be easy to conclude that the state bears direct responsibility for protecting all the conditions that constitute this common good. Such assumptions are, however, unwarranted. This becomes apparent when we reflect upon a principle much articulated in Catholic social teaching: the concept of subsidiarity. This idea was partially formulated by Aquinas when he commented, 'it is contrary to the proper character of the state's government to impede people from acting according to their responsibilities – except in emergencies' (ibid.: III, ch. 71, n. 4). A fuller definition of subsidiarity was articulated by John Paul II, following Pius XI, in his 1991 encyclical *Centesimus annus*: 'a community of a higher order should not interfere in the internal life of a community of a lower order, depriving the latter of its functions, but rather should support it in case of need and help to co-ordinate its activity with the activities of the rest of society, always with a view to the common good' (CA 48).

The interventions of higher communities, such as the state, in the activities of lower bodies ought therefore to be made with reference to the common good: i.e. the conditions that enable all persons to fulfil themselves. Subsidiarity thus combines axioms of non-interference and assistance. It follows that when a case of assistance and coordination through law or the government proves necessary, as much respect as possible should be accorded to the rightful autonomy of the assisted person or community.

The significance of this principle thus lies not so much in the autonomy that subsidiarity confers upon people, but in the fact that this autonomy is essential if people are to choose freely basic moral goods. Subsidiarity has therefore less to do with efficiency than with people attaining perfection under their own volition. A basic requirement for realising this perfection is to act and do things for ourselves – as the fruit of our own reflection, choices and acts – rather than have others do them for us. The principle of subsidiarity also reminds us of the fact that there are a host of free associations and communities that precede the state and which establish many of the conditions that assist people to achieve perfection. They thus have a primary responsibility to give others what they are objectively owed in justice, tempered, Catholics will add, by mercy.

Provided that the political community's common good is understood in the terms stated above, we can be confident it will not become the basis for authoritarian tendencies. For one thing, the state's responsibility for the political community's common good is to help people to make choices for virtue – not to force them to do so. Secondly, the common good, properly understood, does not necessarily require uniformity. It actually creates room for pluralism insofar as it seeks to enable as many people as possible to pursue basic moral goods in a potentially infinite number of ways.

## Prudence, sin and love

This understanding of the political community and its common good provides us with the basis for reflecting upon the principles that determine what state authorities may do in a society that values human freedom and human flourishing. Far from constituting an open-ended invitation to expanded government, it points in the direction of limited government. It indicates, for example, that the political community is only one of a number of communities and should not therefore displace or absorb the proper responsibilities of other individuals and associations. Considered in this way, the Catholic understanding of the political community's common good is incompatible with totalitarianism of any kind, precisely because the totalitarian state attempts to absorb all other groups within itself.

The state's ability to perform this assistance role is complicated by a number of factors. One is the knowledge problem. Attempting to determine the conditions that constitute a political community's common good is a difficult exercise. Though some elements are constant – such as the protection of innocent life – the totality of these conditions is never static. The state authorities cannot know everything about all the conditions that constitute a political community's common good at any one point in time. Neither legislators nor judges are, for example, in a position to know the number and particular character of obligations incumbent upon all individuals and associations.

Another significant problem is the fact that the people occupying positions of state authority, be they in the executive, legislature or judiciary, are not perfect. From a Catholic standpoint – not to mention everyday human experience and the lessons of history – state officials are also fallen creatures marked by the stain of original sin and, like the rest of us, sometimes choose evil rather than good. They are just as prone as anyone else to making mistakes, to acting outside their area of competence, or even to abusing their position for personal interest. There is a tendency on some Catholics' part (though the problem is hardly confined to Catholics) to imagine that state officials, be they elected or appointed, will always act in the interests of the common good. The lesson of every study of bureaucracy from Max Weber onwards is that the real, as opposed to stated, goals of such organisations and officials often have very little to do with the common good and far more to do with the bureaucracy's self-interest and its desire to preserve and expand its powers.

We are thus faced with dilemmas. If we are to flourish as human beings, we need to act under our own volition. Yet we cannot do so if our decisions are constantly pre-empted for us by the state. On the other hand, our opportunities for free choice may be unreasonably limited if certain prerequisites such as the rule of law which rely heavily upon state authority for their efficacy are absent. At the same time, we know, given man's fallen nature, that a considerable proportion of those people in positions of political and legal power have little interest in the common good and, in some instances, have ceased to be able to distinguish between their own self-interest and a given society's common good.

On one level, the sheer difficulty of resolving these dilemmas is a good reason to ensure that the powers of state institutions are defined as unambiguously as possible and limited in their application. This may limit, to some extent, the effects of the misguided, mistaken and sometimes sinful choices of state officials. At the same time, the same dilemmas underline the importance of the Church reminding government officials that they have a special responsibility to cultivate a special type of human wisdom if they are to perform their responsibilities for a society's political common good. This wisdom consists of discerning what the political community can reasonably contribute towards the liberty and flourishing of its members, and what it cannot (Finnis, 1998: 186). Aquinas underlined this point when he specified three levels of prudential wisdom: individual *prudentia*; domestic practical reasonableness; and political practical reasonableness. 'The good of individuals, the good of families, and the good of civitas', he wrote, 'are different ends; so there are necessarily different species of *prudentia* corresponding to this difference in their respective ends' (Aquinas, 1963: II, II, q. 48).

One way of prudentially discerning the role of government institutions in a given situation is to ask ourselves what the state can and cannot generally do well. This may be determined by identifying other groups' deficiencies and asking when no other community, save the state, can render the assistance that will remedy the deficiency until the ailing non-state organisation can reassume its appropriate role.

Reason and experience tell us that no family is capable of securing public order or administering justice within a political community. Nor can any private person, local association or church successfully undertake such a role. The same reason and experience suggest, however, that the state is a very inadequate child-raiser. In normal circumstances, this function is properly performed by a family that knows and loves its children. When the family experiences problems beyond its control, it should normally be the case that the extended family or neighbours are the first to render assistance. When no other group can render the appropriate form of assistance, it may then be necessary for the state to act.

Hence the fact that children are best raised by their families does not rule out, in principle, any possibility of state intervention in particular circumstances. Examples might be when the police are summoned to stop an incident of spousal abuse. The urgent need to protect the goods of life and health in such cases makes it imprudent to wait for other family members or other intermediate groups to intervene. Normally, however, direct state intervention in family matters is unwise because it involves the application of political wisdom – and power – to a sphere where domestic wisdom and authority ought to prevail. The state's responsibility to maintain an order of justice will nevertheless occasionally necessitate such intervention, precisely because failure to act coercively against spousal abuse may contribute to a deterioration of the public order essential for a political community's common good. Though it is impossible for the state to prevent all cases of, for instance, stealing and intentional killing, such actions should always be prohibited by state authority. Unless such practices face the ultimate sanction of state punishment, a fundamental condition that assists all to fulfil themselves will not prevail.

This principle is central to Catholic teaching concerning, for example, the subject of intentional abortion. The Catholic Church teaches that it is neither possible nor desirable for the state to forbid all evil acts. The Church's teaching in favour of legally prohibiting intentional abortion is, however, partly derived from its awareness that the common good is directly damaged by the removal of any protection from lethal force from innocent human beings who, though *in vitro*, enjoy – as science and reason demonstrate – the same fundamental characteristics of being human as all other members of the human species.

This suggests that, in principle, state institutions may act in ways that contribute to the moral–cultural dimension of a society's common good. Yet the same common good demands that the state should not attempt to protect or alter a society's moral ecology in ways that seek to force people to acquire virtuous dispositions. This point is well explained by the Catholic theologian Germain Grisez. Though recognising that a political community will not be well ordered unless most of its members are encouraged to freely choose acts that contribute to human flourishing, Grisez insists that it is not the state's direct responsibility to demand virtue in general:

> even though a political society cannot flourish without virtuous citizens, it plainly cannot be government's proper end *directly* to promote virtue in general ... both the limits of political society's

common good and its instrumentality in relation to the good of citizens as individuals and non-political communities set analogous limits on the extent to which government can rightly concern itself with other aspects of morality, especially insofar as they concern the interior acts and affections of heart rather than the outward behaviour which directly affects other people. (Grisez, 1993: 850)[1]

The important word in Grisez's reflection is *directly*. This indicates that the state's legitimate concern for public order is not limited to upholding the law and procedurally adjudicating disputes. Rather it is a question of state institutions indirectly supporting the efforts of individuals to choose the good freely.

In his first encyclical letter, *Deus caritas est* (2005), Benedict XVI integrated many of these points into a reflection upon the role played by the Christian theological virtue of love in limiting state power. The state – and, by extension, law – is, Pope Benedict noted, primarily concerned with the realisation of legal justice. But Pope Benedict reminded his readers that 'There is no ordering of the State so just that it can eliminate the need for a service of love. ... There will always be suffering which cries out for consolation and help. There will always be loneliness. There will always be situations of material need where help in the form of concrete love of neighbour is indispensable' (DCE 28). *Deus caritas est* also explains that a state attempting to take care of all problems would inevitably degenerate into a soulless bureaucracy

---

[1] Emphasis added.

that treats people as things rather than persons: 'The State which would provide everything, absorbing everything into itself, would ultimately become a mere bureaucracy incapable of guaranteeing the very thing which the suffering person – every person – needs: namely, loving personal concern' (DCE 28). This does not mean, Benedict maintained, that society does not need a state. What, the encyclical comments, '[w]e do not need [is] a State which regulates and controls everything' (DCE 28). Instead society requires 'a State which, in accordance with the principle of subsidiarity, generously acknowledges and supports initiatives arising from the different social forces and combines spontaneity with closeness to those in need' (DCE 28).

The encyclical's emphasis on the state's supporting and assisting role is thus linked by Pope Benedict to the priority that ought to be given to the spontaneous activities that emerge from the rest of society. This, the Church teaches, should shape the state's activity in the economic realm. While John Paul II's *Centesimus annus* noted that one of the state's tasks 'is that of overseeing and directing the exercise of human rights in the economic sector', the encyclical immediately added that 'primary responsibility in this area belongs not to the State but to individuals and to the various groups and associations which make up society. The State could not directly ensure the right to work for all its citizens unless it controlled every aspect of economic life and restricted the free initiative of individuals' (CA 48). Reflecting on this point, the Catholic moral theologian

Joseph Boyle suggests 'there is a significant limit on the extent to which the polity can provide welfare rights' (Boyle, 2001: 218).

## Conclusion

Much more could be written on the Catholic case for limited government than the preliminary analysis contained in this chapter. What is perhaps most striking, however, is the extent to which its argumentation differs from contemporary secular arguments for limited government. Though not indifferent to issues of efficiency and utility much stressed by economists, the Catholic case for limiting the state proceeds primarily from concerns for human liberty, human flourishing, the instrumental nature of the political community's common good, the demands of Christian love, and the critical moral and social importance of non-state organisations (ranging from the family to intermediate associations), as well as a deep awareness of the power of sin and its effects upon our fallen world.

At an even deeper level, Catholicism rejects the notion that the state – or any other human institution – constitutes the final horizon of human existence. The Church refuses to place its hope of each person's ultimate salvation in the state. Though Catholicism's fundamental attitude to government and law is not negative, the Catholic Church points to a hope that goes not just beyond the state but beyond political activity in general. 'Fear God and honour the Emperor', proclaims the First Letter of Peter (2:14). And yet, as Joseph Ratzinger once preached in a sermon for Catholic German politicians, 'Christian faith has destroyed the myth of the divine state, the myth of the state as paradise' (Ratzinger, 1988: 151). Put more simply, the infinite necessarily limits the finite.

## References

Acton, J. (1948), *Essays on Freedom and Power*, ed. G. Himmelfarb, Boston, MA: Crossroad.

Aquinas, T. (1948), *De Regimine principum ad regem Cypri*, Taurini: Marietti.

Aquinas, T. (1963), *Summa Theologiae*, London: Blackfriars.

Aquinas, T. (1997) *Summa Contra Gentiles*, Notre Dame, IN: University of Notre Dame Press.

Boyle, J. (2001) 'Fairness in holdings: a natural law account of property and welfare rights', *Social Philosophy and Policy*, 18(1).

Brodrick, J. (1950), *Robert Bellarmine*, 1541–1621, London: Longman.

Charles, R., SJ (1998), *Christian Social Witness and Teaching: The Catholic Tradition from Genesis to Centesimus Annus*, vol. 1: *From Biblical Times to the Late Nineteenth Century*, Leominister: Gracewing.

Finnis, J. (1980), *Natural Law and Natural Rights*, Oxford: Clarendon Press.

Finnis, J. (1998), 'Public good: the specifically political common good in Aquinas', in Robert P. George (ed.), *Natural Law and Moral Inquiry:*

*Ethics, Metaphysics, and Politics in the Work of Germain Grisez*, Washington, DC: Georgetown University Press.

Gregg, S. (2007), 'Legal revolution: Sir Thomas More, Christopher Saint Germain, and the schism of Henry VIII', *Ave Maria Law Review*, vol. 5:1.

Grisez, G. (1993), *The Way of the Lord Jesus*, vol. 2: *Living a Christian Life*, Quincy, IL: Franciscan Press.

More, T. (1931), *The English Works of Sir Thomas More*, ed. W. E. Campbell et al., vol.1, London: Eyre & Spottiswoode.

More, T. (1969), *The Yale Edition of the Complete Works of St Thomas More*, vol. 5, part I: *Responsio ad Lutherum: Latin and English texts*, ed. John M. Headley, New Haven, CT: Yale University Press.

More, T. (1976), *The Yale Edition of the Complete Works of St Thomas More*, vol. 13: *A Treatise upon the Passion*, ed. Garry E. Haupt, New Haven, CT: Yale University Press.

Pinckaers, S., OP (1993), *Les Sources de la morale chrétienne*, 3rd edn, Fribourg : Université de Fribourg.

Ratzinger, J. (1988), *Church, Ecumenism and Politics: New Essays in Ecclesiology*, Middlegreen: St Paul Publications.

Ratzinger, J. (1996), *Salt of the Earth: The Church at the End of the Millennium*, San Francisco, CA: Ignatius Press.

Ratzinger, J. (2006) *Values in a Time of Upheaval*, San Francisco, CA: Ignatius Press.

Suárez, F., SJ (1944), *Selections from Three Works of Francisco Suárez, S.J.: De legibus, ac Deo legislatore, 1612. Defensio fidei catholicae, et apostolicae adversus anglicanae sectae errores, 1613. De triplici virtute theologica, fide, spe, et charitate, 1621,* Oxford: Clarendon Press.

# Appendix

## MAJOR CHURCH DOCUMENTS TO WHICH THE AUTHORS REFER

| Author | Document | Date |
|---|---|---|
| Benedict XVI | *Caritas in veritate* | 2009 |
| John Paul II | *Centesimus annus* | 1991 |
| Benedict XVI | *Deus caritas est* | 2005 |
| Second Vatican Council | *Dignitatis humanae* | 1965 |
| John Paul II | *Dives in misericordia* | 1980 |
| John Paul II | *Ecclesia in America* | 1999 |
| John Paul II | *Ecclesia in Europa* | 2003 |
| John Paul II | *Familiaris consortio* | 1982 |
| Second Vatican Council | *Gaudium et spes* | 1965 |
| Second Vatican Council | *Gravissimum educationis* | 1965 |
| John Paul II | *Laborem exercens* | 1981 |
| Second Vatican Council | *Lumen gentium* | 1965 |
| John XXIII | *Mater et magistra* | 1961 |
| Pius XI | *Mit Brennender Sorge* | 1937 |
| Paul VI | *Octogesima adveniens* | 1971 |
| John XXIII | *Pacem in terris* | 1963 |
| Paul VI | *Populorum progressio* | 1967 |
| Pius XI | *Quadragesimo anno* | 1931 |
| John Paul II | *Redemptor hominis* | 1979 |
| Leo XIII | *Rerum novarum* | 1891 |
| John Paul II | *Sollicitudo rei socialis* | 1987 |
| Benedict XVI | *Spe salve* | 2007 |
| John Paul II | *Veritatis splendor* | 1993 |

Documents can be obtained from the Vatican website: www.vatican.va